D1481489

persons and their growth

PERSONNALITÉ ET RELATIONS HUMAINES
(PERSONALITY AND HUMAN RELATIONS)

growth

persons and their growth

persons

*The anthropological
and psychological
foundations
of PRH education*

A collective work realized by PRH-International

January 1997 edition

This first edition was translated into English,

Spanish, Italian and Flemish.

Acknowledgments

This book is the result of a collective effort carried out under the auspices of PRH-International. It could not have been written, translated and edited except for the talented and unselfish contributions of many people.

The invaluable contribution of its principal author, MICHEL LAMARCHE, must be emphasized. His multiple abilities and his availability were of inestimable value. We offer him our most special thanks.

Several committees collaborated in the preparation of this book:

A PERMANENT ADVISORY COMMITTEE,
responsible for writing and finalizing the manuscript.

- PIERRE LACOMÈRE *(France)*
- MICHEL LAMARCHE *(France)*
- ANDRÉE LUMEAU *(France)*
- GILLES PASQUEREAU *(France)*
- CLAUDE ROUYER *(France)*
- ITALIA VALLE *(Italy)*
- with the collaboration of LÉONE BRÉARD,

Angèle Charbonnier and Madeleine Jaunasse.

An Internal PRH Reading Committee,
entrusted with general rereading and supervision.

— Ana Azofra *(Spain)*
— Colette Bergeron *(Canada)*
— Arturo Cecchele *(Italy)*
— Micheline Gagnon *(Canada)*
— Cécile Lefebvre *(Canada)*
— Marie-Anne le Guyader *(France)*
— Maureen McAlduff *(Canada)*
— Marie-Claude Merlet *(France)*
— Thérèse Nadeau *(Canada)*

A Reading Committee, External to PRH,
composed of specialists in the Humanities and other disciplines from many countries. Their capable contribution helped us to compare the contents of this book with other approaches or psychological movements, confirm our thinking and make the work accessible to a larger readership. We especially wanted to point out this assembling of skills and impartial commitment, at the service of a collective work.

One could say that this book was written in the same way PRH was formed: with a lot of generosity, patience and effort. It was inspired by passion and love of people and of humanity. It is intended to serve their growth and their advancement.

This book was translated into English by Rita and Jack Lynch *(Canada)*.

The translation was revised by Albert Fournier *(Canada)*. It was finalized by a PRH reading committee composed of Thomas McMahon *(USA)*, Mary Frances Roberts *(USA)* and coordinated by Albert Fournier.

To all those who have taken an active part in the production of this work, we wish to express our most heartfelt thanks.

PRH-International

To our readers

It was more than 25 years ago that the PRH Organization was created and almost 30 years ago that its founder, André Rochais, began the research in psycho-pedagogy which constitutes its base.

The publication of this first reference text on the anthropological and psychological foundations of "PRH Psycho-pedagogy" stems from our desire to offer the result of those 30 years of research to anyone interested in the human being and to compare ourselves to other schools. Added to this are the repeated requests received from groups and professionals in the Humanities.

This book is the expression of an experience and a practice which have been long observed, patiently considered and carefully examined from contact with "human reality". That reality is represented by the thousands of persons who have practised this psycho-pedagogy on themselves and with whom we have been in constant dialogue. Nothing set down here was written without first having been certified through observation.

Readers who have some experience in PRH education will rediscover a world they already know. They will recognize the indicators suggested for knowing oneself and one's functioning, and for leading a successful personal, professional and social life. They will be able to certify, as they go, to what degree they have been able to integrate the "theoretical frame of reference" in the course of their growth journey.

Readers who have no practice in PRH training will become acquainted with this same theoretical framework. They should take care to note that it is but a "framework" which works - as does all theoretical knowledge of humankind – only if they "appropriate it internally" by challenging themselves personally through an exercise in self-training.

Readers will not be surprised to find convergences with other authors, other approaches, other research. The essential characteristic of PRH research is to centre first and foremost on the growth of the person. Thanks to a specific pedagogy this research opens one up to self-discovery, usable by all human beings, whatever their culture, education level or professional and social position.

This collective work is intended as a first attempt to present this psycho-pedagogy to anyone interested in the human being and seeking to delve without respite and as deeply as possible into the mystery of Humankind. Our aim is to help them to live better and "be better" at the service of a more and more human Society.

CLAUDE ROUYER
President, PRH-International

Summary

"In the absence of a theoretical frame of reference, human beings feel their way along, with only intuition to guide their progress. They are only capable of approximation even though they do their best".

ANDRÉ ROCHAIS
Founder of PRH

Foreword

There is something unusual, even paradoxical about PRH psycho-pedagogy.

It was born from the research of a man (André Rochais), who was passionate about the growth of persons, to be sure, ... but who never planned to form a school.

It has spread like wildfire to all continents ... without advertising.

It has already reached hundreds of thousands of people ... different people: from the Western World, Africa, and the Far East, intellectuals, some of them highly placed, blue collar workers and even illiterates.

It has been the object of a major written work of synthesized observations and pedagogical documents ... without any formal publication.

Even today, PRH psycho-pedagogy is not known to the general public or the world of the Humanities ... and yet it could be called a school. Its anthropology has been developed starting from a rigorous observation of human reality, perceived from the standpoint of personality growth and taken in its universality and totality (that is, including and linking the different dimensions of the human being: psychological, physical, social, spiritual ...). It thus offers an original and profound reflection on persons and their growth. Its pedagogy, based essentially on self-discovery using a specific method of analysing one's own experience, is also new in the world of psycho-pedagogy.

One could go on describing this paradox between the scope, the originality and the productivity of a work on the one hand and its unobtrusiveness on the other.

It is understandable and even desirable that any creation in this area of the Humanities not appear in the marketplace too soon. If a psycho-pedagogy is to be guaranteed a solid foundation, with full knowledge of its limits, including any indications of what might not be accurate or helpful, one cannot skimp on the time required for it to mature, to accept challenges and adjust its observations and methods.

Today, PRH psycho-pedagogy has proven itself in the field. It contributes to the basis of self-knowledge which is an indispensable aid if human beings are to understand their own behaviour, develop their personality and live out their choices and their relationships in harmony with their conscience.

The origins
of PRH psycho-pedagogy

PRH psycho-pedagogy (also called PRH education) was born from the merger between a man, André Rochais, and a group which formed around his thinking and research.

Born in 1921 in Les Deux Sèvres, this Frenchman of simple origin took a very early interest in teaching, in education and in the relationship between the individual and society. First as a teacher, then as a school principal, he had a passion for the "discovery method" of teaching. As his contact with other teachers and the parents of students went on, he became aware of his more marked interest in the education of adults rather than of children.

At about age 30, he felt a calling to the priesthood. He returned to his studies and was ordained, following which he enrolled at L'Institut d'Études Sociales de Paris, where he was introduced to social psychology. From 1962 on, he devoted himself entirely to the education of adults. He started by teaching social psychology, then developed training courses in political life, economic life, international relations and social psychology. Right from the beginning they were highly successful.

In the course of his teaching, he noted that he was particularly taken with all that concerns humankind and its development. This led him to devote himself to a systematic research on the subject. From the time he started teaching, he had the inkling that in the depths of every individual there exists a healthy zone from which persons can discover their own personality and live harmonious lives. In 1966, he came across the work of an American psychotherapist, Carl Rogers. This confirmed him in his thinking and sent him back to his own research on the human psychological structure.

This intensive work of observation, coupled with constant interaction with his public, eventually gave André Rochais a clear view of the human personality, its functioning and the mechanisms of its growth. His ambition was to describe "the universal human being": the basic structure observable in all humanity, regardless of cultural background. According to him, this understanding of the profound nature of humankind would provide access to an ideal way of functioning with respect to one's development and social productivity; in short, personal fulfilment. Bit by bit, an explanatory system of the human being in the process of growth was taking shape.

A profound humanist, André Rochais sought a way to make his discoveries accessible to all. He wanted his research to be able to help people aspiring to live a better life, whatever their education level. Pedagogue that he was, he then set out on a quest. He went in search of everything that might help people to know themselves, take themselves in hand, find meaning in their life, and free themselves from all constraints preventing them from living an existence in conformity with their personality and their deep conscience.

Thus was the pedagogical creativity of André Rochais set in motion and the first workshops centred on the knowledge of oneself were born. Those first workshops, very general in nature, contained the basis of all that would be developed later.

In view of the success achieved by his workshops and the range of requests pouring in from France, Canada and other countries, he offered a course for people interested in conducting the workshops he was giving. In 1970, together with the "educators" of that time, he created an educational and research Organization called PRH (Personnalité et Relations Humaines), to diffuse the psycho-pedagogy that the Organization was putting in place. His fondest wish was that the educators become competent professionals within an educational enterprise. He was spontaneously interested in the lived experience of his educators and in his own experience as a founder. Based on these observations he began to research on the characteristics of this type of group.

From then on his life was closely linked to the development of the PRH Organization which his team of educators was helping him to build. He remained at the head of the PRH Organization, not sparing himself in spite of a physical condition sorely afflicted by illness. He delegated his powers as soon as he could, devoting himself only to what he considered to be his mission, namely to work with others to create the pedagogical tools conducive to personal growth. The growth of persons represented for him a privileged and inescapable way of contributing to the humanization of society. That was his dearest wish and one which best unites all the elements of his person: the man, the priest, the Humanities researcher, the pedagogue.

Until his death in 1990, he worked without respite, in close collaboration with his team of educators, extending the range of their research to include group life and life in the business world, the relationship of humans to a Transcendency, life as a couple and the education of children.

Throughout his entire life he proved himself to be a humble man, deeply honest, authentic, consistent within himself, and unselfish. He sought neither to appropriate his research to himself, nor to profit from the discoveries he made, giving all of it to the PRH Organization.

André Rochais had a passion for the success of men, of women and of humanity.

Part One

Psychological and pedagogical research at PRH

Part One of this book describes how the PRH psycho-pedagogy was elaborated and how this work gave birth to a methodology of specific research.

The psychological and pedagogical research at PRH was initiated by André Rochais. This research, indelibly imprinted with his original thought, has continued to develop over the years within the educational Organization known as "PRH".

Important note:

In the Glossary at the end of the book the reader will find the definitions of concepts and expressions specific to PRH psycho-pedagogy, as well as some other common terms to which PRH gives a particular meaning.

Early PRH research:
the hypotheses of André Rochais

Many questions filled the mind of André Rochais as he began his research. They were a driving force, constantly spurring him on in his investigations. Two among them were most basic.

The first question appeared very early: *"Where in a person can one go to set in motion the process of growth (of one's personality) and of establishing good order (in one's way of functioning)?"*[1]

Three anthropological suppositions arise from this question, each of which André Rochais set out to certify :

– "where to go" implies the existence of a "place" in the person which, if it were found, would allow for development and good order. From this came the hypothesis on a topology of the human psyche;

– the "process of growth" appears in this hypothesis as a natural human phenomenon, capable of setting itself in motion from a specific place in the person. It contains the beginnings of a dynamic conception of the human being, in whom the emergence of the personality is evolutionary;

– and finally, the "process of establishing good order" evokes a notion of internal order to be acquired in the person – one could say a hierarchy which has to be respected - for proper functioning. This hypothesis is at the base of the psychology of the healthy, "in

[1] The quotations which are not footnoted in this work
come from texts that are internal to the PRH Organization.

order" person, which the entire PRH explanatory system would eventually develop.

When, in the course of his studies, he noted how much humanity is socialized, a second basic question followed close on the heels of the first: *"What is personal in an individual ... and what is socialized?"* His aim was to diagram the structure of the person delimiting what is proper to the individual and what is the result of one's social conditioning. Behind this question, the old "innate vs. learned" debate is easily recognized. Therein lies the foundation of the "Personnalité et Relations Humaines" Organization. It is that permanent interaction between the specific personality of individuals and the human environment to which they relate. Those two questions form the very basis of PRH research.

Human relations also aroused his interest. He questioned himself on the role affectivity plays in these relations. Can one envisage human relations without taking into consideration the important role played by affectivity?

A fourth question prompted his research: how exactly to help people who came to him with their problems? Instinctively, he had a tendency to give advice, to seek what seemed to him to be the best solution, and to suggest it. But this procedure was not in harmony with what he had learned through the discovery method of teaching, where the person is party to the research. He therefore went looking for a more appropriate and efficient way to help others.

Challenged by the wide range of audiences he faced, André Rochais also quickly posed the question of one's relationship to the Absolute, to a Transcendent reality – to God, for those who accept the term. At the time, he was not only training believers in search of themselves and coherence in their lives, but also atheists, opposed to all forms of religion. He was looking for a link between the values held by the latter and an Absolute. He wondered if openness to a Transcendency could be experimentally perceived by all human beings. He also wondered about the link between the phenomenon of growth and relationship to a Transcendency.

There was one final basic question: could human research, using an analytical tool to decipher the inner person, be a road toward what some people call God?

The influences on André Rochais

His surroundings

André Rochais was strongly influenced by the working milieu from which he came. His father was a factory worker and, in the bistro operated by his mother, the young André mingled with the people in all their material and human problems. He liked that world of simple folk. He was determined that they, too, should have access to something that could help their existence and growth. Intentionally, he expressed himself in the simplest possible terms, understandable by the greatest number of people.

His religious affiliation

Right from birth André Rochais was steeped in the Christian and Catholic ethic of his family and surroundings. His entrance into a religious congregation of teachers and his studies in theology reinforced this religious cultural immersion. He was particularly influenced by the social doctrine of the Church. He concurred with its very humanistic vision of the human being and society, a fact which fed his social thought.

His association with the discovery method of teaching

André Rochais was very much taken by the new post-war pedagogical current held by people like Maria Montessori and Célestin Freinet ... This new way of looking at children and their education was exactly what he hoped to accomplish with his students: make them become "active participants" in their own training; help them to discover life for themselves.

His studies, notably in social psychology

His training at the Institut d'Études Sociales influenced him, among other things, in everything concerning the relationship of the individual to society. He learned about group living from Fichter's book titled *"Sociology"*. These studies had a major influence on the first courses he gave in social psychology.

The social movement of the time

It is not by chance that André Rochais started his systematic research during a period of strong social unrest. He felt the disillusionment of the time. People were faced with dehumanizing materialism and aspired to a new way of life, based on different values, more in harmony with their essential aspirations.

The influence of Carl Rogers

Two books that André Rochais read at the beginning of his research were: *"On Becoming a Person"* and *"Psychotherapy and Human Relations"*, both by Carl Rogers. These readings would have a determining impact on his research. Here is what he would say about it a few years later :
"Four things struck me :
— his statement: the depth of the human being is positive;
— his declaration that we can trust our intuitions;
— his distinction between what is known (the intellect as he put it), and what is felt or lived (the organism, in his language); and
— his method of helping people.
"I had my answers :
— to put things in order, people must be reached in the depths of their being, where the positive is found;
— to be oneself, one must trust one's intuitions;
— his distinction between what is known and what is felt helped me to create my own diagram; and
— my way of helping others to develop was the same as his: a helping relationship based on human relations, where we have faith in others and strive to stimulate their growth."

Other influences

His reading of Sigmund Freud had a notable effect on his research about the superego and the notion of the unconscious.

Victor Frankl, in his book *"Psychotherapy and its Image of Man"* confirmed his belief in the importance of a relationship to the Absolute and the meaning of life for psychological health.

He read Carl-Gustave Jung.

Alfred Adler's approach interested him greatly, because of the educational psychology dimension in his work.

Abraham Maslow's *"Toward a Psychology of the Being"* also reinforced him in his own research on what he has called one's being.

He was also inspired by Max Pagès' work *"L'Orientation non directive en psychothérapie et en psychologie sociale"*.

On the philosophical and anthropological side, he was marked by the personalist trend of Emmanuel Mounier, by Jacques Maritain and by Pierre Teilhard de Chardin. He had an open mind and trained himself in disciplines such as Characterology and Morphopsychology. Throughout his life he was interested in anything published in the field of the Humanities.

His attitude toward these influences

Beliefs, thought processes and ideologies which have been imbued from a very tender age, are not abandoned just like that. It is obvious that in his research, André Rochais was influenced by his past. Christian anthropology, in particular, led him to some of his questions and hypotheses. His intellectual honesty as a researcher, on the other hand, constantly reminded him to be aware of these contributions and cultural conditioning, to question them, to look at them in perspective, ultimately to reach human reality as objectively as possible. *"Reality is my master"*, was not only his motto; it was his way of understanding the phenomena which he described.

If he was influenced at the outset by researchers like Carl Rogers, André Rochais quickly diverged from them. His preferred method was direct observation. His ambition was to explore the human being as precisely as possible. He wanted everyone, regardless of culture, regardless of ideological, philosophical or religious persuasion, to recognize from their own experience, all the elements of the explanatory system he was decoding.

The specific niche
of his research
and of PRH research

André Rochais was first of all an educator. He was in search of the most efficient way to introduce people to self-knowledge and personal growth. How could people be helped to see their lives clearly, to understand the "why" of their behaviour, to no longer be at the mercy of their uncontrollable and unconscious reactions? How to become oneself, with one's own personality, free of alienations? How to find one's life-work and pursue it effectively? How to encourage an awareness of the meaning of one's life? ...

His first preoccupation was therefore educational in nature, with one main objective: to foster growth. It was this educational intention which pushed him into a psychological type of research. He wanted to understand the "human machine" in its different workings and try to decipher the "operator's manual" of the universal person.

The specific niche of his research - PRH research - can thus be pinpointed as: a *psycho-pedagogy of growth;* growth of persons, growth of couples, growth of groups. Included in the latter category is growth in a specific type of group which he called the "Foundation", because of the congregation of its members around an innovative insight on society, carried by a founder.

Psychological research at PRH

The methodology

There are different ways to approach reality, each with its own specific research methodology. André Rochais was intuitive. His research followed his *"instinct of being"* as he called it. His creativity could be compared to that of an artist, moving him by inspiration. The stringency of his work was always present in the outpouring of intuitions to observe and decipher, then to certify and validate. In addition, he was driven by a desire to serve humanity, offering people a way to develop their potential and to heal their wounds. Thus, applied research was his field of endeavour.

At the outset, as we have seen, he had no preestablished research plan; only questions which obsessed him, and one intention, to foster growth, to hasten it, if possible. It was only much later, when PRH research was sufficiently developed, that he became aware of the instinctiveness with which he conducted his investigations and he explained this in his notes. He thus set down the different stages of what has become the PRH research methodology.

– Stage one – an observation of internal reality and an attempt to understand the observed phenomena

He practised this observation first of all on himself: his behaviour, his reactions, his sensations, etc. He then observed others, the countless people he met in helping relationships and the workshops he conducted. He would constantly examine his own lived experience and that brought to him by others; to define it, then explain it as precisely as possible and finally, get to the root of the phenomena he was witnessing.

– Stage two – A decantation

The work of observation brought him a store of data, all of which he retained somewhere in himself. Then began a period of decantation which produced what he called an *"internal alchemy"*. Elements were assembled, connected to each other, to other experiences or to other established facts. All this internal work was done very naturally, almost without his knowledge, in preparation for the next step.

– Stage three – emerging insights

At some point in this internal work, a phenomenon *"like a bubble breaking on the surface of the water"* emerged in his consciousness. More often than not it was a series of new intuitions which had the force of certitudes, or perhaps some mini-syntheses, which would come upon him suddenly, in some way crystallizing the many previous observations. These insights were turned over once again to his *"internal alchemy"*, from which they subsequently returned in broader and broader syntheses.

– Stage four – a questioning of his discoveries

André Rochais would submit all of his discoveries to the crucible of criticism before accepting them as elements of his own explanatory system. This confrontation took three main forms:
– First of all, he put himself to question by verifying, with the critical eye of his intelligence, the accuracy and coherence of what

he was advancing. He thus compared his discoveries with what he already knew and especially with reality. He did this until he felt his certitude to be accurate and well-founded. He also sought to distinguish what could be generalized from what could be termed as "special cases".

– Secondly, he shared his intuitions. At the outset he addressed himself primarily to his public, then to his colleagues. He was then on the look-out for any reaction without discrimination. The contestations and questions he received challenged him to a closer analysis of the realties he had observed, and this broadened his own field of awareness. The assents consolidated his perceptions, especially when they were accompanied by converging or complementary observations.

– Finally, from the very beginning of his research, he had another way to test the validity of his discoveries, thanks to the international nature of PRH. Numerous testimonies reached him, coming from widely diverse cultures. They corroborated his affirmations and often even showed astonishment at the fact that a Frenchman could describe human psychology with so much fidelity and universality.

Little by little he was filled with unwavering certitudes.

– Stage five – writing syntheses
Once his discoveries were sufficiently matured and verified and his unwavering certitudes sufficiently emerged, it was time to synthesize these observations in writing. These syntheses were already in him in a latent state, in the form of *"sensations with knowledge content"*, structured in such a way as to tie the elements together. He analyzed the content methodically to express it as strictly and completely as possible. He tested his writing until it expressed reality with accuracy and precision. He arranged his thinking with a care for clarity of communication and pedagogical progression. Then these syntheses, provisional at first, were read and criticized by third parties whom he chose with a view to the objective he was pursuing. He then reworked them, always taking into account the feedback he had received.

"From provisional syntheses to definitive syntheses; from syntheses on

one phenomenon to syntheses on other phenomena, I came to the point where I was able to elaborate an explanatory system which is broad, coherent and more and more complete".

The main characteristics of psychological research at PRH

From the manner in which André Rochais conducted his work, one can deduct certain characteristic elements of this research, begun by him and now practised in the PRH educational Organization.

– The object of the research concerns "internal reality", the lived experience, (i.e., sentiments, sensations, reactions ... in brief, intrapsychic experience and its consequences in terms of behaviour, relationship, action, meaning ...). Observation of the mechanisms of growth is central to the study of one's lived experience. This experience is analyzed in relation to persons, groups and couples. The research also relates to the genesis of that lived experience, to understand it, integrate it in the consciousness and own it, eventually to modify it.

– The population being observed is made up of adult men and women of all ages and cultures, not showing serious psychological problems.

– The objective of the research is to promote growth. It is applied research.

– It considers the intuition of the researcher to be very important. Such intuitions must be analysed methodically and the analysis must be compared to the perception of others, with constant care being taken to limit the spread between the subjectivity of the perception and the reality observed.

This type of research calls for intellectual discipline. The researcher must submit to the newly discovered reality, even when it is disconcerting and causes previous images to be questioned. It also calls for humility. The reality will always surpass the limited perception currently held by the researcher. Moreover, the researcher has no control over the time it takes to become aware of some elements.

– It is a phenomenological type of research close to the methodology of C. Rogers, who said: *"The source of all authentic knowl-*

edge rests on an immediate experience of oneself and others, an expe-
rience which, starting from daily living, frees itself from the prejudices
and distorted intellectual limitations contained therein ..."[2]

– It is a rigorous type of research. Only the generalizable reality is retained to constitute the explanatory system.
– It is in constant evolution, due to the infinite complexity of human reality.
– It is validated through continuous feedback from people of all nationalities and also in the successful progress seen in those who have followed PRH education.
– Its results are published in "Observation Notes".

To date, PRH research has not used nor induced experimental situations or methods of quantification.

Pedagogical research at PRH

PRH pedagogical research follows the André Rochais line of thinking. When he discovered an important element of the explanatory system of the human being in the process of growth, he instinctively sought a way in which others could profit by it. He did this in order to help them know themselves better, understand themselves better, behave more efficiently and thus progress more rapidly. Pedagogical research was thus begun in parallel with his psychological investigations. His familiarity with the discovery method of teaching, as well as his own experience, had taught him that the most efficient and fruitful way to self improvement lies in personal discovery. For that to happen, one must put oneself in a state of research, that is, ask oneself questions. His pedagogical research therefore related to the types of questions which could promote this approach to self-discovery. It also dealt with the progressive and methodical sequencing of these questions. With that he could more easily achieve an increasingly refined, deep and complete perception of any given phenomenon that he observed.

One can say that his method of pedagogical research generally followed a very similar line to that of his psychological research. For example, to construct a workshop he proceeded in two stages:

[2] L'Orientation non directive en psychothérapie et en psychologie sociale, p. 6

M. Pagès Dunod, 1967

– first of all, it constructs itself within me;
– then, when it has matured, I construct it.

In the first stage lay the internal work where all of his observations were concentrated. A sensation would develop in scope and richness of content within him. He would then start perceiving the various connections and constituent elements of what would become a workshop. This stage could last from a few months to several years. Then a second stage would start. He would try to find a sequence of questions, (the GPA's: Guidelines to Personal Analysis), corresponding to the internal logic of the sensation he had of the workshop. Feeling his way along, he would gradually come to a point where all the elements fell into place and the whole structure followed, smoothly and coherently.

Two more steps would be needed to complete his work. First came an experimentation of the workshop with a public, for verification and fine tuning. He wanted the questions to be simple to understand and interesting to the participants, so that people could easily get into the process. Finally, in the light of his many observations and the feedback from participants, it became possible to write a pedagogical document which the educators would use to give the workshop.

As much as intuition dominated his research on humanity, it was his logical and methodical side which prevailed in this area of education.

"That was how the pedagogical tool developed. Its magnitude surprised me. But there is so much to observe, especially since, with time, the internal scan becomes sharper and the analysis digs much deeper."

Interaction between André Rochais and his collaborators

Most of the time André Rochais worked by himself in his office. The deciphering of his intuitions required that type of solitude. However, he greatly appreciated the collaboration of the educators, which he deemed indispensable in many respects. First of all, he liked to hear the observations of others on phenomena he was studying himself. These observations contributed to his *"internal alchemy"*, enlarged his perception, stimulated him and provided him with research trails in areas as yet unexplored. A significant number of his discoveries came as a result of this interaction with the educators and their research. Nothing that concerns the human being left him indifferent, even though he himself felt limited in the study of areas where he had little personal experience.

When he felt that a person was very enthusiastic about a subject on which he himself had done little work or in which he had little experience, usually he would react by encouraging that person to go ahead. He was interested in the progress of their work. That is how some educators explored certain phenomena (e.g., guilt, the relation to the body, the meaning of life ...) and created educational tools with him. These he watched over to safeguard their pedagogical coherence with the other means available to the public. Thus he experienced this complementarity of research and creation during his lifetime.

Moreover, he felt the need for others to react to the fruits of his research. He had built up a network of readers of the Observation Notes in order to receive feedback. He had also perfected a method of integrating the texts used by the educators, who were urged to react to the writings they received. He examined these reactions critically with the greatest interest and always answered any questions that were raised. He also asked the educators to report on the reactions of participants in workshops: their questions, their difficulties. The users of PRH education were of great value to the research. During these experimental workshops he would often modify the pedagogy to take the remarks of participants into account. He appreciated any suggestions made to improve the pedagogical tool or clarify a way of formulating. He had the gift of turning the people he associated with into researchers. With all these contributions he created files which he would go back to, reworking the existing tools or creating new ones.

Convergences with other research

PRH research attempts to observe and describe human reality as faithfully as possible. Other researchers in the Humanities are doing (or have done) the same thing, with the same requirement for accuracy. The object of the research: the internal reality of the person; and the method of approaching this reality: by clinical observation,[3] are the same. Therefore, one can expect that a certain convergence in viewing persons and their functioning would appear naturally, even though there might be variations in the application of these concepts. There is no denying that significant anthropological and psychotherapeutic differences exist, as between the psychoanalytic and behaviorist schools, for example. Nevertheless, certain convergences are starting to manifest themselves and there is every reason to believe that they will intensify in the decades to come. More and more researchers, who do not know each other, who come from different countries and cultures, and who have different philosophical and religious group affiliations, arrive at similar and sometimes complementary conclusions. These include points as fundamental as the positiveness of the profound nature of humankind or the use of personal histories to understand the root symptoms of psychological disturbances. Other similarities arise in the process of developing potentialities, the healing of psychic traumas, etc. Edmond Marc, in his book *"Le guide pratique des nouvelles thérapies"*, talks of this trend in humanistic psychology. The following passage illustrates this proximity without excluding particular differences :

"The different processes which claim to belong to humanistic psychology ... each have their specificity. They have in common a certain 'philosophy', a certain vision of man which expresses itself in concepts like: respect for the person, responsibility, freedom, growth, experience, encounter, authenticity ... They also tend to reject the idea of too marked a difference between health and illness, addressing themselves to "normal" persons just as much as to 'neurotics'. Their objective is not so much to nurse or cure an 'illness' as to allow people to develop and broaden their potentialities, enrich their lives and experiences, and make their relationships more intense and more harmonious."[4]

[3] Clinical Psychology: "Science of human behavior founded mainly on the observation and analysis of individual cases, normal as well as pathological, which can be extended to group behavior. Concrete in its base, and complementing experimental methods of investigation, it is capable of producing valuable generalizations." *Vocabulaire de la psychologie* p. 352, H. Piéron PUF 1968.

[4] *"Le guide des nouvelles thérapies"* p. 10 E. Marc. Ed Retz 1988.

In PRH psycho-pedagogy we find points in common with these values as well as this concept of the human person and the development of human potential, all proper to humanistic psychology.

This common basic perception of the human being, enriched by the specific contributions of each approach, is extremely valuable. It brings one closer to human reality. It is a factor which validates these discoveries and the methods used. In particular it represents an indispensable point of departure to approach the areas of life where people get involved, such as in politics and the organization of society, education, work, health, etc. It thus opens a path toward an increasingly satisfying and humanized way of conducting life in society.

The evolution of research at PRH

Many stages mark the course of the research done by André Rochais and PRH.

– A first period extends from 1961 to 1966. André Rochais had just completed his studies with a thesis on the theme: "La formation des adultes", (Education of adults) and he was starting to teach social psychology. What mobilized much of his attention at that time was the influence that society exercises over the individual. In giving his courses, however, he realized that his vision was slowly changing. He was shifting away from the social part to focus on the psychological experience of individuals. He was searching for that which could be personal in an individual, prompting his search for a diagram which could indicate the socialized part of the person, distinguishing it from the personal aspect.

– In 1966 he discovered the work of Carl Rogers, ushering in a new stage that would continue until 1973. During that period, André Rochais laid down the fundamental tenets of his explanatory system and the pedagogy of self-discovery. The first training workshops on personality as well as a diagram of the person made their appearance.[*] At the same time, he was conducting research in five different fields: the person, the group and its government, the helping relationship, affectivity and relationship to God. In

[*] Cf. p. 54

1973, he felt that he had, in his own words, "completed a research project". The cornerstones of the foundation of PRH psycho-pedagogy were in place. An enormous task of thorough study and application of his discoveries remained to be done.

– The next period – from 1973 to 1980 – was marked by intense pedagogical creativity. André Rochais created many new educational tools, more and more in association with his collaborators. They perfected a method of analysing sensations. They worked on the mechanisms of growth and identified the principal laws of personal development. It was also a time when PRH broadened its field of research to include life as a couple, the relation of persons to their body. In 1979, the explanatory system was enriched by discoveries concerning the aspiration to exist and the phenomenon of non-existence.

– From 1980 until his death ten years later, André Rochais worked essentially at perfecting tools already in use, recasting many workshops and applying the already completed explanatory system. Examples of the latter include workshops on the education of children, on life in the workplace and on the method of discernment and decision-making.

How André Rochais approached his research

The way in which André Rochais conducted his research often impressed his contemporaries. A moment should be taken to examine it.

Even though he invested all of his energy in his research work for more than twenty years of his life, he always considered it to be a way to serve humanity, not as an end in itself or a source of personal satisfaction. He was keenly aware of the responsibility that his gifts placed on him, but at the same time he never appropriated the merit of being their holder. He lived a humble life. He considered that he was only deciphering intuitions which were given to him internally and was always astonished at their presence and at how enlightening they were. He often experienced a sort of wonder in face of these discoveries. This surrender of any credit for his work dictated a rule of conduct which he applied without fail; he delivered everything that was given to him to produce. It even led him to entrust all the fruit of his personal research to the PRH educational Organization. He did this totally and unselfishly, since he always explicitly considered PRH to be the proprietor of the concepts he discovered.

Another attitude characterized his approach to his research. It was a constant vigilance relative to the manner in which his research was taken over, used and continued. He was greatly concerned that what he had thus perceived should be respected. He protested against anything which could distort the pedagogical tool which he discovered by associating it, for example, with methods used in other research. Paradoxically, as was stated earlier, he opened himself willingly to being challenged when he was in a state of research and showed a true capacity for self-questioning.

Research after André Rochais

During his lifetime, he encouraged all the educators to put themselves in a state of research. He did not want others to be content with repeating what he had said or written. He wanted the educators to get to know what they were teaching from their own personal research and experience. He also wanted them to enrich PRH research with their personal discoveries. To help them, he created tools that promote research specific to the growth of persons.

Since his death, this state of research has carried on. New workshops and mini-tools for personal development have been created or reactivated.

To ensure that the value of this enormous pool of observations and knowledge of the human being would be recognized and used to the best possible advantage, a coordination of the personal and group research was gradually put into place at the international level. This constant research is one of the fundamental characteristics of the PRH Organization. The growth of persons and human relationships are realties so complex and evolutionary that an approach aiming at the greatest possible precision requires this type of on-going investigation. (This is true, even though the Humanities will never attain the scientific character of the so-called pure sciences).

The research of André Rochais may have been a personal way of thinking, but it was developed and continues to flourish within the PRH Organization. He wanted PRH to be the place where research born of that intuition would develop and where pedagogical tools would be produced.

Thus the PRH psycho-pedagogy of growth, as it exists today, is truly the realization of the initial intuition of André Rochais, deepened, developed, and implemented by and in the PRH Organization.

Part two

The PRH explanatory system

The research conducted by PRH under the impetus of André Rochais has yielded a vision of the human person, of its ways of functioning and a concept of human relations. This section on the explanatory system of the human person in the process of growth presents the principal elements of both the anthropological concept and the psychology upon which the PRH psycho-pedagogy is based.

Chapter 1

An overall approach to the person

The principal characteristics of PRH anthropology

A first axiom

Persons are born with a specific genetic heritage at both the physiological and psychological levels. Innately, their personalities are already in germination. *"Our genetic baggage is made up of a certain number of potentialities which are not independent from one another. They are interconnected and orderly."*[5] They also have their constituent limitations, which show up only upon full development of these potentialities.

Human freedom

Freedom is fundamental to human nature. *"Freedom is part of my genetic makeup."*[6] In a state of potentiality at the outset of life, this freedom awakens gradually, is educated and exercises itself within the constraints of the genetic makeup and the surroundings which are proper to each individual.

The uniqueness of the person

Each person is unique. Some commonality certainly exists among all humans, but personality and the subjective lived exprience are particular to each individual.

---

[5] O.N. *"The Emergence of My Essential Course of Action"* p. 2, 1991
(O.N. = Observation Note).

[6] Idem.

A dynamic and evolutionary concept of the person

This is the keypoint of PRH anthropology: persons have a capacity to evolve throughout their entire life. An aspiration to exist, driven by a dynamism of growth, constantly impels them to open up, to actualize their potentialities, to free themselves from obstructions and to seek to accomplish that for which they were made. The psychological health of a human being can be brought about only in this forward movement, that is, through change. Nor can balance and harmony be considered as established facts. They must always be the object of research, taking into account both personal and environmental development.

Three basic elements contribute to growth. One must bring the lived experience into consciousness through analysis; make decisions in agreement with one's conscience, and then implement them; and, equally important, choose a favourable environment for oneself.

A positive perception of the foundation of personality and a key to understanding negative behaviour

On the basis of its own observations, PRH affirms the fundamentally positive nature of the human personality. In this, it agrees with Carl Rogers,[7] and differs from approaches recognizing the existence of a "fundamental brutishness". For PRH, the most basic aspiration in human beings is the aspiration to exist and consequently, to protect one's existence from anything that threatens it. It is not an aspiration to destroy.

Note : The affirmation that the foundation of the human personality is positive in nature could give the impression of a "Utopian" vision of the person. Yet PRH distinguishes itself from the somewhat idealistic anthropological conception which is usually attributed to Jean-Jacques Rousseau. For PRH in fact, human beings are born neither good, nor evil. They are born driven by a powerful aspiration to exist. They are born with a more or less extensive potential of capabilities. They are already marked at birth by their intra-uterine history. The latent positive foundation of their personality will reveal itself only if they find in their surroundings the necessary elements for development: security, recognition, love, etc. In other words, human beings are born with all the requirements to be "good", but they will effectively become good only if favorable surroundings allow them to develop that potential positively and if their free will consents to the actualization of that potential. If such people fall upon negative surroundings or

---

[7] "On Becoming a Person" pp. 73-74, C. Rogers, Houghon Mifflin - Boston 1961.

if they refuse to make use of their potentialities, the energy contained in their aspiration to exist might well be turned toward defensive, destructive or self-destructive behaviour.

Disharmonious behaviour, "disproportionate and recurring reactions"[*] are symptoms of traumas which usually originate in the childhood past, or result from acquired disordered functioning; they are not attributable to the deep nature of a person. Criminals, in voluntary recollections, for instance, always mention serious traumas which occurred in their past, clearly explaining their subsequent deep disorders.

When people take the means to heal from their traumas and put order back into their lives, their positive foundation gradually reappears, they adjust their behaviour, they radiate a basic harmony and their social productivity enriches their environment. Many individuals, seriously engaged in working on themselves, have made this observation. If the negative were constituent in the person, people could not free themselves of it and would remain condemned to seeing their dysfunctionings, and the consequences thereof, perpetuate themselves throughout their entire life.

The affirmation that the foundation of human nature is positive does not preclude an acknowledgement of its limitations, its vulnerability and the resulting necessity for vigilance; neither does it deny the major role played by the environment and education in promoting its actualization.

Thus, in spite of the current weight of numerous negative aspects in humanity – atrocities, wars and other abominations, injustices of all kinds, the tragedy of many human beings, etc. – PRH views humanity with optimism. It has faith in the capacity of humankind to evolve and find solutions to the problems it encounters; faith in its humanization. This faith is reinforced through observation of the depth of resources present in all human beings, and the fact of undeniable progress in the humanization of persons and groups. Society is in some way driven toward an enhanced-being. Even so, the inner freedom of persons must be sufficiently awakened to adhere to and cooperate with this natural evolution toward humanization.

The very relevance of PRH action with persons, couples, parents, groups and business firms rests on this faith in humanity

[*] The phenomenon of disproportionate and recurring reactions is studied on pp. 104-105 and pp. 183-185

and the progressive humanization of society. A basic option follows : that of committing oneself concretely to promoting this attainable humanization and treating the deep root of all social ills. At PRH, this commitment takes the form of in-depth work, with those who wish to do so, to free the huge accumulation of potentialities that they possess, to help them discover the meaning of their life, to educate their deep conscience, to heal the wounded areas of their personality, to equip them with the necessary knowledge to become themselves and to make their life as sucessful as possible, in relationship with others.

The relational and social dimension of the person

Human beings are not by nature self-sufficient. They are made for relationships, for exchanges and communication. They aspire to give and need to receive. Their humanization and growth are achieved thanks to human relationships. Thus, independence, in the sense of seeking to cut oneself off forever from others and protect oneself from their influence, is not healthy behaviour for one's personal development. On the other hand, there exists in everyone a capacity for psychological autonomy which should be encouraged, allowing them to live their decisions in reference to their deep conscience and not in alienation to others or to events.

The place of the aspiration to love and the need to be loved

The need to be loved and the aspiration to love occupy a central place in the person. The satisfaction or frustration of that need and that aspiration condition psychological development, color actions, thoughts and relationships, and are integral to the meaning of one's life and one's humanization.

Openness to a Transcendency

In the very depth of all human beings one can experimentally perceive an *"openness to a Transcendency, that is, to a reality greater than oneself, infinite in some way and, at the same time intimate to oneself."*[8] Observation shows that bringing this dimension of transcendency into consciousness and developing an intimate and personal relationship with this reality, constitute a fundamental source of growth and promote the fulfilment of the person.

It is at the heart of this relationship to a Transcendency, and to

[8] O.N. *"The Being"* p. 4, 1990

values which emanate from it, that people discover a meaning to their life.

A hierarchical vision of the psychological structure

Persons are perceived in their entirety, interconnecting the physical, the psychological and the spiritual; and taking into account both the human and material environment.

PRH psycho-pedagogy describes the person in the process of growth as being composed of five pivotal centres: the being, the "I", the sensibility, the body and the deep conscience. These pivotal centres are autonomous and at the same time in constant interaction with one another, either in convergence or in opposition to interests or needs. Actions originate from the aspirations or needs of these pivotal centres. Each of them plays a particular role in the growth of the person, but they do not all have the same importance. A hierarchy exists.

The hierarchy which ensures the healthiest and best adjusted functioning in an adult places the being and the deep conscience above the others. The "I", the body and the sensibility follow. When this order is not respected, disharmonious behaviour perturbs the person's general functioning.

The place of the unconscious

The unconscious is approached as the qualifier of an active psychic reality which escapes consciousness and thus conceptualization, rather than as a pivotal centre such as conceived at first by Freud.[9] In fact, *"there is unconsciousness at all levels of the person".*[10]

In the PRH approach, this unconscious part of the psyche cannot be reduced only to *"repressed contents which were denied access to the preconscious-conscious system through an act of repression"* (cf., *Vocabulaire de la psychanalyse* by J. Laplanche and J.-B. Pontalis). In addition to such repressed contents, people can find many potentialities about which they will become conscious only as they mature. Also found there are instinctive inner drives, *presumptions,* images, etc. In other words, that which remains

---

[9] "We often speak of two Freudian concepts, the first in which the major distinction is made between Unconscious, Preconscious and Conscious; the second differentiating the three pivotal centres: the id, the ego and the superego". *Vocabulaire de la psych–analyse,* J. Laplanche and J. B. Pontalis, PUF 1968

[10] O.N. *"Diagram of the Person"* p. 4, 1994.

unconscious in a person is linked to many factors, among which are the following:
– a dynamic of growth and emergence into consciousness of inner contents (potentialities, limitations), which require time to appear in the field of consciousness;
– a host of educational and cultural conditionings, which persons have absorbed and often become aware of only if they work on themselves;
– instinctive drives or habits, often to satisfy primary needs;
– a defense system which keeps needs, aspirations, desires or events in the unconscious, to protect the individual from suffering linked to a past wound.

The growth of individuals and their humanization takes place by progressively bringing the unconscious into consciousness. This is one of the foundations of personality development. Everyone is equipped with the ability to analyze themselves, which allows them, little by little, to push back the boundaries of their unconscious.

One of the main objectives of PRH psycho-pedagogy is to help persons to partake in this self-knowledge, a source of true interior freedom and healthy mastery of oneself.

As opposed to other approaches, the method advocated in PRH education to investigate these unconscious personal aspects, does not call for an exercise in interpretation or placing oneself in a particular situation. Instead, it calls for a method of self-analysis, dealing with sensations which have a psychological content.

The importance of bringing sensations, into consciousness and analysing them

"Sensations are internal realities".[11] In other words, they are the lived experience of persons, their truth at a given moment, what they experience, often independently of their will. (For instance, someone could decide not to be afraid and yet still be trembling).

That lived experience is never fortuitous. It originates somewhere in the psyche of all individuals. There are two types of sensation that persons experience internally. It is important to distinguish them because their origin and their impact on growth and

[11] O.N. "PRH Analysis" p. 4 1992.

the conduct of one's life are not the same:

– there are ephemeral sensations, most of which are immediate reactions of the sensibility to a stimulus which is external to the person. (A circumstance, an event or someone's attitude, can awaken transient sensations of annoyance and fear, or calm and pleasure.) The person has no difficulty establishing a cause and effect relationship and spontaneously seeks no further for its origin. It is important to learn to live with and handle these fluctuations of the sensibility;

– then there are more durable and deeper sensations whose direct relationship with immediate circumstances is less obvious than in the first category. Their origin is elusive at first glance, but one has the idea that their analysis could lead to a better knowledge and understanding of what goes on in oneself.

For example, analysis of an ab-normal and recurring sensation of fear can help one discover a link between this fear and a traumatizing event of the past which has unconsciously introduced an insecurity in the person's psyche. The intensity of the experienced sensation and the ensuing disproportionate reaction can thus be rendered intelligible and less dramatic.

By the same token, the analysis of an agreeable sensation of peace could lead one to be aware of a richness of being, such as confidence or serenity.

Permanent sensations exist which are perceived in the inner depths of oneself. They are present the moment one reflects on oneself sufficiently and pays attention to them, whereas other sensations disappear gradually as wounds heal or the causes of their origin disappear.

The self-knowledge approach proposed by PRH rests on becoming aware of the presence of these sensations within oneself and analyzing the ones which seem to be conducive to growth or to a better functioning. This analysis is proposed as a methodical deciphering of the message contained in these sensations to determine their origin. Having thus diagnosed what triggers the sensation being experienced, one is better able to handle one's life by remedying it or, in the case of positive realities of the being, by finding an enhanced way of living.

The analysis of sensations that one experiences is a privileged path to self-knowledge and consequently to the healthy management of one's psychological life, particularly one's freedom. The suppression of one's interior sensations, or simple failure to take them seriously, deprives people of the information they need to lead their lives as coherently and harmoniously as possible.

Note : To take the presence of these sensations seriously does not mean that the subjective lived experience is absolute, nor does it deny the positive role of reason. One could be tempted to consider this lived experience, felt in the first stage, as "absolute truth". Another danger could be to become a slave to one's sensibility, by letting oneself be led by it and justifying one's actions on the sensations of the moment. This is why it is so important to analyse the content and roots of one's sensations and to compare the results of the analysis to external reality, to reason, and to the deep conscience.

The diagram of the person in the process of growth

A major contribution of the PRH explanatory system to the Humanities is its clarification of the psychological structure of the person considered from the angle of individual growth, and its topographical visualization of that structure for educational purposes. (This topology is obviously not to be taken as a reification of the psychological life of the person.)

This presentation by diagram, well integrated and linked to one's own lived experience, has proven to be very helpful in distinguishing many levels or pivotal centres in the person. With the diagram, the internal lived experience can be understood and localized more clearly. It can take actions, behaviour, interior drives born of aspirations or needs, experienced sensations, etc. and link them to the places where they originate in the psyche.

In this diagram (notably the one in current use, (cf. p. 53) three types of elements can be distinguished which intervene in the make-up of the person:

– elements which are external to the individual, such as the human and material environment;

– internal elements linked directly to biological functions. These are "the I" with the brain, the sensibility with the nervous system and the body; and

– internal elements of a metapsychical nature, the being and the deep conscience.

It is obvious that this visualization of distinct pivotal centres in the person, as clarifying as it may be, does not allow one to account for the permanent influences of the pivotal centres among themselves. Nor does it show their ontological links (body/being, sensibility/body, "I"/being, etc.). If it is accurate to consider these places as autonomous on the one hand, with specific characteristics for each one, one must add that they are interdependent and never function without the support of the rest of the person. (How could the pivotal centre of the being, for instance, function without the other pivotal centres?). For a more accurate perception of the functioning of the person, one must never forget to understand it in its entirety.

First diagram of the zones of personality (1969)

	BEHAVIOUR	
Knowledge *Rational intelligence or intellect*	Socialized knowledge	**Cerebral conscience**
	Personal knowledge	
Lived Experience or Felt Experience *Intuitive intelligence or intuition*	Zone of superegos	**Socialized conscience**
	Zone of disturbances	
	Deep zone	**Deep conscience**
	THE INNERMOST SELF	

Influenced by the work of Carl Rogers at the start of his research, André Rochais developed a first diagram which he entitled *"Diagram of the Zones of Personality"*. He identified two principal zones:

– that of knowledge, of the intellect where ideas, judgements and theories - both personal and inherited from one's surroundings - are located; and

– that of the lived experience or the felt experience, in which he incorporated a zone of superegos (the place where the demands of significant other individuals and groups are recorded), a zone of disturbances (where negative tendencies, shortcomings, faults, etc., are concentrated), and a deep zone (where the best of oneself, the riches which make up the innermost self are found).

Second diagram of the person (1977)

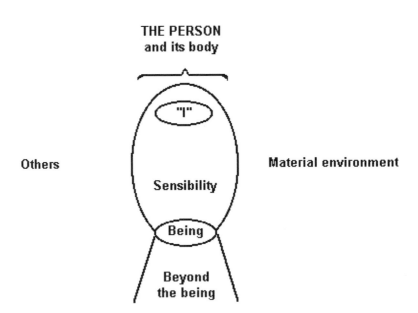

The first diagram contains almost all the essentials of the PRH explanatory system. Subsequently, in continuing its analysis, PRH refined, simplified and perfected its perception of the person. New concepts appeared. The zone of knowledge was replaced by the pivotal centre called the "I" (the place where the intellect, freedom and will function). The zone of the felt experience was clearly subdivided between the "sensibility" which can be peaceful or perturbed, and the being (home of the nucleus of the personality). A zone called "beyond the being" was added (the place where non-expressed potentialities reside and where one perceives the dimension of a Transcendency of the being). The body is mentioned only in the title. "Others" and the "material environment" are now portrayed. Thus, since all these elements play a role in the process of human growth, the person is understood as a totality, psychological as well as physical and social, in relation to the material environment and open to something more (beyond the being).

Current diagram of the pivotal centres of the person (1985)

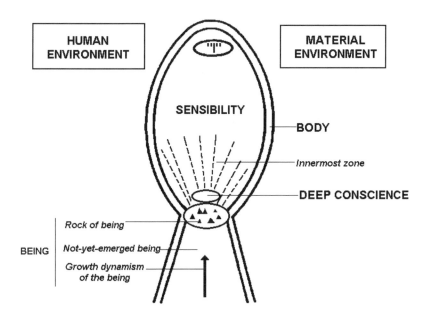

Note : This very refined diagram is intended to highlight the existence of the different pivotal centres of the person. Its is not intended to represent persons in their entirety, nor in the complexity of their psychological life.

The current version consists of the complete 1977 schematic structure, with:

– three modifications : the body is integrated with the person; the "beyond the being" is replaced by the "unemerged being", thus giving greater emphasis to the unconscious and non actualized aspect of this zone; "the human environment" supplants "others" and thus it is put in parallel with the "material environment", to constitute the surroundings within which the person lives in continual interaction.

– a precision : the deep zone of the sensibility irradiated by the being is distinguished from the "rock of being", that solid part of oneself, made up of certitudes – both habitual and unwavering; and

– with two important additions : on the one hand, the "deep conscience" (reference point next to the being, where one experiences faithfulness to self and which is assumable by each of the pivotal centres); and on the other hand, the "dynamism of growth of the being" which drives persons to become progressively what they can possibly become.

The person is composed of these 5 pivotal centres, coordinated and brought into consciousness as a unit. The personality is what specifies and differentiates a particular person from other human-beings. It reveals the person that one is.

Chapter 2

The five pivotal centres
of the person and their
different ways of functioning

We have covered the overall anthropological approach taken by
PRH psycho-pedagogy and the diagram of the person in the
process of growth which gradually developed from it. Now it is
necessary to present a more detailed description of the essential
workings of the personality, as constituted by the five pivotal
centres of the person. The objective is to better understand their
characteristics, their different ways of functioning and their role in
the growth of persons.

The term pivotal centre evokes two aspects of the inner workings of one's personality. There is the topical and structural notion
of autonomous places within the person on the one hand, and a
dynamic notion of power over the rest of the person on the other:
power to trigger actions and to influence (positively or negatively)
the inner lived experience and growth of the person.

The being

Description

The being is a dynamic and positive pivotal centre, located in the
inner depths of the person. It makes up the nucleus of one's personality. In the PRH explanatory system, the being is considered
to be the principal pivotal centre of the person as seen from the
perspective of one's growth. There are four major reasons for this:

– *"it is the bedrock of the entire personality"*[12], its "foundation";
– *"it is inhabited by a dynamism of life"*[13], by a fundamental aspiration to exist, it is there that one finds the deep motivating forces for all growth;
– the other pivotal centres of the person are subordinated to the being and at the service of its fulfilment. In fact, actions prompted by the needs of those other pivotal centres must be in harmony with the being if they are to contribute to the growth of the overall person;
– this is the level at which one can experience the most fundamental joys of existence, whereas the satisfactions and pleasures linked to the functioning of the other pivotal centres are not as intense, durable, fulfilling or stimulating.
In other words, *"it is the most important place"*[14] for the personalization, the growth and therefore the happiness of human beings.

This notion of the being as a central and fundamentally positive reality of the person can be found in many anthropologies. The soul for Christians, the hara for people of the Far East, the innermost self for Carl Rogers, the being for Abraham Maslow, Graf Durckeim, Erich Fromm, etc. are among the approaches that present analogies with this reality observed at PRH.

The components of the being

The identity of persons, their "essential course of action" and their essential bonds all reside at this "bedrock" level of the personality. Openness to a Transcendency also lies at this level. Let us look at these four concepts:

√ **The being is the place where the identity of the person lies**
This identity is comprised of potentialities particular to the individual, that is to say the capabilities, qualities and gifts of each one. *"There is where we find the root of all that is positive within ourselves: our qualities of heart, of action, of the intellect, etc."*[15] These qualities taken together make up the riches of being of the person.

[12] O.N. *"The Being"* p. 2, 1990.

[13] O.N. *"Diagram of the Human Person"* p. 2, 1994.

[14] O.N. *"Educating Children and Youths and the PRH Explanatory System"* p. 3, 1988.

[15] O.N. *"The Being"*, p. 2, 1990.

Examples of capabilities specific to the identity of the person :

– manual abilities (dexterity, do-it-yourself gifts ...);

– intellectual capacities (capacity for abstraction, analysis, synthesis, concentration, imagination, comprehension, discernment, memory, observation ...);

– relational and affective capacities (capacity for openness, altruism, gratuitous love, kindness, communication, tenderness, generosity, forgiveness, tolerance, trust ...);

– capacities for action (capacity for taking up a task, organizing, managing, bringing a task to fruition, for dynamism, for will, for perseverance ...);

– artistic capabilities;

– physical capabilities (skill, endurance, strength ...);

– aptitude for happiness, capacity for wonder, joy, faith in life, sensitivity to beauty ...;

– capacity for truth, acceptance of reality ...;

– capacities for sensibility, for intuition ...;

– etc.

A person's identity is also composed of boundaries, that is to say limitations which are proper to each positive aspect (not to be confused with inhibitions, blockages or simple immaturity, which curb or even arrest the actualization of the positive). To become aware of these boundaries, one must exercise one's gifts as much as possible. Certain signs then announce the threshold of the limitations of the being. These would include an abnormal tension in acting, a disproportion between the effort expended and the results obtained, a sensation of not being able to be more or do more ...

Examples of constituent limitations :

– intellectual limitations (limitations in the comprehension of some phenomena, limitations in the ability to memorize, to concentrate, limitations in the perception of details ...);

– artistic limitations ...;

– limitations in the ability to act (limitations in rapid execution, limitations in dynamism, patience, perseverance, audacity ...);

– relational limitations (limitations in accepting the presence of others, limitations in the capacity for conviviality ...);

– etc.

What differentiates human beings among themselves and specifies the identity of each individual are hierarchy, inner order and the prominence of riches of being, as well as the threshold of constituent limitations. Each person has positive aspects which are characterized by their potential, intensity, limitations and form of expression. On the other hand, one could say that all the essential potentialities of the human species can be found in every person (for example, freedom, love, truth ...).

Note : How can one prove that negative aspects are not part of the identity of the person when most people attribute them to their deep nature? There are certainly many explanations for this. Negative feedback and exaggerated expectations coming from one's surroundings, added to the often repetitive and habitual nature of certain faults or dysfunctions, in all likelihood have induced many people to identify in this way with their negative aspects. "I am lazy, I am clumsy ...", the person says, convinced that it could not be otherwise. Some cultures have also been subjected to the influence of a negative view of humankind, Jansenism in the Western world being one example. In fact, an analysis of behavioural disharmonies shows that they do not originate from what is most profound in human beings. Humans are characterized by the fundamental aspiration to be enhanced and the sensation of being truly one's self. No person in their right mind aspires to become more and more clumsy or lazy, or feels that they are becoming more and more themselves by living that which they call their clumsiness or laziness.

The being is the locus of the person's "essential course of action"

Innately, all individuals have an identity and an "essential course of action" inscribed in their being which they instinctively seek to actualize. The expression "essential course of action" means that for which individuals feel they are made, their journey, their vocation, the niche of activity corresponding to what they are in their inner depths. In fact, even though people have various aptitudes, not all activities exert the same attraction for them or generate the same enthusiasm. People aspire to a specific course of action, where their time and effort can be put into what is most important to them.

Examples of "essential courses of action" : include educating children, creating (artistic creations, crafts ...), researching (scientific research ...), teaching, administrating, cultivating, promoting exchanges (commercial, intellectual ...), manufacturing, helping, curing, directing, serving the community (defending it, organizing it, managing it ...), etc.

People become aware of this course of action over time. Once a variety of efforts has been tried, people are gradually drawn to a general line of activity that brings out the best of themselves. As the being emerges and more experience is gained, this "essential course of action" defines itself more precisely. The potentialities of being are gradually directed toward the actualization of this vocation.

Four criteria can be used to identify the direction of one's "essential course of action":

– a sensation of existing, of being oneself, of being more conscious of one's identity, a sensation of unity between the doing and the being;

– a sensation of giving one's full measure, of living fully without being stifled, of contributing to society;

– a sensation of being profoundly happy, without any after-taste of dissatisfaction;

– a sensation that one's life is meaningful.

As people discover that for which they are made, they commit to it totally, to the point of reorganizing their life and commitments according to that vocation. It then becomes a new phase in their advancement, marked by the presence of a powerful inner strength, abundant creativity, maximum efficiency, and a focus on the essentials of the contribution they can make to society.

Note : One can question whether this new phase, which PRH calls "mission of being", is inscribed in the genetic potential of every individual:

"We observe that very few persons actually reach the phase we call a mission of being. Why?

– Is it because of a growth journey that has not gone far enough?

– Or is it the fact that the essential course of action inscribed in their genetic makeup does not include this "inner rocket" that would thrust them forward once its fire was lit?

We do not have an answer to that question. Of course, one can believe that in all human beings the essential course of action is destined to open up on a "mission of being". The hypothesis is enticing. It would allow us to say that all human beings have a mission of being. But the actual state of our observations does not allow us to believe that with certitude."[16]

The being is the locus of the essential bonds of a person

Two dimensions can be distinguished in the internal structure of the being:

[16] O.N. *"Three Phases in the Emergence of One's Essential Course of Action"* p. 5, 1985.

– a strictly personal dimension, made up of the identity of the person and the "essential course of action". This is the nucleus of the personality. There, each individual has the feeling of being alone.

– a community dimension, as an *"inhabited space"*[17] where people feel profoundly bonded to others in the realization of their "essential course of action". It is the locus of one's essential bonds, bonds of being or bonds of mission. There, people feel bound together, as by constitution, in a more or less extensive social grouping having the same essential values and aiming at social progress. Such groupings extend from the couple, to the family to foundations.

"The bonds of being are rooted in similarity and complementarity at the level of the essential course of action"[18] They are thus distinguishable from other types of bonds which proceed from sentient, intellectual and affective affinities. Bonds of being can even be distinguished from affinities of being, which are due to common aspects at the level of the being, without, for all that, engaging the persons in a common essential course of action. Essential bonds are characterized by their depth, their durability, their variations in intensity in different persons and their source of energy and efficiency in the realization of the "essential course of action". They can exist independently from sentient affinities. They provide a sensation of inner breadth and depth of unity.

More generally, this "community dimension of the being" moves people away from self-centredness and opens them to others and to society. Their perception of the collective dimension is awakened and develops. Individual responsibility for the common good comes to life in concrete commitments, often through the "essential course of action". Thus one can affirm that the being is not egocentric but, on the contrary, contains a powerful potential for altruism.

The being is the locus of openness to a Transcendency

Other than the personal and community dimensions cited previously, the being has a capacity for openness to a "Transcendency". Everyone can experience in their own intimate selves the presence of realities which are of the same nature as their being, but are also experienced as infinite, absolute and permanent

[17] O.N. *"Community Dimension of the Being"* p. 2, 1985.

[18] O.N. *"The Being"* p. 4, 1990.

realities, non-reducible to what the persons are, to what they do, nor to what is in their consciousness. This can be said of Truth, Love, Life, Freedom, Justice, the Dignity of the person, Wisdom, Beauty, etc., assuming that these realities are perceived in the depths of oneself under the form of sensations, not as abstract ideas or ideals. People, for instance, who devote themselves to the cause of justice or who live an interior relationship with their God, experience this contact with reality that is beyond them while at the same time remaining alive and acting within them.

People who have a conscious relationship to these realities which transcend them are transformed. It is as though they were attracted, drawn, expanded and brought to their ultimate humanization by the Absolute or the Perfection of these realities. The relationship to a Transcendency contains an astonishing potential when one thinks of all those people who devote their lives to this Transcendency which attracts them and calls them (the case of monks or people engaged in humanitarian causes, for instance), or of all those who freely prefer to give up their lives rather than deny that which constitutes the Essential of their existence (the case of those who die so that Liberty, Justice, their faith in God or human Dignity may be respected ...).

It is through contact with this recognized and identified Transcendency that human beings discover the deep meaning of their existence and the strength to advance toward their fulfilment. Personality development, in the fullness to which individuals can reach, is not realized solely through the harmonization of their ways of functioning, nor only through efforts of the will. It requires an openness to that which transcends them (available to all human beings), and eventually to a relationship with that Transcendency (assuming that one experiences it, recognizes it and lives it as the Source of life and development). This relationship keeps the person in a constant drive toward an enhanced being.

This explains why, in PRH psycho-pedagogy, this dimension of openness and relationship to a Transcendency at the level of the being is seen to be very important for personal growth. The PRH approach thus diverges from other anthropologies, where the notion of Transcendency is understood differently. Some see it as a metaphysical abstraction, others as an unconscious projection of ideals, or a form of sublimation, or again as an answer that human beings give themselves to escape from their existential anguish, etc. Even though some people live their lives under different conceptions, a thorough analysis of the human lived experience makes it possible to affirm the primary role of openness to a Transcendency in the person's growth journey.

The emergence of the being and its growth

At the beginning of life, the being is a totally unconscious reality. But it is also an evolutionary reality, driven by a dynamism of growth which constantly impels it to actualize the potentialities which constitute it and to appear in the consciousness of the person. The phenomenon of the emergence of the being proceeds from two interactive drives: actualization of the riches of being and awareness of them. This emergence will therefore take place only at a certain maturity level. Awareness comes with the maturity of the intellect, while maturity of the body gives way to action.

Observation shows that people have no direct power over the emergence and growth of their being, in the sense that they are not the ones who can create their own potentialities and order their growth at will. Nor can they foresee or decide on this growth with their intellect or freedom. Human beings are subject to a reality beyond their power (their genetic makeup, the natural laws of growth, interactions with the environment ...). However the emergence and development of one's potentialities can be promoted by knowing and accepting this reality, by a stimulating environment (vitalizing relationships of being, for instance) and by action. Even though people may perform acts and live attitudes which promote the emergence and growth of the being, the results are to some extent beyond their control. The fact remains that these actions and attitudes are never neutral.

Three stages can be identified in this phenomenon of emergence:
– A stage in which persons perform actions which put to work potentialities as yet unknown to them. They rely on an often fragile and not very conscious intuition that the task is perhaps not outside their reach. At this stage they depend heavily on the

people in their surroundings who have faith in them and in their capability to succeed.

Example to illustrate this first stage : People who have never done so before, decide to organize a sports tournament. They have an idea that they can bring the project to fruition, but cannot affirm it with certainty.

– A second stage, where persons become aware that they have a capability. Positive experiences serve as references to confirm them in the certainty of their aptitude. Positive feedback from outside sources confirms these perceptions.

Example : Having succeeded in organizing the tournament, persons become aware that the capability to organize is part of themselves. They can start to rely on that certitude to dare to undertake other things which call for this organizational capability. They are more reassured.

During that second stage these persons identify the action taken as being constituent of themselves, their identity. They realize that this faculty belongs to them. It is a passage from "I do" to "I am capable of doing", and to "I am capable, therefore I am". This identification is fundamental to growth and self-confidence. It is the basis of all certitudes and therefore is at the heart of psychological strength and a feeling of responsibility with respect to the riches which life has given them. This identification promotes a self-image which is more in conformity with reality.

– A third stage arrives when persons have acquired long experience in the exercise of this gift and are confronted with the constituent limitations of this positive aspect of themselves. It is then that they experience the *"boundaries of the territory of their being"*[19] and no longer doubt their capabilities within the limits of those boundaries. An unwavering certitude that this aptitude is part of themselves thus sets in like an undeniable reality. Failure, mistakes, criticism or simply difficulties in getting something done no longer generate self-doubt or the doubting of one's real possibilities. They bring questions of where adjustments or necessary changes can be made, but no inhibition, self denigration or guilt.

[19] FPM *"Growth Guide"*, p. 3, 1994.

The inkling, the habitual certitude and the unwavering certitude constitute the three phases in the emergence – and thus of the experimental knowledge – of the realities of one's identity, "essential course of action" and essential bonds, including the bond to a Transcendency.

The three zones at the level of the being

At this deep level of the person, three zones can be distinguished, which are differentiated from one another by their nature, their substance, their ability to be brought into awareness and their effects on the sensations.

The zone of the "rock of being"

The "rock of being" is composed of the habitual certitudes and deep unwavering certitudes mentioned in the previous paragraph. It is the solid zone of the personality whose strength and scope are dependent on the degree to which the being has emerged into the consciousness of the person. The "rock of being" is where profound intuitions originate, providing enlightenment and impelling toward action, often demanding it, as constructive requirements of the person. Intuitions emanating from the "rock of being" are a source of advancement, innovation and creativity. There is nothing static about this zone of the being, it is constantly animated by the dynamism of growth of the being.

The zone of the unemerged being

This is a zone still in the unconscious, corresponding to latent potentialities which will be revealed as personal growth and opportune circumstances occur.

Examples : potentialities of paternity or maternity sometimes appear only with the arrival of one's own children; the capacity to accept responsibilities often emerges during the course of a professional career; potentialities such as tolerance, wisdom or realism often come with advancing age and life's experience. etc.

Because human resources are so abundant, this zone seems to be bottomless. (In the diagram of the person, that is what the opening of the truncated cone toward the bottom is intended to illustrate). Although unconscious, these potentialities are nonetheless active, in the sense that they can push and orientate individuals on their identity axis, their "essential course of action" and their bonds of being. Thus, "an instinct of being" or "reflexes of being" lead one toward personal development with an intelligence and coherence that is discovered only afterwards. This "instinct of being" can also manifest itself when the being or some of its aspects are threatened from without, particularly in childhood, (e.g. the risk of bothering others, of being rejected ...). The instinct of being then releases a protective system in defense of its integrity, repressing the desire to act upon those aspects of self which are not well received by one's surroundings.

The deep zone

This zone, located in the deep sensibility, is sensed as close to, and irradiated by the life emanating from the being. Immersion in this zone brings a person well-being, peace and life. It affects the functioning of the intellect, providing more hindsight and objectivity. It affects the functioning of the body, making it more relaxed. Finally, of course, it affects the functioning of the being, which can make the best of every given moment.

The core of self and the periphery of self

All realities are not equally important at the level of the being. There is a hierarchy which ranges from what is least essential for the person, the periphery of self, to things concerning the most essential, the core of self.

The periphery of self

The periphery of self is formed of riches of being which are felt as constituent of self but not as central as those which are found at the core of self. Included in the periphery of self can be certain relational gifts such as kindness, willingness to help, humour, certain artistic, manual and intellectual capabilities, certain gifts of action such as organization, efficiency, etc. Experiencing these riches brings contentment, but it is less intense than that resulting from the actualization of gifts related to the core of self. The aspiration to exist loses in intensity as one goes toward the periphery of the being. This means that some gifts will never be developed to their full potential without the person feeling a loss, for all that.

The core of self

Elements composing the core of self include the most essential traits of personality (such as truth, love, liberty, justice, creativity); factors concerning one's deep vocation; the deepest bonds shared with persons who have the same "essential course of action"; and one's relationship to God or to a Transcendency. The aspiration to exist is very powerful in this core of self. To live it is to experience a deep fulfilment. Interference with the actualization of the core of self can cause deep wounds.

It is not always easy to determine the boundaries between the core and the periphery of self. It varies from one individual to another. Some people stress the actualization of peripheral gifts because they gain recognition from them, others do not dare to let their essential gifts come alive. What is peripheral for one individual, such as a gift for music or painting, can be essential for another. All the same, the two may invest similar efforts in pursuing the gift. When individuals engage in their "essential course of action" and are confronted with choices to be made, the difference between core of self and periphery becomes more distinct. People can eliminate activities that concern peripheral potentialities, but they cannot abandon the actualization of riches coming from the core of themselves.

"Experiential" approach to the being

It is not easy to observe and describe this pivotal centre of the person. The being participates directly in the very mystery of each individual, in the sense that this reality is so vast and profound that researchers will never finish discovering it. Actually, since the being is by essence a reality that is subjective, evolutionary and perceived in the depths of self, it is not directly accessible. Often it has not emerged enough to be perceived consciously. Moreover, it can easily be confused with other pivotal centres such as the "I" or the sensibility, especially at the beginning of a process of self-knowledge.

Reflection, readings, action or the reflection of others can be paths of approach and awakening for knowledge of the being. However, if one wishes to account for the reality of this pivotal centre in all of its profundity, flavour and dynamism, such knowledge can only be experiential (*"immediate experience"* as C. Rogers would say). In other words, access to the being is gained through the sensation of a profound and clear inner experience which has been properly tested and separated from other psychic manifestations. In fact, the being reveals itself in the form of sensations which emanate from the very depths of self. Often tenuous, sometimes strong, these are always carriers of energy and perceived as positive. Neither purely cerebral reflection nor simple affective emotions of the sensibility will permit access to this level of being, let alone grasp or describe it.

The other pivotal centres of the person are able to participate in this approach to the being. This can happen :
– when the "I" emerges from ideas, images or worries which preoccupy it, when it becomes attentive to this level of the person and puts itself in a receptive state, suitable to capture the sensations coming from that locus;
– when the sensibility is peaceful, relieved of painful or agitated sensations which can encumber it, or also when it is free from any defense mechanisms which anaesthetize or harden it;
– when the body is relaxed.

External conditions can help bring about an internalization and awakening of deep sensations which make knowledge of the being possible. These include silence, nature, reflective reading, music, relationships... Such favorable conditions do not suffice in themselves to know the being. An analysis of the awakened sensations is necessary.

Some approaches have been prescribed to facilitate access to the being and make knowledge of it possible. These include :

An approach through self-image

Among the positive elements of the image one has of oneself, some are felt as being part of one's deepest self in a very personalized way. These elements are part of the being of the person. "I believe I have a sense of responsibility", or "I see myself as someone sociable", people will say, in expressing the content of their image. More deeply, in describing how they experience their identity, the same people will say, often with a more reflective intonation, "I feel that I am myself when I am responsible and sociable". Or they may reverse the thought: "When I live irresponsibly or avoid relationships, I feel with a certain uneasiness that I am not truly myself, I am not being faithful to myself."

An approach through important choices

Among the motivations which prompt someone to opt for a certain type of education, profession, state of life, social or religious commitment, etc., one can detect, among other things, fundamental aspirations which arise from the being. Behind these aspirations there are potentialities of that being which seek to be actualized.

Example : The choice of social work can express potentialities such as altruism, a sense of human justice and dignity, care for the underprivileged, willingness to help, the desire for human contact and communication, the capability to help, to educate, a sense of responsibility, the capacity for teamwork, etc.

An approach through actions

Actions are also a valuable indicator of the profound identity of persons and that for which they are made. In analysing what they do, people learn what they are capable of, what they like to undertake and realize. Potentialities of the being that are already being actualized can be identified this way.

Examples : Persons who play musical instruments often actualize potentialities such as a taste for the beautiful, a sense of harmony, sensibility, will power, courage, perseverance, the ability to learn, the joy of creating or performing, etc. Persons in business can embody the gifts of service to their clients, communication, observation, intelligence, discernment, counsel, honesty, kindness, etc.

An approach through people who are positive influences

On the one hand you have the mirror principle: positive feedback, when it is accurate, is an aid to knowledge of the being; on the other hand you have the phenomenon of deep attraction exercised by people whose being is similar or complementary to one's own. Moreover, some groups or circles (social, professional, associational...) allow positive aspects of oneself to be implemented. Becoming aware of what is awakened in one's inner depths and what is actualized thanks to these persons, groups or circles, leads to the discovery of one's identity traits.

Example : A political leader can awaken a passion for serving the common good, for generosity, a sense of commitment, moral integrity, a concern for unity and coherence, etc. Some youth movements may have revealed potentialities such as the pleasure of working with others, the ability to adapt, courage, a sense of discipline, respect (for nature, for others...), a sense of celebration, of social interaction, etc.

An approach through reactions under great stress

Certain aspects of the being remain solid in moments of hardship (confidence, will, a sense of responsibility, deep certitude that there is a meaning to what one is living, patience, etc.). Other aspects come into play in these circumstances (hope, internal strength, "with trials comes courage" says the proverb...). These solid elements of personality are part of the "rock of being". They can be depended upon when facing such trials, or to get over them when a person has been inundated by them.

An approach through deep aspirations

The potentialities of the being seek actualization. This is manifested in the person though an aspiration to be oneself or to achieve something in life. People thus learn who they are by stating what they could make of themselves by realizing these aspirations.

Example: behind the dream of becoming a linguist, one can express personal aspirations, such as openness to the world, as opposed to, a taste for communication, a thirst for novelty, curiosity, research, etc.

All of these approaches could remain very theoretical or external to the person. In other words, they would be useless for promoting growth through self knowledge, if care were not taken to experience each constituent element of the being as part of oneself and thus integrate it into one's self-image. The experience of this deep zone of the being lived within oneself, personalizes an individual, awakens the feeling of self-confidence which propels one forward.

The manifestations of the being

By observing one's lived experience, a person can discover many ways in which the being manifests itself. These inner expressions are perceptible thanks to the sensations they produce in the sensibility. It is fundamental to the conduct of one's life and growth that these manifestations of the being and their dynamism be taken into account.

The aspiration to exist

The aspiration to exist is the most important of these manifestations. In the inner depths of all individuals, the latent desire to be oneself, to be faithful to what is felt to be the best of oneself, becomes particularly evident when the opportunity to actualize one's potentialities occurs (when making a choice, for example, or on the contrary, when that desire is frustrated). The aspiration to exist takes many forms, which can be active or reactive.

Deep intuitions

The being manifests itself though insights (inner enlightenments or inspirations which inform the intellect). At times these intuitions can be hardly perceptible they are so tenuous. In some cases they are produced in a way that is unexpected, strong, concise and full of meaning (for instance, in the case of an "event of being" concerning the choice of a mate, orienting one's life...) Note that deep dissatisfactions can be the being's way of protesting in some situations, when it cannot live or grow, for instance.

Internal invitations

The internal invitation to take action or express an attitude (for

instance: invitation to say something to someone, to take steps ...;
to be patient, considerate, firm...).

Imperatives

An imperative for action to be taken that imposes itself on the
"I" as an unwavering certitude (for example, to break off a bad
relationship, to embark on a personal growth program...).

Determination

The phenomenon of determination lies close to invitations and
imperatives. It is not a question of performing an immediate
action, but an orientation, a direction to take, which is imposed
from within (for example: to take charge of one's life, to pursue
some studies, to get involved in politics...).

The instinct of being and the reflexes of being

The instinct of being and the reflexes of being are manifestations
of the being which are unconscious at the time they express themselves. Only later, is their coherence gradually discovered. They
allow the being to develop according to a logic and coherence
which are proper to it. They make the being adapt and fulfill itself
in reaction to the environment. (For instance: in certain choices,
in face of dangers, or again under the form of protests, refusals...).

The functionings of the being

The being is a pivotal centre which lives, functions and expresses
itself naturally through actions. This is more easily done when it
is well emerged, when the person lives in energizing surroundings
and when nothing bothers or thwarts this spontaneous drive
toward actualization.

The functioning of the being is autonomous and is free, at least
in some part, from the power of the "I". However, it is influenced
and at times even constrained by the state of the other pivotal
centres and the environment. It presents a certain number of
characteristics once a person experiences it.

When people function from their being, they live in faithfulness
to themselves, in their inner depths, in coherence with their

habitual and unwavering certitudes, and docile to their deep conscience which is like *"the voice of the person in the process of growth"*.[20] This requirement of faithfulness to oneself results at times in uncomfortable aspects for the "I", for the body or for the sensibility. It can frustrate these pivotal centres in some of their needs. From another view, the functioning of the being individualizes a person and accentuates one's difference from other people. In this sense it constitutes a richness. When traces of fusion or dependence subsist in relationships, however, it brings on suffering.

In this type of functioning, people experience peace, a sense of being authentic and a solid and quiet happiness which is able to coexist with a painful sensibility. It is at this point that people attain a sensation of fullness of existence. Their actions are stamped with assurance, strength, tenacity and patience, making them particularly efficient. People who experience this functioning of the being remain open and free in relation to others, sure of themselves but flexible.

At the start of a growth journey this type of functioning is sporadic. With the emergence of the being, this functioning becomes more and more familiar and spontaneous.

Note on the term "to exist" : This term needs clarification, since it is used in everyday language to mean types of behaviour which are sometimes contradictory, often leading to confusion.

When the being manifests and affirms itself, one has the sensation of existing. One's functioning is then characterized by its soundness, its strength and at the same time by its moderation, its absence of an after-taste of dissatisfaction. One is master of oneself and acts in faithfulness to one's deep conscience. This way of existing is constructive, creative, even though at times it might be disturbing. In PRH terminology, the term "to exist" qualifies only that adjusted functioning of the being which implies the exercise of the inner freedom of the subject which takes others into account without becoming alienated to them. (Freedom in this sense is taken as docility to the deep conscience.) However, some actions can give only an illusion of existence to those who behave that way. Such actions include being beside oneself with anger, taking an action of counter-dependence toward one's surroundings, or displaying a lot of assurance thanks to specific capabilities. In these cases, sensations of release or self-affirmation can be confused with a sensation of existing.

[20] O.N. *"Determination - Wish or Desire - Project of the 'I'"*, p. 5, 1988.

The dysfunction of the being
or non-existence

While the functioning of the being is dynamic, non-existence is characterized by a loss of energy, leaving one unable to actualize all or part of the potentialities of being.

This dysfunction can take many forms. For instance, some people live without being conscious of their being. They have the feeling of not knowing who they are, of not having personal references, a feeling of being inexistent, without personality, with an inner emptiness. Others doubt their capacities or are inhibited from actualizing them, they cannot affirm themselves. Still others are paralysed by the fear of existing, by shame or by guilt from taking their place among others. Others present an appearance of existence behind which hides great insecurity, etc.

At the origin of this non-existence are wounds. Individuals have not felt sufficiently recognized in their right to exist such as they are or in certain aspects of their personality. They expected this recognition from their significant others, at a time of their growth when it was vital that they receive this right to exist. This non-recognition prevented confidence from emerging or broke the confidence that they were beginning to acquire, whence the dysfunctions. This point will be studied in the chapter concerning the healing of past wounds.[*]

The place and role of the being
in the growth of persons

This place is central by the very reason of the essential position the being holds in the person and the presence of the dynamism of growth at this deep level. Personal growth is first and foremost the development of one's being into its diverse dimensions: identity, "essential course of action", essential bonds, relationship to a Transcendency, *"There is no growth of personality except through the being"*. The other pivotal centres develop only to serve the fulfilment of the being.

The role of the being in this growth is especially a motor role. A

[*] Cf. p. 179 Chapter 6.

determination to progress comes up from the inner depths of oneself and prods the person toward an enhanced being. Profound motivations underlie this determination and impel one to exist, to affirm oneself, to push back the limitations fixed by others or by oneself. It is also a directing role in the sense that, by emitting intuitions or sometimes demands for action, the being will impart a direction, an axis, according to what is in harmony with it and its fulfilment. Thus growth will take place in conformity with the direction given by the being and the inner order of its potentialities. By taking decisions and acting along this axis the person achieves harmonious development.

The "I"

Description

This pivotal centre is so named because "I" is the expression commonly employed to evoke this level of the person: "I think that... I choose to... I want to..." Other psychological approaches speak of the ego, the me, the mental, the cerebral zone, the spirit, the consciousness, etc.

The "I" is the governing centre of persons. It is from this centre that they conduct their lives, handle and invest their resources and decide on their actions. It is a pivotal centre sensed at the level of the head.

It is also an autonomous centre which has its own life with specific requirements (rationality, coherence, logic, truth, feasibility ...), its needs (to understand, decide, act...), its mechanics of development (mainly through learning...), its centres of interest (not everything retains its attention or strikes it in the same way), its memory (cerebral memory). It has its view of things, its representations, its theories, its aims, its ambitions, its projects ... to the point that many people who have not become aware of their deep inner life and developed it, or have hardly done so, see in the "I" their only centre of reference, their "identity". They identify and confuse their "I" with their being. With them, "reason" dominates.

The "I" is therefore a locus of reference where people have ✓ recorded those principles, laws, patterns of thought, standards and images which influence their thought and action. The principles or laws decreed by persons themselves, from their own experience or reflection, constitute the references of their cerebral conscience; those acquired from their education and surroundings form the references of their socialized conscience.

Three groups of faculties function independently at the level of the "I". They are :
– the intellect, with its capacity for awareness, analysis and understanding, reflection, conceptualization, reasoning and imagination, all the cognitive faculties as well as a reflective capability which permits the "I" to be conscious of itself...
– freedom, which brings the capacity for discernment and choices, the deliberative and decision-making faculties...
– the will, covering the capability to mobilize and orientate energy, the volitional faculties...

People govern their lives and handle their growth through these three functions.

In the evolution of living species, it is with this reality that the maximum level of complexity and evolution has been attained. In fact, it is the functioning of one's intellect, freedom and will that make the human being distinct from the animal kingdom totally conditioned by its instincts.

Note : This typified and personal aspect of the intellect, freedom and will is part of the initial potential with which people are born. These realities also have their constitutional limits, their "threshold of incompetence" as Dr. Peters would say. Like the other realities of the being, they may or may not be recognized and lived as part of oneself, integrated into one's self-image. Thus, persons with a normal intelligence quotient, able at times to succeed in very difficult matters, can feel that they are unintelligent. It is therefore important to distinguish: 1. the potential contained in the realities of the being (intellect, freedom, will); 2. one's awareness of it and its integration into one's personality (which constitutes the "rock of being"); and 3. the functioning of these faculties. The latter can combine and harmonize with the functioning of the being or remain apart from it, even oppose it. For instance it can act in support of personal ambitions, appearances, the pleasures of action or the juggling of ideas. In our observation of the "I", these intellectual, decision-making and volitional faculties are examined solely from the angle of their functioning and their involvement in the overall growth of the person.

The principal phenomena of the "I" and the growth of persons

The self-image

The self-image is a subjective representation that the intellect has of the physical and psychological reality of the person at any given moment. It is the way in which one perceives oneself. This image is made up of elements experienced as positive (qualities), as negative (faults, limitations not yet accepted) or as constituent limitations perceived as unchangeable.

Children construct their self-image starting from the "mirror" effect of their close acquaintances: what is said about them, their attitudes, as well as from unspoken messages that they get and interpret for themselves. This representation evolves over time and is enriched with life experiences. However, first impressions, accurate or not, have a tendency to be engraved at the level of the "I", structuring the judgements people make of themselves. Attempts to modify an image formed in this way often come into conflict with unconscious resistance to adjust to reality. The intellect has difficulty opening itself up to new perceptions when it already has an idea of a given reality. For instance, it is difficult for individuals to see themselves as being determined if they have always considered themselves to be indecisive. This resistance to change in the self-image constitutes one of the principal impediments to growth.

Many factors influence the adult self-image :
– the way one has been (and is) perceived by others and what they say about it;
– the way one receives and interprets the reflections or attitudes of others;
– the way one interprets the causes of failures or mistakes, as well as the reasons for success; in general, what an analysis of actions reveals about one's capabilities, dysfunctions or limitations;

– the intuitions that individuals can have about themselves and how they analyse them;

– the social stereotypes in relation to which persons situate and compare themselves, or in which they are situated and compared ...

All these elements lead to a self-perception that is either somewhat realistic or somewhat deformed, but individuals always consider it to be their truth. This perception reassures them. Consciously or not, one starts out with a self-image when making a decision or taking action. The individual identifies with this self-image, often finding it normal to be that way and to organize their existence in conformity with that idea. If persons see themselves as capable, they will undertake things, reinforcing the faith they have in themselves and in their capabilities. If they consider themselves to be "good for nothing", they will not act, resulting in the maintenance or even the accentuation of the false image they have of themselves. In other words, the self-image plays a preponderant role in the process of everyone's actualization and personalization. One cannot say "I" except in reference to a representation of oneself.

When individuals tend toward a faithful representation of themselves, reconciling their lives to what is said about them and integrating their positive and negative aspects, as well as their limitations when these appear in their field of consciousness, we speak of a realistic self-image.

When individuals perceive mainly their negative aspects, or magnify them, (their faults, deficiencies, incapacities, failures, errors, the gap which separates them from what they would like to be or do...); when they see their constitutional limitations as negative elements, and when they have almost no access to an awareness of the positive in themselves, we speak of a negative self-image. This partial and deformed representation is a significant handicap to a healthy relationship with oneself and others and to growth. It destroys self-confidence, thus inhibiting people in their relationships and in their actions. The first step toward healing is to become aware of this phenomenon and its origins and to accept with humility that currently one has a deformed view of reality. The second step in this long journey toward the restoration of a normal self-image is a patient and tenacious reeducation of one's intellect to capture those aspects which are positive and assimilate them into one's self image. It is to be noted that few individuals are exempt from this negative image of themselves, at least at certain times in their life and/or for certain aspects of their person.

Finally, when persons have a lot of difficulty recognizing their negative aspects and limitations, when they justify their errors and failures, and magnify their positive aspects and accomplishments, we speak of an over-rated image. At the origin of this type of image, under which there is always a negative image, there can be self-doubt, insecurity and a profound non-existence experienced in the unconscious. The latter is somewhat concealed by a compensatory outward appearance, thanks to real peripheral accomplishments which give the individual an impression of existence, making it difficult to be aware of that overvaluation. There again, the consequences on oneself and on relationships are important to note. There is a tendency to take on tasks beyond one's means, to change course in case of failure, to protect oneself in power struggles where one dominates, to be psychologically dependent on well-known people, etc. This phenomenon often appears among people whose social success or sensitivity to "what will they say?" override the invitation to be simply and fully themselves.

The ideal self

This is a particular form of self-image toward which people try to gravitate. It is what they would like to become. At the basis of the ideal self are aspirations seeking to express themselves and needs waiting to be satisfied. This ideal is in fact the result of wishes coming from different regions in the person :
– the potentialities of the being aspire to live and develop, generating a self-fulfilment ideal, to become more and more oneself. It is a stimulating and realistic ideal;
– social stereotypes presented as models, an often conformist type of education, as well as the expectations of the people around a person, suggest the ideal of what one should be to "be great". This creates an ideal image aimed at the satisfaction of the needs to be recognized and loved, it is the social ideal;

– the ambitions of the "I " also construct an ideal, especially when they are aimed at compensating for a negative image or an underlying guilt. This is the "ego ideal" to use a Freudian expression. The content of this ideal is often marked by ideas of perfection and/or omnipotence.

The ideal self therefore originates concurrently in the fundamental aspiration to exist and in a narcissistic attention to and affective dependence on others, each individual having a tendency to single out a form of ideal according to one's background and stage of development.

The effect on growth will not be the same, depending on the emphasis placed on one type of ideal over another. An ideal founded on the potentialities of the being is very stimulating. It acts as a magnet which constantly attracts people to develop and become themselves. An ideal founded on social stereotypes is also stimulating but it keeps one in a state of dependence, sustaining a mechanism of comparison. It is a source of insecurity and guilt: one never is "as one should be to satisfy the whole world" ! Finally, an ideal created by the "I" is a source of tension, of intolerance vis-à-vis oneself and others. It tends not to take limitations into account, often leaving individuals in a state of deception in relation to that which they would like to be or to achieve.

A realistic ideal might be defined as follows: *"To be oneself, that is, what one discovers oneself to be in one's inner depths, and not what others say, wish or expect. To be only oneself, that is, not to exceed one's limitations and not to be taken in by the ambitions and enticements of the 'I'. To be totally oneself, that is, to leave nothing uncultivated of that which one is, to be attentive to all that emerges from the deep level, in order to implement it with intelligence and tenacity."*[21]

The principal ways in which the "I" functions

Because of its very place and role[(*)], the "I", through the functionings of the intellect, freedom and will, has considerable influence over the growth of persons as well as over their

[21] O.N. *"The Ideal Self"*, p. 6, 1994.

[(*)] Cf. p. 90.

acquaintances and their environment. The ways in which the "I" functions will be approached from this "personal growth" point of view.

At this level, most of the ways a person functions result from cultural acquisitions (education and cultural surroundings). One has learned to function in certain ways and hold certain attitudes (for example, voluntaristic, cerebral or even autonomous functioning, openness to reality, etc.). Other ways in which the "I" functions come from self-education, possibly reeducation, as one attempts to ensure coherence between principles, ideas and deep aspirations on the one hand, and behaviour and actions, on the other.

The functionings of the intellect

The function of the intellect is to know and understand reality (one's own and that of the surrounding world), to reflect and to reason. Informed by sensations, the intellect deciphers the messages conveyed by the sensibility, and puts into words what the person perceives and feels. This is how a simple impression, intuition, need or sensation, experienced but not expressed, passes into the field of knowledge, into clear consciousness.

– The well-adjusted functioning of the intellect

When the intellect works according to the requirement for an accurate expression of perceived realities, it is called a well-adjusted functioning of the intellect. There is no discrepancy between sensations and the words or expressions used to describe them. C. Rogers uses the term "congruence" to depict this appropriateness. When it functions this way the intellect is both exacting and open. It does not lock reality into the perception it has of it today. It remains open to all that can enrich its knowledge of reality, even at the cost of questioning representations acquired previously and from which a person may have made decisions and taken actions. The well-adjusted functioning of the intellect is thus always accompanied by humility in face of reality, the content of which one never perceives completely. Reality rarely presents itself as one had (or would have) imagined it, anticipated it or wished it to be. To function in a well-adjusted manner, the intellect must readjust to reality as it presents itself. To do this, it is frequently confronted with the task of laying to rest past images of oneself, of others, of life or of any reality. This discipline of the intellect to really stay in contact with reality makes interpersonal communication particularly efficient, since it filters out the projections and interpretations that are the source of many misunderstandings.

"This well-adjusted functioning of the intellect is of paramount importance to a well-conducted life. Using the image of an automobile, one could compare the intellect to the headlights. It has to seek reality, to know it better and better, so that freedom can decide with full knowledge and advance on the solid ground of reality."[22]

Note : An important part of the education offered by PRH consists in developing this healthy rapport between the intellect and reality. One learns to interpret its components as they reveal themselves, to integrate these discoveries into the entirety of what is thus far perceived as reality and to relinquish all that is not in conformity with reality. It is a school of truth with oneself, with others and with external reality.

– Cerebral Functioning

There are times when the intellect does not use this direct contact with reality in order to know it. It works with ideas received from others or stemming from previous analyses, with thought patterns, interpretation grids, prejudices or logical arguments. This is called cerebral functioning. The intellect is no longer in contact with the reality it evokes or seeks to know. It is disconnected from reality. Some people draw satisfaction and self-affirmation from talking about reality without sensing it. For them, functioning in this way has become habitual. They are not aware that distancing themselves from the immediate experience is a dysfunction and/or a form of flight from certain aspects of reality, which have become inaccessible because of a weight of suffering repressed in their unconscious.

– The lethargic intellect

There are circumstances too, when the intellect can fail to function. It can no longer analyse or understand. It capitulates, not because of complexity or a low level of intelligence, but because of a blockage which paralyzes its proper functioning. In

[22] O.N. *"The Intellect and Its Functionings"*, p. 3, 1988.

that case we speak of a lethargic intellect, symptomatic of a wound at this level of the "I".

Examples : In some individuals, blockages of the intellect occur when they are faced with figures, forms to fill out, the analysis of their sensations, theoretical questions or ideas. Others react this way when faced with a practical problem like the handling of apparatus, etc.

The functionings of the freedom

Unlike other functions, free functioning, the expression of the faculty to choose and decide, appears only later in the development of the person. It is, as it were, an ultimate function in the humanization process of an individual, challenging one to exist and take responsibility.

– *The dependent functioning*

Early in life, others make all the decisions. Children, particularly when they are younger, are not conscious enough of what goes on inside of them. In the seething whirl of needs, desires, ideas which cross their mind, their reactions and the messages from their deep conscience which are starting to come to them, children cannot distinguish what is good for them and what is not. They are, in fact, not very conscious of the validity of what they are being told to do. Not being able to provide alone for their vital, physical and psychological needs, they depend on the people around them. They therefore function in dependence, conforming to what is dictated to them by others, and thus receive what they need: affection, recognition and security. At the adolescent stage, freedom takes the form of, "I do what I want or what I feel like doing". It is a necessary step of counter-dependence with respect to laws which have been imposed from the outside and the people representing those rules. At the same time, the functioning of dependence remains. The sensibility, the body and the "I", or the reactions of submission and revolt vis-à-vis others, reign supreme and rule the person's behaviour. This functioning of dependence, normal in childhood and adolescence, can extend into adulthood and become a dysfunction. It appears when teachers or other responsible people do not ensure that the reference to the deep conscience is developed. They maintain their guardianship, on principle, through habit or from insecurity. As long as the subjects themselves find a benefit in having others decide for them or prefer to be led by the tyranny of their needs, a dysfunction of dependence occurs.

– *Indecision*

Indecision constitutes another form of dysfunction of freedom. It is a more or less total inhibition of the faculty to choose and decide, usually accompanied by great anguish. Leading up to this indecision, one finds either a form of immaturity or, more commonly, a psychological wound. Instances of the former include individuals who have a hard time indicating their preferences or resisting the desire to do everything. The latter can be identified from symptoms such as fear of failure, fear of making a mistake, fear of being duped, fear of the reactions of others, guilt for existing, insecurity, etc.

– *Free or autonomous functioning*

Free or autonomous functioning appears with the emergence of the deep conscience, with the capability to exist at the level of the being and free oneself from alienations which hinder the exercise of one's freedom. It is seen more often in the psychologically adult subject, but can also be found in some choices made by many young people or by adults who are not very mature. It corresponds to the normal functioning of freedom which follows the phase of dependence and counter-dependence described earlier. This functioning is characterized by :
– consideration of all of the elements involved in making a decision: the expectations, points of view, current or foreseeable reactions, etc. of others, the situation with material events and conditions, one's own reactions, the needs and potential of each pivotal centre;
– standing back from these various elements to feel the intuition of the decision which will be constructive for the being and, at the same time, assumable for the overall person, adapted to the actual situation and to others as they are;
– a sensation of self-mastery, of not letting oneself be run by others;

– a sensation of profound peace and satisfaction at the level of the "I";

– a sensation of faithfulness to oneself and of personal growth.

In this free and autonomous functioning, the intellect plays a fundamental role. By accepting all the elements of reality with openness, impartiality and humility, the inner freedom of the person is already established. Some enticements for the immediate gratification of one of a person's pivotal centres are so attractive they make this intellectual discipline difficult to maintain. That is the price of freedom, the supremacy of "the principle of reality over the principle of pleasure", in the words of Freud. The joy of growth obtained from this submission to the voice of the deep conscience compensates abundantly for any frustrations endured.

The functionings of the will

– *Voluntary functioning*

The will is that faculty persons have to mobilize their energies, to make the effort to achieve what they have decided. The will is thus distinguished from automatic reactions, reflexes and impulsiveness. The normal functioning of the will, called voluntary functioning is dependent on the potential of the will, which is different for every individual, on the education received, which is a more or less awakening force, and especially on the nature and strength of one's motivations. These can originate in the different pivotal centres of the person. (The affective and the sensible incite one to do what is pleasurable, what one feels like doing; the rational and principles push the will to do what must be done; the being and the conscience invite one to act as oneself and be faithful to oneself.) Usually, when the validity of the action to be taken is sufficiently brought into consciousness, voluntary functioning is experienced without tension and without exaggerated requirements. At times, circumstances call for a more sustained and more costly effort, a "shoulder to the wheel". The energy expended then needs to be recovered afterwards if one's system is not to be in a deficit position.

– *Voluntaristic functioning*

Voluntaristic functioning is a deviation of this faculty. It is not always identified as a dysfunction by people who live this way. Their education, their surroundings or simply their active and enterprising nature, have conditioned them to consider this constant and exaggerated call upon their strengths as normal. In this type of functioning the will no longer seeks to serve persons and their growth. It loses respect for the limitations of the body which is abnormally tense. It becomes subject to the "I", and the satisfaction the "I" draws from action for action's sake, to its ambitions, to its value system, where effort, performance, duty, "perfection" take precedence. Relationships with others are established in terms of domination and a refusal to accept their "weaknesses". Behind this voluntaristic functioning one often finds a flight from self, non-existence at the heart of oneself and a disproportionate ideal self. These are accompanied by a feeling of guilt for not doing enough, and deficiencies in the need to be recognized, which seek compensation in the self-affirmation offered by action. Not being able to be recognized for what they are, some individuals hope to be recognized through what they do.

– *The loss of will*

The other extreme to this excessive functioning is total apathy or loss of will. The intellect perceives the action to be taken, the choice may even be made, but there is no will to do it, as though the will had lost the power to command the body to act. The person lets things go, puts things off, feels a debilitating fatigue, like a broken spring... This lethargy can be sporadic, resulting either from a lack of vitalisation and motivating stimulation on the part of one's human environment, or from physical fatigue which is easily noticed. But it can also indicate a profound difficulty in coping, which is deeply rooted in childhood when the natural surge of life was choked for lack of acceptance and appreciation. In that case, it has become an habitual mode of "non-functioning".

Some mechanisms of the "I", obstacles to growth

Defense mechanisms

When people feel physically threatened by assault from an individual, a group or a situation, their instinctive reaction is to set up a defense system. (They will, for example, rebel, flee, attack, become firmly entrenched...). This is a normal survival reflex which protects the organism from injury and possible destruction.

What is true for physical assaults is equally true for "psychological assaults". The perception of a threat brings forth a system of defense, whose role is to protect individuals from certain truths about themselves (or about others, about life ...), in particular those which :
– would disturb them;
– would put in doubt the image they had of themselves or of external reality;
– would reveal inconsistencies in what they feel, think, say, or do;
– would confront them with previously unknown sufferings;
– would destabilize them in the well-established convictions on which they depend and which at times give meaning to their life.

Faced with this internal danger, this potential imbalance, individuals can use their "I" to defend themselves, to protect themselves from what makes them insecure. They try to escape the discomfort of the imbalance and anguish, and repress the truth appearing in their field of awareness. Most of the time they do this unconsciously.

The defense mechanisms wielded are numerous and varied, often subtle. They vary, depending on what is threatened (for instance, the mechanism of justification or certain forms of projection or accusation of others, protect an overvalued image. The mechanism of self-depreciation preserves a negative image or an overvaluation, thus rationalizing actual failure or the fear of failure. The mechanism of idealizing one's past is frequently used to keep unconsciously accumulated suffering repressed. The mechanism of negating or minimizing one's needs reduces or hides the suffering from deficiencies), etc.

It is essential not to read these mechanisms in terms of morality or guilt (by judging oneself or qualifying someone else as being untruthful or proud, for example). This type of behaviour must be decoded in terms of psychological functionings linked to past traumas, to be accepted as such, and upon which the task of rehabilitation can begin. These mechanisms are noxious for growth if they tend to become an habitual mode of functioning. While they protect the person from destabilization, they prevent one from having access to an essential condition for stability and psychological health: the knowledge of one's reality and the acceptance of that reality.

Because of their harmful effects on growth, some defense mechanisms have been studied more particularly at PRH. These are self-doubt, guilt, and imaginary functioning.

The mechanism of self-doubt

This mechanism is linked to the intellect. Individuals become incapable of perceiving their riches of being and having faith in their possibilities and intuitions. It can be triggered in specific circumstances or it can be permanent. This mechanism of doubt is also seen in the field of healing. Individuals who have not yet been successful at ridding themselves completely of certain dysfunctions may doubt their ability to improve their psychological health.

Behind this mechanism, one can identify :
– a limited emergence of the being. Individuals have little experience and few certitudes at the level of their being. Because of this, they doubt their capabilities and feel insecure about moving into action. By experiencing the growth of their being and the healing of what hinders that growth, they can overcome these doubts and become established in the security which comes from the knowledge of their real possibilities and limitations;
– a dysfunction of the intellect. It perceives reality but individuals are unable to believe that their perception of reality is adequate. They do not believe what they see or feel. Because of this, no certitude can take root in them. Everything is constantly questioned, generating a negative image, insecurity, anguish and inhibition. As for all other dysfunctions of the "I", this is an

obstacle to growth. It is therefore important to understand its origin (doubt planted by an event or a person...) and to work at reeducation to achieve proper functioning, in this case confidence in the truth of one's sensations and letting the intellect adhere to reality.

The mechanism of guilt ✓

Being aware of one's share of responsibility according to the circumstances, feeling justifiably at fault for a reprehensible act, regretting one's dysfunctions and their consequences, repairing harm done to others: all these things are good and contribute to healthy human relations.

However, the mechanism of guilt is considered to be a destructive dysfunction, harming the growth of those it inhabits, and "poisoning" relationships with others. It is a disproportionate self-accusation, often unfounded, accompanied by sensations of fear or anguish, which can go as far as states of depression or obsession. This mechanism is triggered like a reflex, for example, when the person responsible for an error is being sought, when something isn't going well in the group, or again when one has made a blunder or a mistake. The person then feels abusively at fault, as the cause of everything that has gone wrong. The intellect is incapable of seeing the situation in perspective. It cannot objectively establish its true share of responsibility, nor that of others nor of the circumstances.

The mechanism of guilt often goes back a long way into the individual's past. Its origin can be found in many kinds of cause. Some examples of the most frequent causes are :
— a very moralizing and judgemental education which can induce the sentiment that one is always deserving of reproach;
— a hyper-responsibility or an ideal which one cannot meet, producing a feeling of guilt for not doing enough, for not being equal to the task, for not being able to make it, for not being good enough;
— a prohibition to happiness, under the pretext that others are unhappy, whose consequence is to make one feel guilty for any pleasure, satisfaction, or even a taste for life;
— a link which has been established between the fact of existing and the unhappiness of a loved one. The mechanism of guilt is then triggered as soon as someone suffers;

– more commonly, it is also a mechanism which has been awakened very early in children who have been denied their fundamental needs to be recognized and loved by significant others. They feel unconsciously that if they are not seen or appreciated, it is because they don't deserve it. They therefore feel guilty for not being valuable and not being likeable.

Imaginary functioning as a defense mechanism ✓

There exists a particular type of cerebral functioning, in that it is linked directly to a painful or an exuberant lived experience of the sensibility. It is called imaginary functioning. It is also called imaginative functioning (not to be confused with a capacity for imagination, which is a source of inspiration and creativity). Imaginary functioning is of the cerebral type because it calls for representations, images, ideas, interpretations or projections which are disconnected from reality. The intellect is detoured into the imagination where it draws elements which dramatize or embellish reality. It fabricates a complete scenario starting from a fear or desire of the sensibility, without being conscious at the time that it is a fantasy. The unrest at the level of the sensibility is reinforced by the scope of the imaginary representations, and a kind of synergy is released between the imaginary cerebral functioning and sensitive functioning.

A transient imaginary release is not to be classified in this category of imaginary functioning, since it is of short duration and its intensity remains proportional to whatever touched the sensibility. Imaginary functioning, on the other hand, when it is recurrent, prolonged and seriously adrift from reality, indicates that there is a wound to be healed. Analysis of the need which triggers this way of functioning opens the door to an understanding and then the healing of the disproportionate part of this phenomenon. For instance, imaginary functioning can be at the origin of a disproportionate need for security: one anticipates the situation that one will meet and imagines what will happen, what will be said, thus consciously seeking to have a grip on reality and mastery of the situation.

These various mechanisms of the "I" which are obstacles to growth (and for which the list is not exhaustive) are not mutually independent. Often they coexist and interact within a person. Thus, for instance, the mechanisms of self-doubt and guilt generate imaginary functioning, or guilt brings about other defense mechanisms such as self-justification or accusation of others, etc.

The place and role of the "I" in the growth of persons

If the being and the deep conscience constitute the first pivotal centres in relation to the harmonious functioning and growth process of the person, the "I" is its second reality. This rank is linked directly to the role of the "I" which is to serve the growth of the being and the harmony of the overall personality (physical, psychic and spiritual).

If the "I" elevates itself to first place by imposing its views, its ideal, its principles or its ambitions, the entire individual suffers, as well as the people around. This is because it is severed from what is most essential: the being and the deep conscience. If the"I" lets the sensibility, the body, events or others supplant it, individuals are like a ship without a captain. They will drift, following the prevailing drives or external expectations and influences. In both cases, disharmony and division settle in the personality, becoming in the long run a source of neurosis.

It is thus up to the "I" to know and manage the potential of riches with which persons are gifted, so as to put them on the axis for which they were made, with a view to optimal productivity and the enrichment of society. Its role is to put its faculties of intellect, freedom and will at the service of the best of self, so it can live, develop to its maximum, consistent with the rest of the person (notably one's deep conscience) and external reality. In that sense, the "I" has functions of research, decision-making and investment of the body's energies, of vigilance and control over the consistency and realism of what a person undertakes or does, and also of communicator through verbalization.

Its role consists as well in educating itself to hold attitudes favourable to the growth of the being, for example: to be open to that deep locus of self, to accept what it is, with its riches and limitations, to be confident in its capacities and respect its limitations, to listen to its aspirations or intuitions, to refer to the deep conscience for decisions, to be patient in face of the slow development of the being, etc. To reeducate itself, it also has the parallel role of unmasking harmful attitudes which it has acquired, such as a closed mind, repression, censoring out the positive content of the being, indifference, distortion of reality, depreciation or overvaluation, domination, doubt, outward appearances, perfectionism, comparison with others, in short, all of the dysfunctions studied above.

The place and role of the "I" are not easy to maintain. While it is at a control station of the person, which confers on it the prerogatives cited above, at the same time this power has meaning only when subordinated to the life and growth of the being and is humbly submitted to reality. Yet, it is through this role and this humble attitude that it will find its own development, its greatest satisfaction and efficiency. It is also at this place and in this role that the "I" promotes a path to unity in the person. Instead of ignoring each other, living in rivalry or apart, the two main autonomous centres (the being and the "I") enter into a cooperative relationship which benefits the overall person and everyone around.

The body

Description

The body is considered to be a pivotal centre of the person, that is, a locus from which actions are taken (for instance, to provide for its own needs and adapt to the environment). It is a pivotal centre linked to the sensibility and in direct contact with a human environment and material realties. The body is perceived through its vital "space", its clothing, the things which concern it, its defined lifestyle.

The body is a sexual reality which determines the identity of individuals and influences their choices, behaviour and relationships.

The body is a biological reality which has its specific laws of functioning, of development and of aging. It is a reality which has potential and limitations: resistance, longevity, energy, beauty, health, etc.

It is a *"reservoir and producer of energy"*[23] and vitality of varying degrees, depending on the person. All individuals start out with physical assets which they can maintain throughout their existence or which they can dissipate, causing premature wear and tear of the organism.

It acts as the revealer of the truth of the person's inner lived experience. Each bodily sensation (physical well-being, tension, hunger, warmth, etc.) contains a message which gives information about the physical and/or psychological lived experience. This body language does not fall under the power of the " I". Bodily manifestations can impose themselves without the "I" being able to control them (emotions, illnesses...). By the same token, the body can be considered as a realistic "old sage" that must be heeded.

The body offers a means for individuals to express themselves: their sensibility, their sentiments, their thoughts, their being... (through gestures, looks, attitudes, the voice, sexuality, but also through the choice of clothing, etc.).

It constitutes a privileged means of access to the being and the unity of the person. Muscular relaxation, breathing exercises and certain body positions promote interiorization and the experiencing of deep sensations coming from the being. Moreover, physical well-being is a roadway which opens onto the well-being of the overall person.

There is a constant interaction between the different pivotal centres of the person and the body. Principles, the ambitions of the "I", its submission or intractability with regard to the deep conscience, all have repercussions on the body, stressing it, exhausting it or respecting it. The desires by which the sensibility is carried away, as well as the sufferings that it endures, take a lot of energy. Finally, between the two pivotal centres, being and body, there is an ontological unity. *"We are being and body. The two are so inseparably one that we can call ourselves "embodied beings".*[24] Thus what touches the being reflects and expresses itself in the body. (For example, when a profound joy emanates from

[23] FPM 46 *"Managing My Body"* p. 2, 1988.
[24] FPM *"Growth Guide"*, p. 10, 1994.

someone's being, their face lights up, a deep motivation mobilizes them, the sensation of interior freedom provides a physical relaxation, etc.). The reverse is also true. The state of the body has an influence on the "I", the sensibility, and the being. (Their efficiency is greatly diminished in the case of fatigue, for instance, or on the contrary, is reinforced when the body is in good shape). The growth of the being humanizes the body, allowing more and more of the radiance of the being to show through. This distinguishes the human being from the animal kingdom.

The relationship of persons to their body

This relationship has its own history. We know this history begins in the inter-uterine life and is marked from the beginning by heredity. It goes through a deep upheaval at birth and continues, in a permanent interaction between the state of the body and its lived experience on the one hand and the state and lived experience of other pivotal centres and the social and material environment in which the person lives, on the other. This history ends with declining abilities and death. During the course of this history, the body is transformed. A relationship is established between the individual and the body both in its entirety and in its constituent parts. This relationship, evolving over time, is influenced by a body image which has gradually been formed from personal perception, from the looks and remarks of others and also from the cultural representations of the body which are in style in the society into which the person lives. Each culture has its models, value judgements and taboos in this area. The relationship of individuals to their bodies is dependent on the relationship that others have had and continue to have with the person's body, with their own bodies, with the human body.

This relationship of individuals to their body can be viewed from two angles: how they consider their body, and how they behave with respect to their body.

Everyone lives a particular type of relationship with their body. For some, it is a friend, a partner, a servant, a good companion, whose limitations are accepted and with which a relational harmony has been established. All this brings satisfaction in terms of action, pleasure, relationship, well-being... For others, it is a machine that works more or less in the way they want it to work, a useful object but one which must be looked after... Others see it as an enemy, a traitor, a tyrant, a beast, an object of shame or else as a "killjoy", a source of pain, of anguish... Still others have no relationship with their body. It is an unknown. They seem to live without it. For some, the reverse is true. They have made a God of it, etc.

The way one treats the body and takes care of it depends to a great extent on the way in which the body is considered. Here again, there is a wide and varied range of behaviour. Those who consider it as a friend take care of it, its health, its hygiene, satisfy its needs, respect its limitations, spare it. Those who see it as a useful object have a tendency to profit from its services, sometimes to abuse it, to grant it the vital minimum and to look after it only when the machine is "out of order". Those who perceive it as an enemy despise it, maltreat it, seek to dominate it, at times to anaesthetize or destroy it. They make it pay for the constraints and annoyances that it imposes on them. Those for whom the body is an unknown are not aware of it, do not take it into account, neglect it. On the other hand, persons who deify it have a tendency to overvalue it, to provide it with excessive care and attention, to devote an exaggerated amount of time and money to it...

The needs of the body

These can be classified into two categories: physical needs (basic or not), and psychological needs linked to the body. (The compensatory needs of the body will be studied in the paragraph concerning the functionings of the body).

Physical needs
Physical needs are related to life or to the survival of the body and the human species. They are also related to the well-being of the body. These are the needs to sleep, eat, drink, breathe, move, the need to be well looked after when sick, the need to protect

itself from threatening dangers, the needs for comfort and satisfaction of the senses, sexual needs, etc.

Psychological needs

The psychological needs linked to the body appear very early in children. They are the need to be recognized in one's body, to be seen and appreciated in one's sexual identity, loved through the touch of the mother and father, the need to be secure, the need to be "well", happy in one's body, "feeling good", the need for freedom to express one's body, to release tensions... In adolescence, there is the additional need to feel that one's parents are happy with the transformations of one's body and the need to be able to talk about it simply and freely. In adulthood, some of these needs subside. Others remain, but their dissatisfaction is less serious than in children who establish a relation to their bodies from the way their environment and their acquaintances interact with them. Also, certain needs appear with age, the need to conserve one's energy, to rest, to receive good care, at times to follow a diet.

Disproportionate and recurring reactions of the body

The body, like the sensibility which will be studied in the next chapter, reacts to its environment as well as to what happens within it (biochemical reactions...) These reactions allow the body to adapt continuously to internal and external reality and thus to preserve a certain balance.

Under specific conditions and with certain types of people, some reactions of the body can become disproportionate and recurring in nature. Included among the reactions specific to this pivotal centre are some psychosomatic phenomena (such as headaches, stomach ulcers, lumbago, allergies, lethargy, etc.), tyrannical drives (such as oral drives, sexual drives, destruction drives, death drives, etc.), some forms of uneasiness, emotional troubles, shame vis-à-vis the body of others (men and/or women), some forms of distancing oneself, movements of flight, or its reverse, irresistible attraction to certain persons, the apathy of some functions (loss of sleep, loss of appetite,...). These reactions can become chronic if the deep causes which provoke them are not worked on. In fact, at the root of these reactions one finds wounds linked to the body (acts of violence, affective deficiencies, suspicions, negation of one's identity, depreciation, contempt, mockery, the death of loved ones, etc.). These wounds have been registered in the body under the form of tensions and fears, they are awakened in circumstances which unconsciously recall the original circumstances when the body suffered. They are at the source of certain ways in which the body functions (cf. following paragraph).

The healing of psychological wounds is a matter for specific psychotherapeutic work, especially when they are related to the body.

Note : The symptoms used by the body to display a disorder of a psychological nature have a link with certain weaknesses of the physical system. There is "fertile terrain" for certain anxieties rather than others. It would also seem that there is a link, almost symbolic, between the type of psychological problem and the type of physical symptom. For instance, a sore back could be the indicator of a too heavy moral load.

The functionings of the body

The functionings of the body are directed at satisfying its needs. Four types can be identified:

Instinctive functioning

The most basic is instinctive functioning. It is a characteristic of the membership of humans in an animal world governed by instincts. The instinctive needs of the body seek immediate satisfaction, automatically and impulsively, without the support or control of the "I" or the deep conscience. The acts resulting from this functioning are not necessarily harmful to the being and its growth, but the absence of reflection and decision preceding the action is a loss in terms of freedom, conscious responsibility for one's actions and gestures, and therefore of humanization. This functioning is normal in children, it becomes abnormal in adults when it is an habitual mode of functioning.

Compensatory functioning

All of the characteristics found in instinctive functioning are included in the compensatory functioning of the body. However, as its name implies, this mode of functioning is compensating for an inner void. Here, it is not the simple satisfaction of a need which is at stake, but a compulsive search to fill an emptiness, an ill-being, *"a deep and long-standing non-happiness linked to a wound of non-existence"*.[25] There is either excess or inadequacy in the way needs are answered (bulimia, alcoholism, addiction to smoking, sexual craving, hypersomnia, activism ...). The immediate pleasure felt when an expressed need has been satisfied is not enough to suppress the underlying existential void. By developing the being and healing the latent painful past, this type of functioning can gradually be made to disappear.

Apathy of the body

While the two previously cited modes of functioning are powered, even dictated, by the needs of the body, the reverse can also happen. The body can lose some of its vitality or energy, and lose the use of some senses, the feeling of some needs. This is apathy of the body or its non-functioning. The cause can be ageing or illness, it can be psychological in origin (analgesia, deafness or blindness, sexual apathy, etc.). This non-life of the body, originating as it does in a psychological problem, requires proper help.

Normal functioning of the body

The human body normally functions peacefully. There is self-mastery in the ways used to answer its needs. Individuals take into account their physical needs and satisfy them appropriately and in moderation, without haste or greed. *"One acts according to one's human nature, not dominated by one's instincts"*.[26] For this type of functioning to become habitual and not result from voluntarism, the being must have acquired sufficient maturity and the "I" must take its place at the controls of the person, who then feels a great satisfaction in living so free and level-headed. The dignity of a human being also depends on the way the body functions.

[25] O.N. *"The Body and Its Functionings"*, p. 2, 1986.
[26] O.N. *Idem*, p. 3.

Managing the body

While taking care of one's body and managing one's strength is important and part of the physical well-being and health of the body, there is more to it than that. The management of the body is closely linked to one's final purpose: the fulfilment of the being in one's identity and "essential course of action". To manage one's body is to take the means to accomplish completely that for which one is made. People who are aware of this fact are deeply motivated to take care of their body on a daily basis and to treat it with care over the long term.

Healthy management of the body requires a good knowledge of it: its potential, its weaknesses, its limitations, its needs, its rhythms, its reactions, its symptoms, what regenerates it, what is harmful to it and wears it out prematurely, etc. It also calls for an awareness of one's chosen or imposed principles, the rules of life to be applied in this area, as well as the reason behind them. In truth, not all principles are constructive. Some have to do with what is fashionable, "what is being done by others" but are not necessarily suitable for oneself.

This management will be a matter of balance between what the body expends during work and activity, and its available strength. The latter can come from the original capital or be reconstituted through nourishment, sleep, physical exercise, relaxation, or a favourable lifestyle. The gradual exhaustion of the constitutional capital can be slowed down by a balanced management of one's resources and expenditures.

Heeding and recognizing the body's signals allows one to take it into account, notably when decisions are required for which it will have to supply the energy.

The place and role of the body
in the growth of persons

In the hierarchy of importance which has been established relative to the growth of persons, the body follows the being and the "I". It has to be subject to, and managed by the "I" for the fulfilment of the being. It precedes the sensibility because of its close link to the life of each individual.

Its principal role is to supply the energy which the being needs for the achievement of the person's "essential course of action".

It serves as a "control panel" for the "I", informing it on what is working (sensations of physical well-being, health...), and what is not (symptoms, uneasiness, illnesses...). It is a valuable contributor to conducting one's life with concern for the growth of one's being.

It also has a regulating influence on the "I", which is easily ambitious and lets itself get carried away by action. The body's limitations, which become more pronounced with age, constrain individuals to moderate their physical activity and can promote a turn to reflection and a certain degree of wisdom. A new scale of values comes into being and the body may have been its discreet but efficient instigator.

The body plays a role in the healing process. Like the sensibility, it has recorded everything which has affected the person. The tensions it has accumulated coupled with the energy at its disposal make this slow recovery possible. The former promotes an awareness of the injury, while the latter allows the purging of sufferings and releasing of tensions.

The sensibility

Description

The term sensibility is taken in the sense of a capacity to resonate, to be affected, to be emotional, to resonate and to react to physical and psychological stimuli. The sensibility is considered to be a pivotal centre of the personality. It is very close to the body, to be sure, but where the psychological lived experience (notably the affective) is especially present. This pivotal centre puts the "I" in relationship with the external world through the intermediary of the five senses. Through the sensations, it also links the "I" to the interior world, to the other pivotal centres of the person. The stimuli touching the senses or the sensations coming from the psyche (the being, the sensibility, the "I") and felt in the body, reach the brain through the nervous system, physical medium of the sensibility, comparable to a *"conductive fluid"* for these messages. As scientific discoveries of the last decades have confirmed, the nervous system acts somewhat like a *"tape recorder"*, keeping track of all the events of the subject's lifetime from the time of conception. The sensibility therefore plays a fundamental role in the process of self-knowledge because of its functions: to feel, to resonate, to transmit, record and reproduce messages.

The sensibility is present and reactive from the beginning of life. It is coloured with the individual's personality. On the one hand the potential of the sensibility differs from person to person, and on the other hand, the degree of this sensibility differs according to areas, for example it reacts more in the areas where the being aspires to live, as well as in the sectors where it is hampered in its development. The sensibility is also marked by the cultural context which awakens it by making it resonate to certain values, interest centres, persons or things (beauty, actions, nature, literature, altruism, money, science...). The sensibility is also influenced by the two affective registers: what it likes, what attracts it or gratifies it, and the reverse, what displeases it, offends it, wounds it, frustrates it or repulses it. Finally the sensibility is marked by the joys and sufferings of one's life, which generate reactions and biases that are favourable or unfavourable, depending on the imprint left by previous experience.

Two zones in the sensibility

Two zones can be distinguished in the sensibility based on the depth of what happens in this pivotal centre.

A superficial zone

This is a very epidermal superficial zone, outright reactive, at the very instant that the sensibility is affected. Such reactions are often ephemeral, unforeseeable and amplified as though the sensibility were acting as a resonance chamber of external or internal reality. The annoyances of life barely scratch this zone, at times causing relatively superficial wounds; the pleasures of life gratify it momentarily; the absence of turmoil or pleasure leaves it outwardly peaceful.

A deep zone

This is the deep zone of the sensibility, characterized by more stability. There, reactions are less primary, sensations being felt less superficially, more loaded with psychological content. It is a zone irradiated by the being, where one experiences peace, life, deep aspirations and all of the manifestations of the being. However, when a person is confronted with a harmful environment in which fundamental needs are not satisfied, or hardly so, a suffering or even a wound can be produced at this deep level of the sensibility and a defense mechanism sets in to protect the being.

Also at this level, pockets of suffering can be observed, often not conscious. These originate from past wounds, particularly those which have affected the fundamental aspiration of the being to exist, either in its totality or in some of its aspects. When those wounds are reopened, they generate great anxieties which are propagated throughout both the epidermal and deep sensibility. They hamper, sometimes even block, the actualization of the potentialities of the being.

These two zones of the sensibility include healthy parts, with adjusted reactions due to the absence of traumas, and wounded parts, which have become either hypersensitive or insensitive.

The states of the sensibility

Depending on the zone concerned (superficial or deep), depending also on the nature of what excites it (circumstances, people...) and what is affected (the healthy or wounded part), there are several states of the sensibility. Four categories can be identified :
– peaceful, harmonious, calm, adjusted...;
– excited, thrilled, euphoric, exalted, exuberant, irritated, angry, explosive, highly strung, boiling ...;
– painful, perturbed, torn, bruised, suffering ...;

– frozen, anaesthetized, paralyzed, indifferent, rigid, "armoured"...

These states of the sensibility will induce different reactions proper to this pivotal centre.[(*)]

As the person grows, the states of the sensibility undergo an evolution. It thaws out in sectors where it protected itself by being anaesthetized; it becomes peaceful, more harmonious and more adjusted where a wound was produced; it is revived and refined through the increasing openness of the person toward the exterior. In a sense, it becomes more permeable, more receptive, and therefore more vulnerable. At the same time, the growth of the being makes a person stronger and the development of the intellect helps to see things in perspective. Thus, progress in psychological maturity has a tendency to increase the accessibility of the sensibility to joys and sufferings. At the same time, however, one is less destabilized because of the greater stability of the being and the greater objectivity of the "I".

Note concerning a few concepts such as hypersensitivity, emotionalism, vulnerability, psychological fragility and insensitivity:

– Some people naturally have an extremely delicate sensibility which resonates intensely at almost anything. This type of sensibility can be found, for example, in artists. This form of very intense sensibility, linked to genetic makeup, must be distinguished from hypersensitivity which is the result of a heavy past of suffering and/or deficient defense systems which have not succeeded (or are not succeeding) in sufficiently protecting the individual from suffered assaults. It is very likely that this hypersensitivity develops most often in persons who are already very sensitive by nature.

– Emotionalism is a strong reaction of the sensibility, accompanied by physical manifestations (tears, perspiration, redness, palpitations, trembling, etc.). It is a natural phenomenon in people who have not repressed their sensibility and find themselves confronted by a stressful or unusual situation. Individuals with a very intense sensibility have a tendency to become more emotionally excited than others. If this emotionalism is excessive and uncontrollable, it may come from wounds that have been awakened by some present circumstances.

– Some people associate sensibility with fragility. In fact, to be sensitive assumes that one is open and receptive and can be reached. Thus vulnerability is the corollary to being sensitive. At times, this state of vulnerability leads the individual to employ a healthy

* Cf. p. 105.

defense system to avoid destructive suffering in a way which can be conscious and managed. This vulnerability is not in itself a sign of psychological fragility. It can in fact be accompanied by a basically solid personality, which actually makes the openness and receptivity possible. Vulnerability is a normal characteristic of human nature and of life in general. It participates as much in the riches of life as in its traumas.

However, the sensation of psychological fragility, on the other hand, is linked to its lack of possible support from the "rock of being". Individuals are lacking in self-confidence, destabilized, at the mercy of other people or events, incapable of facing up to things, insecure, anguished. While vulnerability entails a normal prudence, fragility favours hyperprotection because of the insecurity it generates. Only the humility to recognize and accept this fragility can get persons in touch with their truth again, thus regaining access to their stability.

– Hard-heartedness or insensitivity may appear to be peculiar to "strong" people, capable of imposing themselves on others, of facing difficulties without emotion and of enduring trials. In fact, it is a form of hyperprotection, a shell, which masks a basic fragility and/or a non-acceptance of one's vulnerability. In difficulties and trials, it is normal for the sensibility to be touched and for people to experience suffering.

The different types of reaction of the sensibility

The normal reactions of the sensibility

A reaction of the sensibility is said to be normal when what is felt and the reactions that follow are proportional to the scope of the triggering factor (circumstances, events, persons...). Thus, a happy event, awaited for a long time, provides an intense emotion. Conversely, an unjustified reproach, expressed aggressively, hurts a person, prompting indignation, protestation and explanations. These reactions are normal, in the sense that the cause and effect are proportional, a sign that the sensibility has been touched in a healthy, non-wounded part. In this category of normal reactions of the sensibility, one might include vigorous reactions (vivid protests, refusals, bursts of anger ...) linked to the fact that something essential was touched in the person, at the level of the being. The reaction is proportional to the value that this essential represents for the person. In that case, there is no feeling of a loss of self-control, but a strong self-affirmation.

Occasional disproportionate reactions

It can happen that the sensibility will sometimes react too quickly or not enough (moments of nervousness, depression, indifference...), whereas usually, in the same circumstances, it has had a well-adjusted reaction. These reactions do not have their roots in a wound of the sensibility. They can be the result of fatigue, a moment of greater vulnerability linked to circumstances, a health problem, a lack of vitality of the being, etc. It is wise to identify the exact cause in order to find a better mode of functioning.

Disproportionate and recurring reactions

These consist of reactions of the sensibility which are almost always triggered in specific situations, with specific persons or when facing specific events. They can be manifested in three ways :
– by explosion, anger (expressed or internal) aggressiveness, violence, euphoria, excitement, inordinate attraction or rejection...;
– by depression, dejection, sadness, melancholy, moral despondency, withdrawal into oneself, anguish...;
– by insensitivity, indifference, anaesthesia, coldness, apathy ...

The diagnosis of these reactions is not always easy to establish, especially when there are objective reasons, in the current circumstances, to feel pain (an injustice, a misunderstanding, a rejection, a suspicion, a dismissal, a bereavement ...), or when all the people around are reacting in a manner which is far out of proportion. Other than by its scope, one can pinpoint a disproportion by the abnormal duration of the reaction, by the range of the defense system put into place (flight, distancing, aggressiveness, hard-heartedness ...) so as to be no longer confronted with the triggering factor. One can also be alerted by the different reactions of others in the same circumstances.

Once the reaction is identified as being disproportionate, one can go back to the deep cause in the psyche by analysing the sensations experienced at the very moment of the reaction. In fact, observation of that phenomenon has made it possible to establish a psychological explanation. A disproportionate and recurring reaction appears every time the factor which triggers it is analogous to a past situation, event, or person that wounded the person experiencing the reaction. That is what gives it its recurring nature.

Failure to comprehend the deep causes of these phenomena often leads people to make moral judgements, accusing themselves or others of maliciousness, laziness, carelessness, heartlessness, etc., or else to project on the current situation the cause of the reaction. (For example: "I would not have reacted so violently if I had been addressed in a different tone of voice" or, "I am completely depressed because of the weather"). In need of an explanation for experiences they are not controlling, this is how human beings justify their behaviour.

This phenomenon of disproportionate and recurring reactions and their causes will be examined again in the chapter on the healing of past wounds.

The functionings of the sensibility

The sensibility can function in four different ways.

Well-adjusted or peaceful functioning

It can function normally, having reactions that are proportional to what stimulates it. There is no discordance between the internal or external stimulus and the response of the sensibility. The sensibility is usually calm, except in the case of stronger reactions which are justified by a particular circumstance (bereavement, dismissal, accident, or more commonly annoyance, loss of objects, relational difficulty ...). That is why we speak of well-adjusted or peaceful functioning. There is a sort of normal control of the sensibility through the life of the being and the "I", without any repression. The "I" can see things in perspective. It is not submerged, but rather in a position to analyse the sensations as they arise and to situate them in context. One is free and master of oneself. To be acceptably consistent, this type of functioning assumes that the being is sufficiently emerged, to balance the sometimes exaggerated reactions of the sensibility.

Sensitive functioning

Opposed to this well-adjusted functioning, there is "sensitive functioning" where one is carried away by one's sensibility and one's desires, impulses, repulsions, sufferings, fears, excitement. The sensibility dominates and leads the person, without the "I" being able to control it. This is the type of functioning which is manifested in the disproportionate reactions mentioned in the preceding paragraph and which becomes recurring when it originates in past sufferings. Sensitive functioning generates actions marked by impulsiveness, excesses, impatience, and sometimes filled with an intense emotional past. To succeed in reducing this mode of functioning, it is necessary to restore order in the ways of functioning of the pivotal centres of the personality. The being needs to grow and become stronger; the "I" must learn to assume its role of personal manager and control the person's reactions; the sensibility has to heal past wounds, and the body can help through relaxation.

Daydreaming or compensatory functioning

Daydreaming or compensatory functioning is similar to sensitive functioning due to the fact that the sensibility has taken over the primary role and dominates the person. It is also similar to imaginary[*] functioning. It has its own characteristics, however, which distinguish it from both of them. This mode of functioning can answer two needs :
– when the sensibility is hurting, day-dreaming is a way individuals choose to avoid suffering and take refuge in an imaginary world where everything happens for the better, as they would like reality to be. This way of functioning is a survival method which some people use when faced with great trials or a heavy painful past;
– this functioning can also be triggered by positive agitation of the sensibility. Day-dreaming thus makes people disconnect from reality by providing them with abundant pleasure. They build an imaginary world for themselves in which what they experience and what excites their sensibility is prolonged and intensified. All of their desires are fulfilled and they bask in happiness.

In both cases, day-dreaming compensates for a state of latent unhappiness. Although the search for happiness through day-dreaming is illusory, it will have a tendency to continue as long as the person has not found other modes of satisfaction in reality,

[*] Cf. p. 89.

and as long as the "I" has not opted to remain in reality and to resist the temptation to escape. That requires a sufficiently high level of motivation, for the sensibility, in losing its compensation, is faced with frustration and pain. Confronting them represents the only hope to one day heal from these underlying sufferings.

Apathy of the sensibility

Finally, the sensibility can cease to function, not feeling, not resonating, not reacting any more. It is the apathy of the sensibility or insensibility. This apathy can be the outcome of an education where the repression of sensations was valued as a strength and advocated as an efficient and virile mode of functioning. Some people have thus self-educated themselves to not "listen to themselves", to harden themselves so that they gradually have no more feelings. Apathy of the sensibility can also be found in individuals who have had to protect themselves from acute suffering. Dr. Janov in a chapter entitled *"Repression: the lock on the brain and the loss of sensibility"*[27] shows how the organism secretes endorphins with an analgesic effect when it is confronted with physical or unbearable moral pain. The healing of this apathy is possible but calls for a serious commitment by the individual and appropriate help.

Managing the sufferings of the sensibility

The way one reacts when suffering or experiencing turmoil is not without consequences for oneself, one's growth and one's associates and acquaintances.

The first reflex of someone faced with what makes them suffer, is avoidance. Human beings do not like to suffer. When suffering appears they instinctively seek to avoid it, reject it or suppress it. People all have their own register of primary reactions when the sensibility is thus hurting :

− some have rather introverted reactions: withdrawal into themselves, even shutting themselves off, self-accusation, hard-heartedness. They blame their temperament, their heredity, fate;

− some are more extroverted in their reactions, accusing others,

[27] *"The New Primal Scream"* pp. 48-66. Dr. Arthur Janov, Enterprise Publishing Inc. Wilmington, DE 19801, 1991.

assaulting them, reproaching them, seeking a guilty party other than themselves;
– still others break down, either letting themselves be submerged in their suffering or repressing it, ignoring it, anaesthetizing it.

These instinctive reactions are normal and understandable in the first instance, but they do not really disencumber the sensibility of suffering, since the latter has not been accepted. Often, these reflexes even weigh down the painful past with guilt for having had such a reaction.

A second phase is necessary to better manage one's turmoil, in other words, to limit its disadvantages to oneself and others. It is a matter, at the time, of accepting the fact that one is suffering, of consenting to the presence of that suffering within oneself, then analysing its contents in order to understand its origin. When the situation allows, the fact of letting the experienced sensation and its emotional content out in the open, helps to "evacuate" the suffering. The natural way to cleanse suffering is to let it come out, even if it requires crying about it, until it is appeased. Time then does the rest. When suffering originates in the past, an analysis of the current sensation provides the only access to the deeper sensations of the past, still alive and reactive but buried in the unconscious. Gradually, they reappear in the sensibility with their former intensity. They can be analysed and their emotional content can thus be evacuated.

In this management of suffering of the sensibility, the "I" plays an important role. It has the task of accepting the suffering and analysing its cause. It then must decide in concert with the being to react to the urges awakened by the turmoil in order to control the disharmonious reactions which arise.

The place and role of the sensibility in the growth of persons

The sensibility has many roles in the process of growth.

It intervenes at the level of self-knowledge because of its capacity to capture messages and transmit them to the "I", through live sensations that it can analyze. It is the path of access to the being, at the level of the deep zone, and more broadly, to reality.

The sensibility, through the satisfaction of the senses or the sensation of calmness, can be a path to plunge more deeply into the level of the being, where one experiences happiness and a deep peace.

It serves as systemic memory, as a data bank from which one can draw knowledge of forgotten or repressed elements. This role is indispensable to the process of healing. When the sensibility frees itself from tensions it has put away in pockets of suffering, a new lease on life washes over the person and energizes the being.

Through a reactive defense system, the sensibility protects the individual from the sensations of some sufferings, and the being from assaults. This is useful at the time wounds are suffered, but it handicaps the life of the being afterwards.

The more intense, adjusted and harmonious the sensibility, the more it fosters the objectivity and intelligence of the "I", giving it access to delicate and subtle perceptions or intuitions.

Because it is naturally vulnerable and receptive, the sensibility also plays a role in personal humanization. In this sense, it completes the rationality of the "I".

It coats the expression of potentialities of the being with its particular hue, whether artistic, affective, masculine or feminine, with its harmony, etc. It thus enters into the personalization process of the individual.

The sensibility itself develops with growth and healing, along with artistic and cultural education. It becomes refined and vibrates to new realities which before had left it more or less indifferent.

We have just seen that the sensibility, while it is not primary, as are the being and the deep conscience, occupies an important place in individuals and their growth. In many people, this locus needs to be adjusted. In fact, the sensibility can become a handicap to the conduct of one's life if it takes first place on a regular basis, imposing its reactions, its needs, even its requirements on the person (as is the case with sensitive functioning or day-dreaming). The person is thus subjugated only to pleasure and immediate gratification, to the emotional above all else. By giving priority to the sensibility in this way, people remain superficial, harming contact with the depth of themselves and their psychological maturation. A comparable reverse handicap exists if people allocate no place (or too little place) to their sensibility and its manifestations, in which case they impoverish their relationships with both themselves and the people around them. They become prisoners of their own protection, isolating themselves from internal as well as external reality. Their personality becomes rigid and hard.

Thus the sensibility intervenes in the overall growth of individuals, encouraging them but also handicapping them when it does not occupy its rightful place and/or when it is wounded and when it distorts or blocks the messages it receives.

The deep conscience

Before describing the deep conscience it is important to differentiate other types of conscience which persons develop as they advance through life.

Different types of conscience

The Socialized conscience

The concept of good and evil appears very early in life. Parents and teachers, as well as their surroundings, supply children with a foundation of moral values. From these, acts are judged as good or bad, permitted or forbidden, dangerous or safe. In a broad sense, children learn from these values to distinguish good from evil. The sum of these learned moral standards constitutes the person's socialized conscience. This conscience is characterized by the fact that it represents an external reference to self, acquired and legitimized by the good of the person and society.

When these rules are taught intelligently by persons who follow them themselves; when they do not present constraints that are too cumbersome for the expression of the life of one's being, their acquisition and integration within the child pose no problem. The child very quickly feels intuitively that such demands are well founded, especially if care has been taken to explain them, and the necessary delay is granted for apprenticeship in their application.

What often complicates the integration of these rules is their diversity, depending on group membership and surroundings. In the same family, the criteria that define good for one do not necessarily correspond to the criteria of another. Neither do the ethics of some business enterprises, or some scientific and political circles, always coincide with social, religious or family morality. These divergences generate internal conflicts. They foster a phenomenon of personality division, accompanied by inconsistent behavior, such as copycatting as circumstances dictate (going along with the crowd), or displaying a bland spirit of conventionality. Conversely, they can elicit counter-dependence and rebellion, leading to alienation.

On the other hand, rules that are consistent with the depth of self help people to relate to themselves and their environment. They contribute to the awakening of the deep conscience.

This moral heritage coming from others marks people for life and often conditions them. The socialized conscience pervades the "I" of the individual, even at the unconscious level, particularly if the social context is very prescriptive and moralizing.

Subjecting oneself to the demands of one's socialized conscience offers the security of feeling that one is operating within the accepted rules or standards. One has "a clear conscience" as long as one's idea of the expectations of others is met. Behind this search for security there is usually a fear of being unloved by someone or being excluded from a group. As a corollary, the transgression of laws dictated by the socialized conscience creates insecurity and/or a feeling of guilt which is psychologically more or less stressful. This guilt can only be removed through reparation, sanction or a return to accepted or legal ways; or else by a de-alienation from the judgement of others and by reference to one's own proper values, those which come from the being.

The socialized conscience is a characteristic of childhood. It is needed to compensate for the immaturity of children and to pro-tect them and those around them from any harmful consequences coming from their unconscious. It predominates as long as persons have not acquired their own proper reference points from experience and their deep conscience is not yet awakened. Persons thus lack sufficient autonomy to decide for themselves. In that sense, a society cannot do without the interiorization of these ethical references on the part of its members. When they are consistent with the deep conscience of individuals, these moral laws guarantee good social functioning. Their transgression leads to social disorder that can be serious.

In adults, the socialized conscience can become an impediment to their growth. This happens whenever it keeps them in dependence toward others and therefore in a form of non-existence. Moreover, this submission to the law of others often engenders a lack of self-respect. The aspirations of one's being are sacrificed to others; one can abdicate from common sense. One's sensibility and body are tyrannized to bend to the demands of others.

The cerebral conscience

Just as persons begin to acquire this faculty of thinking and deciding for themselves, another form of conscience is awakened. This is the adolescent stage. They now have their own ideas, reflections, experiences, ambitions and needs. They have also interiorized and ratified many of the social standards laid upon them - and rejected others. They set their own rules of conduct and their own principles. These become the good to which they wish to conform. In this way the cerebral conscience of the subject is formed. It is often coloured by reactions of counter-dependence toward the moral rules of childhood. This reference to principles chosen for oneself is a necessary phase in the passage from the socialized conscience to the deep conscience. It is a step toward the exercise of a greater inner freedom.

At the level of this cerebral conscience, the ideal of the "I" can occupy a significant place. Demands are then too great for the real capacities of the individual. The resulting failures or shortcomings leave behind feelings of disappointment, humiliation and bitterness toward oneself. One is faced with a feeling of self-guilt.

The deep conscience

When two conditions have been met, the third type of conscience, the deep conscience, starts to awaken in the innermost depths of the child. First, the mental faculties have become sufficiently mature to recognize the messages emerging from that deep zone; secondly, the being is vigorous enough to manifest itself and reveal what is in line with its fulfilment and what is opposed to it.

The deep conscience is distinguished from other types of conscience in that it is not the result of an elaboration of one's own "I", or anybody else's. It is not a "made up" law, but an internal law "received" and experienced as good for both oneself and others, and favourable to growth. The "I" is free to recognize or ignore this inner law, which is *"a reflection of our identity"*[28]. It promotes an inner freedom and a faithfulness to self, even when it derogates from the habits or rules of the surroundings. Other consciences have a tendency to stifle life, with principles to which one conforms often in a voluntaristic manner. *"Docility to the deep conscience makes one venture onto unknown paths, where one always feels alone before oneself, even though others might be travelling the same route. It is the fundamental solitude of persons who, being unique, find themselves committed on a unique path, with a unique law: that which is inscribed in their being"*[29].

Moreover, deviations vis-à-vis the deep conscience do not make the person feel guilty or condemned, as other types of conscience do. Such infidelities first of all incite a sense of responsibility, notably for wrongs done to others or to oneself. One regrets them, without however, falling into despair. The deep conscience provides the enlightenment needed to repair the consequences of these infidelities. It provides an awakening to greater clarity concerning one's limitations and weaknesses. It prompts one to pursue life with more integrity and realism. It commits the person to a dynamic of openness and progress. The socialized and cerebral consciences, on the other hand, tend to wrap one in anguish and guilt when there is a lapse. They often invite rebounding and self-justification rather than self-adjustment.

All three types of conscience coexist in the person. Because there may be discrepancies of maturity in different areas, one of them predominates, depending on the moment or the area of life concerned. Some areas generate an infantile attitude of social conformity, others provide an invitation to refer to one's cerebral

[28] O.N. *"Three Levels of Conscience"*, p. 4, 1996.
[29] Idem, p. 5.

conscience or to situate oneself in counter-dependence. Other areas, in which one is more unified and mature, call upon the level of the deep conscience. This coexistence is at the origin of intrapsychic conflicts and indecision. People seek instinctively to satisfy everyone around them, as well as all the pivotal centres of their own personality.

Persons wishing to follow their growth axis and know real freedom and inner unity, need a long apprenticeship in referring to the deep conscience in all areas of their life. This apprenticeship is the object of a specific pedagogy in PRH education.

Descriptive approach to the deep conscience

From the very beginning of PRH research, the concept of deep conscience appeared as being fundamental to the growth of persons and the exercise of their inner freedom. It was when the third diagram of the person was being developed[*] that it was differentiated explicitly from the being and given a place in the diagram of the person as a distinct pivotal centre of the personality. In that diagram the deep conscience is purposely located next to the being, attached to it, thus indicating its place in the innermost depths of the person and its particular relationship to one's being. Still, the deep conscience is different from the other pivotal centres of the person. It is not a reality in direct contact with what is external to the person. It has contact with the external environment only through the perception that the other pivotal centres have of it. On the other hand, it is a pivotal centre in direct contact with transcendental realities. Thus, for example, those who live a relationship with a Transcendency perceive its "messages" through the medium of their deep conscience.

The deep conscience is a pivotal centre which guides people in the conduct of their life and the pursuit of their complete fulfilment. It can be compared to the compass of a traveller, always available for consultation, to indicate the route to be taken. It is the internal centre of reference that assesses what is consonant with the being and its growth. *"The deep conscience is the voice of one's being in the process of growth. It expresses the aspirations of the*

[*] Cf p. 56.

being, what conforms to its welfare as well as the welfare of the whole person.[30] Just as the human voice is perceptible only when one is speaking, the deep conscience can only be grasped in its functioning, notably when one refers to it. It is a kind of law of life, of psychological health and growth, inscribed in the innermost depth of self. It is a unique law for each person since it is linked to one's identity, destiny and the reality of one's situation. *"It expresses itself by way of invitations to what we are destined to become in line with our basic identity"*.[31]

The deep conscience is not, therefore, an abstract moral reference which would dictate good and evil "as such". It does not distinguish between the licit and the illicit the way an internalized social ethic does. The deep conscience operates in direct contact with the inner lived experience (with one's desires, needs, aspirations, reactions, limitations and wounds ...). It is also connected to the current situation through what the person is experiencing. In this way it optimizes the perception of how best to conduct one's life in faithfulness to one's being and to one's overall harmony. It is a "locus of synthesis" for other pivotal centres in contact with a given situation. Hence the realism of this pivotal centre. It acts and reacts to what persons are experiencing and/or what is presented to them, guiding their decisions toward their "enhanced" being.

The deep conscience is different from a "superego", which would have a tendency to impose its principles and laws, making persons feel guilty if they did not comply. It demands nothing that the person cannot assume. It takes reality into account and receives the consent of all pivotal centres. This occurs even when its guidance destabilizes the ideals or the principles of the "I", frustrates certain desires of the sensibility or demands efforts of the body. That is why faith in one's deep conscience and acceptance of its dictates is always a path of growth and a true expression of the person's inner freedom. Choosing to decipher this internal law step by step, and submit to it, puts everybody in the best condition to become themselves.

Note : If the deep conscience is looked at as a reference to what is good for people and promotes their growth, would that not risk egocentricity, and even be paradoxical to

[30] O.N. *"Three Levels of Conscience"*, p. 3, 1996.
[31] Idem, p. 3.

altruistic morality or simply the common good?

Only that which is in harmony with the being is considered to be good for the overall person. This principle must never be ignored. How, in fact, could the good of persons be in total opposition to that which constitutes their most essential aspirations? Thus, as was said in the chapter on one's being, the social dimension is one of the major characteristics of what constitutes the essential of a person. The natural drive of one's being impels the person to become open to others, experiencing their values. In that way, the whole milieu is enriched by what persons are and what they do. The deep conscience makes the "I" hear the "voice of the being". Thus the "I" is called to actualize the potentialities of the being, and put one's gifts at the disposition of society. Personal good and the common good are thus paired. In other words, the good of others is included in the reference to that which is good for the person. As a corollary, that which destroys others cannot be good for the person. On the contrary, absolute self denial and exclusive centring on others, without taking one's personal good into account can be considered as dysfunctions (flight from self, search for admiration, fusion with another, unconscious compensation for deficiencies, guilt-ridden reparation, etc.). Such behaviour, although it may appear to be altruistic, is in fact egocentric, creating psychological dependencies and guilt in interpersonal relationships. The risk of egocentricity exists when the "I" centres on itself or on the needs of the sensibility and the body, without taking the being into account and thus without reference to the deep conscience. The deep conscience is a voice of wisdom which forgets no one, neither others nor oneself. It gives persons back their freedom by inciting them to assume their fair share of responsibility.

Reference to the deep conscience

The deep conscience can manifest itself in many circumstances: primarily when it is consulted in the course of a discernment; occasionally when an essential aspect of the person is concerned (for example: one's truth, honesty, life, faith, freedom or bonds with others ...). The deep conscience then sends "messages" to the "I" in the form of sensations, intuitions or even imperatives, impelling it to react for the good of the person or of others. It can manifest itself occasionally like this in a quasi reflexive and unforeseeable manner. It is always dependent, however, on the importance bestowed on it and the frequency with which it is consulted.

Reference to the deep conscience is generally a voluntary and conscious act of the "I", when the person has a decision or choice to make or a problem to solve. The process of conscience consultation that the "I" sets in motion can take two forms :

– a simple and quick pause: to choose an act to perform, or confirm whether or not a projected decision leaves the deep conscience in peace. This almost instantaneous consultation often takes the form of a question to one's conscience (for example: Do I say this or keep it to myself? How do I respond to this request? How can this free time be used? Do I make this purchase? etc.). Guidance then comes from the intuitions or from the favourable or unfavourable reactions of the deep conscience. If the decision or the projected action provokes uneasiness, the contemplated act, decision or project about to be undertaken is probably not totally good. This calls for further research, to discover the root of these uneasy feelings and, if possible, reach a more satisfactory decision. If, on the other hand, there is a feeling of peace at the level of the deep conscience, it is often the signal to decide and/or to act.

These pauses can come very frequently during the day. With time, they become a reflex to make decisions of lesser importance and perform everyday actions. *Thus discernment, which is linked to the instinct of being, is trained. Slowly, through experience and by trial and error, we achieve a reliability of judgement. At the same time an 'intelligent' spontaneity in the face of daily life is released in us*.[32]

– this consultation of the deep conscience can also take the form of a longer and more researched discernment, notably when the decision is important or there is a complex problem to solve. During the process of searching for the best possible decision, there is an interaction between the "I" and the deep conscience. A form of inner dialogue is established. The deep conscience needs the work of the intellect to be enlightened as best as possible on all the elements influencing the choice to make or the problem to solve. The "I" needs this reference to the conscience to make a sound decision.

In a first phase, the "I" is predominantly listening and deciphering the messages coming from the pivotal centres, which have been "invited", so to speak, to this "locus of synthesis". In fact, all the pivotal centres of the person react in times of choice or decision. At the level of the being, one can feel happiness, peace,

[32] O.N. *"Four Types of Decision"*, p. 2, 1996.

dynamism, evidence that one is on the right track. On the other hand, the feeling may be that one will not be able to be oneself or be truly fulfilled. At the level of the "I", one may sense that what is envisaged is reasonable, valid, adapted, realistic, feasible and/or affirming. Conversely, there can be doubts, reservations, questions, etc. At the level of the body, one's latent strength can be felt, available and proportionate to the action to take or, on the contrary, one can feel tired, weighed down, the premonition that there will not be enough energy ... At the level of the sensibility, there may be desire, attraction or on the contrary, repulsion; one may have a feeling of calm, well-being, excitement, or uneasiness, suffering, fear ...

During this initial phase, particularly if important decisions are at stake, it is always useful to consult someone with good judgement regarding the decision to be made. Their reactions, advice and suggestions complete the interior survey. This feedback can bring out overlooked elements. It can also help to provide awareness of more unconscious motives that may have slanted one's perception. Consultation can, at times, make one more comfortable with a decision that would be in accord with one's being, but that one would not otherwise dare take.

The "I" is now aware of the reactions of the different pivotal centres and has received the contribution of external advice. It has the important elements needed to make a decision. One must verify from time to time that nothing in one's field of awareness has been concealed. (New elements may appear, notably aspects of internal or external reality, which have been left unconsciously in the shadows. That can happen with something that the sensibility or the "I" would dearly like to have decided in favour of their own satisfaction.)

A second phase then begins. In face of all these internal and external influences, the "I" takes a step back and puts itself as much as it can in an attitude of free listening, available and impartial with respect to whatever the deep conscience may express. This conscious contact with internal and external reality, carried out as thoroughly as possible, enables this "locus of synthesis", the deep conscience, to express either the intuition or the unwavering certitude of a right decision. (The decision might be to delay a decision which, in the actual state of affairs, would be premature).

Once the right decision to make (sometimes, the least detrimental one) has sufficiently emerged into awareness, there remain three steps for the "I" :
– final verification that the decision is truly in agreement with one's being; (The result of the discernment can be submitted to others and their reactions compared to the intuitions of one's own deep conscience. This way of proceeding is indicated particularly for decisions that are heavy with consequences);
– the responsibility of making the decision, with docility toward the voice of the deep conscience; and
– its commitment to take concrete action on that decision. During the actualization phase of the decision, the "I" must continue to listen to, and be guided by, the deep conscience. This docility of the "I" must be present, even in the practical aspects of implementation. It is not rare, in fact, that new decisions need to be taken during this realization phase. This is when the "I" is often tempted to work out its own action strategy without referring to the deep conscience.

The inner freedom of the person is in direct proportion to the humility of the "I" with respect to this "Intelligence" which leads it. After the fact the "I" can verify the underlying consistency of the whole process. Thus, reference to the deep conscience does not proceed from a purely rational reflection which would dictate what must be done. Even if reason, embodied in the "I", has its word to say and is important to consider, by itself it remains insufficient and restrictive. The deep conscience calls for another logic, another deeper and broader source of coherence. In it, another wisdom is applied, where the intuitive part, founded notably on the "instinct of being" and on values related to a Transcendency, occupies an important place alongside rational and/or affective elements.

Dysfunctions of the "I" with regard to the deep conscience

In expressing itself, the deep conscience relies heavily on the functioning of the intellect, and the degree of knowledge the latter has acquired concerning one's interior lived experience and the different aspects of a given situation. Since the role of the "I" is so fundamental in deciding "with full knowledge", it is useful to note certain pitfalls which lie in wait for it, altering its reference to the deep conscience :

– It can fail to consult the deep conscience and leave the person at the mercy of dominating influences.

– It can flee from the deep conscience when it manifests itself, and turn to other "masters", such as principles, ambitions, ideals, desires of the sensibility or the body, expectations of others, all without seeking any further to see whether or not they contribute to the person's overall growth.

– It can make its conscience say what it would like to hear it say, and argue around its preferred decision.

– It can ab-normally justify certain actions disapproved by the deep conscience. A popular expression speaks of an "accommodating conscience".

– It can suppress shameful and disturbing motives.

– It can engage in a discernment with an already precise idea of the solution to be adopted, and pick up only the elements confirming it in the direction taken.

– It can elude any elements of the situation which do not lead in the direction of what it would like to decide.

– It can focus on an aspiration of the being which impels the person in one direction, without taking into account other aspects of one's being or constraints related to reality ...

Accepting the truth and reality of one's experience, with the help of a methodical analysis, is the only way to foil the numerous pitfalls or dysfunctions experienced by the "I" in its relationship with the deep conscience. The exercise of inner freedom presumes a type of asceticism: submission to truth as it is and not as one would want or imagine it to be. To live this inner freedom, grounded on the humble recognition of reality as it is, leaves the subject in profound peace, whereas to distort the truth leads to uneasiness.

It is to be noted, however, that intellectual rigour and honesty will never be able to convey reality in all of its complexity and content. They do not shelter one from errors of discernment. Some motives remain unconscious. Some elements of the situation can escape investigation. Events arise which modify the data. It is therefore wise to place one's discernments under the scrutiny of persons able to challenge elements which have been insufficiently considered. One must also have enough flexibility in the conduct of one's life to adjust or even review decisions whenever new elements appear. Life is in continuous change. Therefore, following one's deep conscience does not dispense a person from being vigilant, in order to verify whether a decision taken in conscience one day, with the knowledge on hand at that moment, still remains current.

Place and role of the deep conscience in the growth of persons and in the conduct of their lives

The deep conscience occupies a place as essential as that of the being in the approach persons take on their growth journey. This is due to the very fact that its fundamental role is to serve the fulfilment of the whole person, principally one's being, in its identity and its "essential course of action".

Its role can be summarized in a few key points :
– It is a pivotal centre constantly in action, available as much for appreciating small daily decisions or ordinary acts, as for important decisions which orient the life of persons and their actions.
– It takes into account and assembles into a synthesis the diverse internal and external realities of a person, as perceived by the "I".
– It reacts to decisions contemplated by the "I", to the expectations of others by expressing, in the form of sensations, its acceptance or rejection of the decisions or actions to come.

– It expresses intuitions of what is right to decide in accordance with one's being and compatible with the lived experience of each pivotal centre.

– It has an influence on the sensibility through the emission of a sensation of peace when there is agreement between it and the "I"; and a sensation of uneasiness when there is disagreement.

– Its role is subject to the reference it is given and the docility with which its invitations are received.

Chapter 3

Persons and their environment

The Human Environment

An individual is humanized and consequently becomes a person, only in contact with other human beings whose personality, and therefore their humanity, has emerged, and who live in a given society. This shows the importance of the human environment in the process of the personalization and growth of each person.

This environment is made up of all those who gravitate directly around the person: family members, neighbours, friends and work colleagues, the people and groups with whom one is engaged.

It also consists of the surrounding milieu: the social, cultural, ideological and religious setting where the values, rules of conduct, laws, beliefs, ideas about man, woman and children, human relations ... are found. This environment has its own history, its past, its locations ...

The determining importance of the political context also has to be underscored in this environment. The advantages available for becoming oneself are not the same, depending on whether one lives in a democratic country, a state ruled by law, or under the power of a dictatorial regime, not to mention a country at war.

The human surroundings in which individuals are immersed have a profound influence on their personality. They permeate mentalities, foster certain kinds of behaviour and prohibit others. They influence the way people deal with themselves, with others and with the world at large. The reverse is also true. Everybody has an influence on the people around them. This influence can be either helpful or harmful for growth. There is evidence to indicate that most human surroundings contain both helpful and harmful aspects, in varying degrees and at various times.

When they come into the world, children do not choose the human environment which surrounds them, hence their almost total dependence and great vulnerability. For this reason too, there is a need for awareness on the part of parents and teachers to develop their own human and relational qualities with the children. Later on, individuals are better able to exercise their freedom of choice with regard to the company they keep, so that the people around them also participate in their growth.

A favourable human context is composed of people who are reasonably mature, capable of awakening the best in others by their own human quality, capable also of satisfying primary psychological needs. These include the need to be recognized and loved, the need for freedom, the need for security. Such surroundings contribute to the expression of deep personal aspirations and foster their actualization. They are also characterized by the authenticity and the healthy vigour of their members. The latter are solid and free enough to express wisely what they feel and what can help others, even if it means disturbing them in their pseudo-stability. In this context, persons are impelled to exist and affirm their own personality, assured of being accepted as they are, understood in their inevitable flounderings or errors and constantly stimulated to advance. They are thus in a position to give the best of themselves and develop their inner freedom.

A harmful human milieu frustrates individuals in their needs and impedes them in their desire to exist as they are. This can be a too prescriptive milieu, too coercive or conversely, too permissive. It can be a hostile milieu, unsympathetic, unreassuring, pathological, judging negatively, making one feel guilty, egocentric, or simply indifferent, a milieu where deep values such as truth, justice, love, etc. are scorned.

Paradoxically, it can also be a context which is too gratifying or too protective, not allowing people to have access to their desires, depriving them of the initiative to decide how to manage them. In such an environment, individuals are restrained in their natural thrust of existence. Instinctively, they have a tendency to show only those aspects of themselves which are accepted in their circle and to repress the rest to such a point that they may no longer feel the desire to be themselves, unless they rebel by asserting themselves. These are the contexts in which psychological wounds appear.

The material environment

Individuals cannot be dissociated from the territory where they live. It conditions a significant portion of their existence and development. Just as for the human environment, the material environment acts on the process of individual growth, either to help it or to hinder it, even to thwart it.

This environment is made up of the objects or goods which belong to individuals, which are used for their subsistence, or which fill their world (their things, their apartment or house, their furniture, their decorations, their workplace ...). It is also made up of the larger framework in which they live (urban, rural, regional, national ...) and the economic situation. In an even broader sense, it also includes elements such as the climate, the seasons, the cosmos.

Everyone has personal needs pertaining to their material environment. These vary according to their age, their personality with its characteristics, its tastes as well as its wounds. They vary also according to the person's "essential course of action", social membership, state in life, culture, geographical location, etc. People can act on some elements of their direct environment in order to adapt them to their needs and humanize their lifestyle. They must conform, however, to the requirements of other intangible elements, such as the economic situation or the atmospheric conditions of the moment, for instance.

Examined from the specific point of view of the growth of individuals, the material environment has a double function. The first is to assure that one's vital physical needs are satisfied. Freed from preoccupation with their own survival, persons are more available to look after what happens within themselves. The second function of the environment is to contribute to a psychological well-being and even a blossoming of the personality by offering the material means and a frame of life suitable to the fulfilment of oneself and one's essential course of action. Forms, shapes, colors, sounds, flavours, odours, textures, the presence of elements of nature can all participate in energizing individuals and awakening their being.

Chapter 4

Relational and affective life

Human life proceeds from a relationship. It can only subsist through relationships. It can only develop in contact with affective relationships, that is, relationships in which it draws affection and warmth, where it encounters deep and positive sentiments of others in respect to oneself. Hence the fundamental link between life, growth and love; between life, growth and affective relationships. These relationships take various forms (companionship, friendship, blood ties, deep love ...) depending on the aspirations and needs of the people involved. There are different stages to these relationships, going from dependence to autonomy, stages during which difficulties will arise. Finally, the quality of the love experienced in such affective relationships gradually develops during one's growth journey, tending more and more toward unreservedness in the love that one gives, and openness to the love that one receives.

Defining affectivity and situating it in the diagram of the person in the process of growth*

– In the classical sense, affectivity represents the capacity to experience sentiments and emotions (Cf. *"Vocabulaire de la psychologie"* by Piéron). This concept is used in PRH psycho-pedagogy to designate the two inner drives: to love and to be loved.

(*) Cf. p. 56

– The entire personality is marked and colored by the presence and influence of one's affectivity. It therefore permeates the pivotal centres, each of which lives it or expresses it in a specific manner.

– It is at the level of the being that deep affective potentialities are imprinted (a capacity for love, tenderness, wonderment, communion, giving, generosity, faithfulness, altruism, compassion, forgiveness ...). It is there too, that the fundamental need to be loved is experienced, a need whose satisfaction or frustration greatly conditions the capacity to exist.

– Affectivity accompanies the functions of the "I". The intellect expresses affective life, for example, through the choice of tender words. Thoughts on love, and principles which impel to love are also recorded there. Freedom can choose or not choose to love and/or to open oneself to the love of others. The will also plays its role by mobilizing energy in the action of loving or being loved.

– The body constitutes one of the favoured means of expressing affectivity.

– The sensibility is most especially colored by the affective life of a person. It is at the level of this pivotal centre that all emotions are felt.

Different types of affective relationship

When people are able to differentiate among the various affective relationships they experience, they can see life clearly, avoid disillusions and put their personal relationships in proper perspective. Depending on the moment, one can go from one type of relationship to another (from a friendly relationship to a relationship of growth, for instance). Being conscious of these possible transitions makes a person more efficient and avoids foolish mistakes that can harm a relationship. The following are some types of relationship in which affectivity is present:

Companionship or casual relationships

These are simple relationships that take place on a daily basis, with colleagues, neighbours, sport or recreation partners, etc. A current of mutual understanding exists which is noticeably beneficial. They can provide some material mutual aid and solidarity.

This type of relationship does not have the depth of a friendship, since one is involved in it only superficially. These are cordial relationships, linked to circumstances: belonging to the same business firm, the same sport group, the same building ... They cease as soon as the circumstances or the needs of either partner change.

Friendship

These are relationships which are stronger and deeper than "companionship". (They are easily labelled as friendly because one really likes the persons or knows them well).

At least three criteria define a relationship of friendship :
– a suitable degree of affinity and harmony, with expressions of kindred spirit on values, ideas, commitments, shared tastes;
– in-depth communication, in which partners are personally involved, expressing their lived experience, their feelings, their thoughts;
– a reciprocity in the commitment at the communication level. Friendship is a relationship of equality.

As is the case for all affective relationships, a friendship evolves. In some cases it perpetuates itself and is reinforced, nourished by exchanges and a substantial affective content. In other cases, it breaks down due to personal changes, the appearance of important differences, geographical separation or sometimes simply because the partners no longer have profound sharing to nourish them. Some old friendships, seemingly latent, are easily revived when circumstances permit. The partners immediately find themselves back on the same wavelength.

Growth relationships

"In growth relationships I meet the other for my own good: to grow, to be healed, to become myself".[33] The initiative for the relationship begins with the need of the person making the request, who has to express the need as clearly as possible. This need may be to see clearly and to understand what one is going through at the moment, the need to disclose and appease a bothersome moral suffering, the need to share the aspirations of one's being and to be helped in actualizing them, the need to be heard, to be counselled, to be understood, to be supported, etc. These relationships are

[33] O.N. *"Some Affective Relationships"*. p. 1, 1983.

occasional, they last for the time it takes to satisfy the need. They assume that the person who is addressed accepts the request and can answer it effectively.

In this type of relationship, there is always an affective aspect. People are never indifferent to someone who listens attentively, with kindness and understanding, and who is interested in what is happening to them, especially when they have not experienced this type of relationship before. A relationship of growth is not a relationship of equality as in friendship, even if there is a strong mutual affective current. When the person in need of help has serious emotional deprivations, this current of affection can take on exaggerated forms, with attempts to monopolize, to appropriate, with a strong expectation that the other will fill what was missing in the past and which still hurts terribly in times of frustration.

Helping relationships

There is helping relationship when one answers a request to be heard or helped, whether or not that request is expressed explicitly, whether or not it is conscious. The helping relationship can take various forms, depending on the needs of the person who is asking for help and the context of the request. There is helping relationship, for instance, when one agrees to listen to the confidences of working colleagues, who expect advice or a reaction concerning their personal lives. There is helping relationship when one receives someone who explicitly expresses the need to be helped in solving a problem.

Educational and apprenticing relationships

An educational relationship exists when the initiative for the relationship starts with oneself. This relationship can exist without a request from the interested person (this is the case in the parent-child relationship, for instance). The apprenticing relationship however can also start from a request by the learner, (the case in which the apprentice solicits a contract with an apprentice master …). In both cases, a relationship with someone is established in order to educate them, to teach them what they do not yet know, to advise, correct, stimulate them in their growth. There is a sense of responsibility toward the learner. The extent of this responsibility varies depending on whether one is a parent, professor, occasional educator, apprentice master ...

Helping relationships have at least two points in common with educational and apprentice relationships. On the one hand, the objective is the growth of the other person, and on the other hand, both of these types of relationship involve an affective dimension on the part of the person who is helping if they are to be effective. To want to help and stimulate the growth of someone assumes that one has inner freedom, authenticity and real affection toward that person, based on deep understanding, faith in the other, gratuitous love, and respect for the other's freedom.

Relationships of being, bonds of being

These relationships have already been described in the study of the being, with regard to essential bonds[*]. A relationship of being takes form between two or more persons, starting from mutual recognition that a bond of being exists within each of the persons involved. This relationship is ordained to the actualization of a common "essential course of action". An affective portion is certainly present in this type of relationship, but the relationship of being which is involved here goes beyond the positive or negative affective impact. One feels bonded to another by the common commitment which was jointly recognized, and not primarily because of needs of an affective nature.

The most common examples of this bond of being and relationship of being can be found in the relationship of a couple or in the bonds of mission.

These relationships of being are particularly constructive and stimulating for action, but they also demand a high level of commitment to the relationship.

Blood relationships (blood ties)

One can have affective relationships with one's parents, brothers and sisters, children, grandparents, with all of the persons to whom one is related. At times, these blood ties can be coupled with relationships of being, with the characteristics mentioned in the preceding paragraph. Generally speaking, relationships of being are stronger than blood relationships. (One leaves one's family to take up life as a couple, for instance). Blood relationships root the person in a past and a human lineage.

[*] Cf. p. 59

At the root of relational and affective life: aspirations and needs

To understand what happens in the affective relationships just presented, how they are formed, what makes them last, what tests them, how they are undone, one has to go back to the source of relational life: the aspirations and needs of each person. It is in fact to fulfill aspirations (the aspiration to become oneself, to love, to create, to give ...), and to satisfy needs (the need to be loved, to be understood, to be encouraged ...) that affective relations are established and maintained. And it is when these aspirations and needs are no longer satisfied, or not sufficiently so, that tensions appear and relationships wither and die, unless changes are made.

Note : What is the difference between an aspiration and a need?

An aspiration comes from a potentiality of being which seeks actualization. It is an energy, contained in the positive realities of the being, which impels a person to action. For instance, the potentiality for gratuitous love, seeking realization and personification, turns an individual toward others without expecting anything in return. One can also speak of an aspiration to create, to direct, to serve, to enter into a relationship, etc.

A need is a manifestation of the body, the sensibility, the "I" or the being which demands or expects the necessities for a person's physical and psychological equilibrium (for instance, need for tenderness, for calm, for understanding, for recognition, etc.). The need is characterized by the expectation of a return. One approaches others to receive something which will satisfy the need one has. The approach to others is egocentric. Frustration is aroused if the others do not respond in the manner expected of them.

Two kinds of need can be distinguished :

– Normal needs which call for satisfaction, impelling the human being toward persons capable of answering them favourably. (For instance, among normal needs of the being, there are the need to be recognized, to be loved, need for security, for freedom ...). These needs exist throughout one's life. Up to a point, their frustration can be managed peacefully.

– "Deficiency" needs are needs which were normal at the start, but were emotionally deprived in the individual's past. They therefore arise from the manifestation of a normal need, exacerbated by frustrations resulting from shortfalls (lack of recognition, love, security ...). These "deficiency" needs are usually tyrannical in their quest for satisfaction. Any frustration is intolerable, awakening the suffering of the child in them who has missed something essential for themselves. These needs are insatiable and disproportionate. Only the healing of the psychological suffering which is at the root of these deficiencies can appease the excessive part of the need. This topic will be examined and developed in the chapter on the phenomenon of healing.

From dependence to autonomy

The relational and affective life of a person has a history of its own and undergoes an evolution which is characterized by several stages.

Fusion

Infants are born in total symbiosis with their mother. They cannot feel distinct from her. This state of complete fusion gradually fades, due mainly to the presence of the father, the experience of frustration, the acquisition of language and the physiological maturing of the children, who become able to use their intelligence and their mobility. This fused state leaves an indelible trace in the person, who will long remain torn between the wish to grow and the desire to regress to this state of contentment and security which characterize fusion, especially if life is unsatisfactory.

Sometimes in adolescence and even in adulthood, a person can experience a state of psychological fusion in an affective relationship. One does not exist. One is merged with the other, taking up the personality and modelling oneself on the wishes of that person. One erases oneself, becomes invisible, sacrifices oneself. For a while, this state can be pleasant. One finds benefits in it, living through the other, thus concealing a latent existential emptiness and not facing up to one's responsibilities. But this type of relationship is precarious. The awakening of the aspiration to exist in one party and the need in the other to be respected in one's freedom shakes the relationship. It brings to light conflicts which are often painful because, leading to this psychological fusion, there are deficiencies which have generated a more or less total non-existence.

The dependence of apprenticeship

This is a necessary form of dependence which prepares one for autonomy. In fact, before being able to take command of their life by themselves, children and adolescents go through a stage of apprenticeship of knowledge. During this period of acquisition they depend on parents and teachers for their knowledge and experience. The latter can be content just to dispense the necessary teaching, but they can also gradually bring younger people to find internal standards of their own, giving them confidence in their being and promoting their accession to autonomy. It will be more difficult to acquire if adults maintain the children in tutelage, not allowing them to experience things for themselves

Throughout their lifetime, human beings are in a dependence of apprenticeship toward those who have the knowledge they need.

Psychological dependence

Psychological dependence is manifested when individuals do not dare to be themselves in the presence of others. They are somehow constrained internally to respond favourably to the expectations of others, whether those expectations are real or assumed. A fear inhibits or paralyses them. (fear of judgement, fear of rejection, fear of disappointing, fear of punishment, fear of causing suffering, etc.). This is a stage which is often encountered in youth, a stage whose origin can be linked to young people themselves, who still need too much security and love to dare to set off on their own. The origin can also come from educators, too insecure themselves to accept that young people must make this necessary move and stand on their own two feet, without them.

Among adults, this psychological dependence persists when one has been very dependent in one's past and has not taken care of the growth of one's being. It is that growth which enables one to affirm oneself before others, which makes one sufficiently solid to exist in spite of the eventual reactions of others. The growth of the being frees one from alienation.

Counter-dependence

A characteristic of adolescence, this stage occurs when young people are sufficiently ready to make their own decisions, to affirm themselves with their own personalities, and to see the standards of the people around them in perspective. It is a stage where one assumes one's independence. Though they cannot acquire their autonomy completely, even if it were only materially, an aspiration impels them to no longer subordinate themselves to what they are told to do. They want to set their own limits. Not yet having a great deal of faith in themselves, they therefore use opposition and aggressiveness to position themselves and make themselves heard.

The intensity of this counter-dependence is proportional to the ambivalence in which the adolescents find themselves, torn as they are between wanting to be themselves and not wanting to cut off a relationship, to not displease. It is also proportional to the scope of the dependence they have experienced and the strength of the opposition to their autonomy offered by those who have been educating them. The intensity is sometimes violent when internal tensions are strong. It develops rather calmly when parents or educators encourage them to follow their deep intuitions and their conscience rather than conform to what is expected of them, and when these young people are themselves determined to affirm themselves in a way they feel is right.

In adulthood, some people go through stages of psychological adolescence in relationships where alienation still remains. These stages are painful, as much for the people around them as for the persons themselves. They often lead to estrangement, questioning, trying conflicts. This is a necessary passage on the route from psychological dependence to autonomy.

Autonomy

Autonomy is the capacity to exist freely, such as one is, and to decide in conscience what one has to do, while remaining open to others, to their opinions and advice, without alienating oneself to them. Fear of judgement, of rejection or feelings of guilt may still remain, but they are subsiding. The individual is no longer a slave to these inner drives as was the case in the psychological dependence stage. Persons no longer act according to others but have become capable of being close to others while retaining their own inner freedom. They know how to adjust to take others into account, while not denying themselves. In these relationships, real harmony is possible. Made up of profound esteem and unity, this harmony is far more satisfying than fusion. Harmony takes root in the freedom and profound existence of the persons, whereas fusion takes root in the non-existence of at least one of the two partners.

A certain autonomy is relatively easy to achieve when dealing with people with whom one is not very closely linked emotionally, or who are not close.

However, autonomy takes longer to acquire vis-à-vis significant others, that is, those who have been invested with power over oneself, whose approval is sought and whose disapproval or negative criticism one would like to avoid. With these people, one must seek further inside for the motivations which impel to be oneself rather than as others want one to be.

"The test of real autonomy is the capacity to be close to these people while remaining free".[34]

To love
(gratuitous love, possessive love, dutiful love)

At the core of one's being and affective life, there is the aspiration to love and the need to be loved. This term "to love" can be ambiguous, covering many different meanings. An observation of the actual experience underlying what we call love, makes it possible to differentiate at least three very specific cases: profound and gratuitous love, possessive love and dutiful love.

Profound and gratuitous love

This is a love which emanates from the inner depths of oneself in the presence of the qualities of being that one encounters in others, which assumes that one must go beyond appearances. An attraction and wonderment are then produced in the presence of the inner beauty of these persons. A sort of warm current, forceful yet serene, is awakened, accompanied by profound esteem and

[34] O.N. *"Others"* p. 2, 1990.

affection. Often at the same moment, two sentiments arise. There is a deep desire that these persons become fully what one intuits them to be, plus an inner proviso to respect their freedom so that they may live as they see fit and grow at the rhythm they feel is right for them. This respect for the freedom of others is not indifference toward them, nor an endorsement of everything they do. Love does not leave others in their dysfunctions without trying to help them get rid of them, but leaves them free to accept or reject this help.

It is a unique love since it is linked to the way one looks upon the being of the other. (Parents, holding this profound love with respect to each of their children, feel this love, different for each one).

This profound love is a gratuitous approach to others. There is no expectation of return. One is not frustrated if there is no reciprocity. If the love given is returned, it is beneficial, an aid to full existence, but there is no dependence on this exchange of love for one to exist and to love.

It is a "creative" love, in the sense that it brings to others a form of energy which promotes the growth of their potentialities. *"It allows others to exist freely, without denying anything of themselves. It allows them to follow the path of their own existence, without renouncing any of their aspirations, in the knowledge that they will be loved and even appreciated for affirming themselves this way"*[35].

In order to reach others, this profound sentiment of love must be expressed both verbally and non-verbally. Words which translate the sentiments one feels, tender gestures, a gaze in which others can perceive affection, esteem and admiration, time given, services rendered, attentions given, thoughtfulness, are all parts of this communication, which is as important for the giver as for the receiver. When it is done appropriately, without excitement, it is a source of growth for both parties. To love as profoundly and gratuitously as this, brings out the best in a person; to be loved with this quality of love brings confidence and encourages one also to give one's best.

The capacity to love gratuitously can appear very early in childhood. But, because of deficiencies in one's past, which generate contradictory behaviour, even giving rise to ambiguities, most of the time this profound love without expectation is more or less

[35] O.N. *"Different Kinds of Love"* p. 1, 1992.

mixed with possessive love. Affective relationships then tend to become complicated.

When individuals are sufficiently healed from their own affective deficiencies and have released their potential for profound love, this quality of love and gratuitous gift of self intensifies and is communicated more and more freely. Such people, not centred on themselves, with their profound heart left open to others, have an undeniable social influence. The relationships they create are clear, honest, warm, reassuring and energizing. These persons are humanizing influences wherever they go.

Possessive love

This is a form of love directed toward others, in which attention, esteem and affection may be manifested, but it is not gratuitous. If one loves, it is to receive. While the approach to others might have been gratuitous at the start, it is in fact egocentric, or becomes so. There is an expectation to be loved in return which generates frustration, suffering and even aggressive reactions if it is not satisfied. This is why love and hate alternate so often in affective relationships characterized by possessive love.

This form of love constitutes a normal stage in the affective development of children. In adults, possessive love originates in a wounded sensibility or else reflects affective immaturity. This possession of the love of others, which slips into the way they are approached, is generally symptomatic of the presence of deficiencies. When one has not received sufficient gratuitous love and recognition in the past, the aspects of self which have not been recognized or which have been rejected cannot be actualized. As we have seen, a gap has been created in the normal need.[*] There remains an unconscious expectation of being able to meet someone who will make up for this initial deficiency so that the aspects of oneself which were repressed, but which still aspire to live, can be actualized. When this meeting takes place the aspiration to exist is greatly awakened at the same time as the fear of not receiving or not receiving enough of what had been previously lacking. The expectation is excessive. Possession and domination are then manifested as reflexes of survival in order to keep the other, upon whom one depends to live.

[*] Cf. note p. 132.

These possessive drives which spoil deep and gratuitous love, disappear as the healing of sufferings of non-love and non-recognition take place. Even though possessive love is frequent and intense in a person, it is rare that one cannot detect expressions of gratuitous love in them. For instance, choosing to respect the freedom of the other when one has expectations from that person, is an act which makes real love grow and heals one's egocentricity.

Dutiful love

This form of love stems from a demand of the "I". *"It is more an act of the will than a heartfelt experience"*.[36] One wants to love because one believes one should do so. There is an implicit reference to a commandment which was internalized in the social conscience of the person, as a duty to fulfill: one must love one's parents, one must love one's children, one must love others, one must love one's enemies, one must serve others, one must forgive … The profound and warm affective surge which stems from the being is almost absent, which gives a cold tone to this love. There is no joy, no tenderness, no wonderment, no complicity as in profound love, and yet the gift of self is present, sometimes in an heroic manner.

In dutiful love, there is an unconscious expectation of recognition, the expectation of a return. It is not gratuitous. The common expression "after all I have done for you …" justifies the expectations that one has from those to whom one has given out of duty. Starting from a good intention, this form of love often proves to be blameworthy, even alienating, for those who receive it. They have a sort of debt to pay for the efforts lavished, for the constraints and trouble endured on their behalf.

It is a love which is neither deeply energizing for the one who gives nor for the one who receives it. It salves the conscience of the giver and is certainly not without advantages for the one who benefits from services rendered. But it deprives both of something essential: the warm, spontaneous and happy empathy of a heart that truly loves.

---

[36] O.N. *"Different Kinds of Love"* p. 1, 1992.

Sexual relations in affective life

Depending on the times and cultures, the conception of sexual relationships changes thoroughly and totally. For some, these relationships are the object of taboos, despised or even associated with moral misconduct, and thus blameworthy; conversely, in others, sexual relationships are lived without any moral reference, sometimes in an unbridled way. They are overvalued by some, considered commonplace by others, often removed, even dissociated from a deep affective relationship. For others, they correspond to a particular and preferred form of expression of their love. Still others choose not to have sexual relationships, and to express their affective life in other ways.

Beyond times and cultures, there are also the vicissitudes of a person's life, including the psychological consequences of some experiences.

All these ways of looking at and having sexual relationships are not neutral in the affective life of a person. Experience shows that a sexual relationship can have its real meaning only when it is at the heart of an affective relationship where gratuitous love dominates. It offers real fulfilment through the expression of that deep love, the shared pleasure and the resulting effects of oneness between individuals. The entire person and the relationship have thus grown in stature. A sexual relationship, experienced outside of this profound affective life, can certainly bring physical pleasure to the partners. However, it does not enrich the personality or the relationship with additional love and happiness, the latter remaining in an egocentric mode which is often not lasting.

It is to be noted that, if it corresponds to a life choice in harmony with one's being, the absence of sexual relationships is not in itself a handicap in the progression to affective maturity, nor is it an impediment to living life to the full.

Relational difficulties

Human relationships, particularly those with great affective content, have their more difficult moments, with interpersonal tensions. This is a normal and inevitable phenomenon, about which one must neither feel guilty, nor accuse others.

In fact, the development of individual relationships is brought on by a search to satisfy needs and aspirations. No one can satisfy others as much as they would like to be, nor at the very moment their needs are expressed. Every relationship therefore contains more or less uncomfortable moments of frustration, depending on the type of unsatisfied need or the strength of the thwarted aspiration.

All normally functioning human beings are equipped with a capacity to accept these interpersonal tensions, and the ability to understand the reasons which prevent others or themselves from being gratifying. They are also capable of seeking solutions to make the best of the discomfort or to alleviate it.

Egocentricity

Egocentricity is central to relational difficulties. While a harmonious relationship is established on a basis of openness to others and mutual exchanges, egocentricity somehow denies others, with their needs and aspirations. There is place only for oneself in relationships with others. Everything is lived in reference to oneself, in a constant search for one's own good, using the relationship with others and others themselves to satisfy one's needs. This egocentricity is harmful for relationships, because it is counter to the true source of life: gratuitous love. The love one takes from others will never be fulfilling. Only love which is received from a person whose freedom one has respected can be fulfilling.

The symptoms of this egocentricity can be found in drives such as possessiveness (the sensibility "hungers" for others and takes them over), domination (the "I" imposes its views and wishes on others), appropriation (the "I" establishes itself as the owner of others and uses them as it pleases) and also in imaginary functioning (everything is interpreted in reference to oneself and one's own needs).

To get out of the confinement stemming from egocentricity, a decentralization of self is necessary, accompanied by a choice of openness to others. In this way the person once again establishes a relationship with others and gradually becomes able to give and receive.

Fears

Another characteristic of relational difficulties is the presence of fears and their consequences: the phenomenon of distancing and power struggles.

When one has been subjected to basic deficiencies in relationships as vital as those with one's parents or significant others, the psyche is profoundly marked with suffering, even though, under the effect of repression, it now seems absent. This suffering leaves its trace: fear. In relationships which could be analogous to the initial and hurtful relational situation, the fear of others, of their judgement, rejection, incomprehension, indifference, violence ..., is awakened, generating a reflex of distancing. This fear appears in the form of either a withdrawal: one withdraws from the relationship; or by a show of aggressiveness: one enters in a power struggle, ultimately resulting in a dominated person and one who dominates. These power struggles, in which pressure is exercised on others so that they will think or behave as one would like them to, is a path of relational imbalance and causes new wounds. Problems cannot be resolved on a long-term basis with this type of functioning.

Interpersonal communication plays a key role in improving these potential sources of conflict. For dialogue to be established under good conditions, it is essential that the persons involved first come to see things in perspective and that their sensibilities be appeased. They can then engage in a dynamic of mutual comprehension instead of continuing in a fruitless exercise of confrontation. When people thus succeed in communicating, they have a better chance of reestablishing their relationship and often come out of it enhanced in stature.

The stages of growth toward affective maturity

Affective maturity is the result of a long growth journey, continuing to evolve throughout one's life, even after certain thresholds have been crossed.

– The first stage of this affective journey is characterized by the preeminence of the need to be loved. Receiving this love is vital for one's psychological development and more particularly for the emergence, in turn, of one's affective potentialities. The first experiences of gratuitous love can then appear, marking the end of this first stage.

– A second stage follows, in which the need to be loved and the aspiration to love coexist in the person. When one is loved, one becomes loving. Unloved or poorly loved, one has a more difficult time to continue feeling and expressing one's love for others. A deficiency need to be loved can already be present and, because of the egocentric expectation which it generates, hinder the actualization of the aspiration to love. The growth of the being, coupled with the healing of affective deficiencies, make a person evolve toward a threshold characterized by the emergence of the capacity to love everybody one meets. One's outlook on others then takes on a positive bias, where previously there was a tendency to be defensive. One no longer feels threatened by others.

– A third stage gradually appears, resulting from the disappearance of the unhealthy need to be loved and the growth of one's capacity for gratuitous love. The love experienced for others is no longer conditioned by self-gratification, but results from the unfolding of a profound gaze one has on the being of others and the ability to put in perspective what upsets the sensibility. One loves others because in one's inner depths, a source of love has been freed and asks only to be expressed to others. At this stage, the normal need to be loved remains but is no longer as vital for one's existence. A certain affective autonomy has been attained. The fact of feeling loved remains and will always remain an important energizing factor for the being and thus increasing self-fulfilment. But frustration of that need no longer handicaps the affirmation of self as it did before. Because of this, one can confront more unfavourable surroundings and exist there, whereas previously one did not dare exist other than in the presence of acquaintances by whom one felt recognized.

The means to promote affective growth

Affective growth is the result of both an internal maturity linked to the dynamism of growth of the being and the means which one takes to advance. Among the principal means that have a favourable influence on the acquisition of affective maturity are :
– associating with persons who love gratuitously, because in their company an awakening and a growth of being take place;
– training oneself to get in touch with the best of self, so as to feel one's love for others and become imbued with it, tasting the peaceful joy and freedom that come with this way of loving;
– expressing one's profound and gratuitous love, and taking concrete steps to demonstrate this deep surge of affection toward others;
– working to become aware of what one experiences in this area of affectivity and, when together with a loved one or a person by whom one expects to be loved, seeking to put into words what is happening in one's inner self;
– being attentive to the symptoms of wounds one has suffered, to gradually heal from these affective deficiencies, by evacuating the suffering which is still present from having been deprived of these signs of gratuitous love;
– listening to and deciphering the body signals which help to identify the affective lived experience (compensatory needs, etc.).

These means will be that more efficient if they are supported by inner attitudes such as :
– an openness to everything happening within oneself, whether it is pleasant or questions the image that one has of oneself;
– the search for truth as it is and not as one would like it to be, and the humble acceptance of that reality which one experiences, whether it is positive or negative;
– the determination to progress in order to develop the positive and to reduce the negative.

The place and role of relational
and affective life in the growth of persons

Human relationships, in which there are positive affective exchanges, have a key role in awakening, then constructing the personality. Otherwise, when there is no love shown and there is rejection or simply indifference, the negative impact of these relationships is a real handicap to harmonious growth.

During childhood and adolescence, it is especially under the gaze of significant others and the attitudes that they have, that one feels whether one is lovable or not, valuable or not, whether one's existence is a gift or a burden, whether one has the right to be oneself or not. In other words, the way one is seen by others constructs one's self-image. In this respect, the first relational experiences are very important, imprinting in the individual's psyche either confidence, security, well-being, or conversely, fear, insecurity, suspicion, guilt. Very quickly reflexes are formed giving way to free and authentic communication, to openness and supple existence, or to protection, to being closed to others and to non-existence.

Throughout one's life, affective relationships will either contribute to the advancement of the person or hamper it. They will never be neutral, even if their influence is less determining in adulthood than it was in the first years of life.

Chapter 5

The phenomenon of growth

The growth of persons occupies a very central place in PRH psycho-pedagogy: *"The growth of persons is the number one value of a human Society. We say the growth of persons, not simply the persons, is the number one value of a human Society."*[37] In fact, if the possibility of becoming oneself were cut off, would a person remain a "human person"? Could a Society whose members did not develop be "human"? The phenomenon of growth, common to all living species, takes on a particular character in the human being, who can cooperate in it. All psychological research and its application in the field of education pursue this objective of promoting and even "accelerating" growth. It is therefore important to define the concept of growth and to describe its mechanisms, its manifestations and the factors which foster it, as well as the obstacles and even the "impairments" on this path of growth.

The PRH concept of growth

Growth is the natural tendency toward the overall development of the individual personality. More specifically, it is the dynamic of the ever possible emergence of one's being, its awareness, its affirmation and its actualization.

The term "development" is used for the "I", the sensibility and the body; the term "growth" is preferred when speaking of the being and the person. Growth is considered to be a transformation, a

[37] O.N. *"How to Facilitate the Growth of Persons"*, p. 2, 1991.

progressive maturing of the person, a process of personalization, self-direction and openness. In a word, it is a process of human-ization and insertion into society. It brings individuals from a state of instinctivity, lack of differentiation, dependency and unaware-ness to their dimension as human beings which becomes more and more personalized, harmonious, and lived in self-awareness. They reach a state of being where, in their dealings with others and real-ities which transcend them, they are capable of exercising their free will and taking their life in hand.

The growth of individuals is not linear and constant, but dis-continuous, with progressions, stagnations, sometimes regres-sions. It goes on throughout the person's existence.

The phenomenon of growth and the five pivotal centres of the personality

The growth process concerns all of the pivotal centres of the person.

The being

First of all it concerns the being because, during the life of individuals, their original constituent potentialities undergo a considerable evolution making them conscious of their riches and limitations and enabling them to undertake more and more things. One could compare this mutation to the seed of a tree whose growth process allows the progressive development of the trunk, the branches, the leaves, then the fruit. Thus, the dynamism of growth of the being constantly impels the subject throughout its existence toward an "enhanced being", toward fulfilment.

The "I"

The "I" experiences a development of its intellectual and cognitive functions (learning of spoken language, reading, writing, calculating, development of memory, of the capability for analysis and comprehension, of reflection, reasoning and judgement, etc.); its decision-making functions (development of the capability to make distinctions and choices, etc.); and its volitional functions (development of the capability to strive, to manage one's energies, etc.).

The sensibility

At first, the sensibility is awakened to external and internal reality through the intermediary of the five senses. Then, a development is produced through the refining of the sensorial and perceptive capacities of the person. The latter picks up external and internal messages with more and more finesse and subtlety, allowing the faculties of intuition and knowledge to progress at the same time.

The Body

The body also has a potential for development: physical development in the early years, development of capacities such as suppleness, dexterity, strength, endurance, adaptability, relaxation, etc.

The deep conscience

As the "locus of synthesis" of the other pivotal centres and the "voice of the being in the process of growth", the deep conscience emerges as the growth of the being and the development of the "I", the sensibility and the body all take place. In order to best serve the fulfilment of the being and the conduct of a person's life, the deep conscience is dependent on the evolution of the pivotal centres of the personality. More particularly, it depends on the emergence of the being and the development by the "I" of its reference to this "locus of synthesis". The development of the action of the deep conscience and its manifestations, comes as a result of the maturing and harmonious functioning of a person.

The mechanism of growth

At the root of the mechanism of the overall growth of persons, lies the dynamism of growth of the being, felt internally as a fundamental aspiration to exist. A vital energy animates the potentialities of the being and impels the subject to actualize them. This dynamism of growth is inseparable from the phenomenon of existence.

In other words, the process of growth is rooted in the potential contained in the being of the person and in the actualizing force which inhabits this positive potential.

This dynamic, which presides over the growth of all living species, is a necessary but insufficient condition for the mechanism of growth to function harmoniously. Two other phenomena intervene :

– the fundamental role played by the functioning of the other pivotal centres of the person (the "I", the body and the sensibility). Growth, defined as a natural trend in the overall development of an individual's personality, requires the participation of the three functions of the "I": the intellect, to bring into awareness the aspirations and the potentialities of the being and to conceive their actualization; the freedom, to adhere to this internal dynamic of the being and to cooperate in it; and the will, to put this potential of riches into action. The mechanism of growth also requires the participation of the body's energy, along with good reception and true transmission of the messages put out by the sensibility;

– the important and at times decisive role of the human and material environment. Experience shows that the surroundings count a lot when it comes to helping individuals to exist according to their being, chiefly in the initial phase of the emergence of the latter. A minimum of material conditions is also necessary, on the one hand, for the person to be no longer polarized by the vital needs of the body, and on the other, to promote the life of the being (vitalization through nature and the arrangement of one's living space; physical well-being through a minimum of comfort ...).

Thus, the mechanism of growth results from the interaction of three factors :

– the dynamism of the growth of the being;

– the capacity of the "I" to be aware of this dynamism of life, to accept it and to actualize this potential with the energy supplied by the body, the adjusted functioning of the sensibility; and finally,

– a favorable environment.

This assumes that, at the same time as natural potentialities of the being emerge, individuals :

– surround themselves with a stimulating milieu for their being;

– put order in the functioning of the pivotal centres of their personality. In fact, the latter are spontaneously inclined to satisfy their own needs, in the best and quickest way possible, without necessarily preoccupying themselves as to whether this satisfaction is in harmony with the being and its growth. Often, reeducation turns out to be indispensable, for few people have learned to function normally, that is in reference to their being;
– heal the wounds which hamper the actualization of their being.

We thus have the three axes of the personal growth mechanism:
– blossoming of potentialities, resulting from their coming into awareness, their actualization, and the way they are received and taken into account by the surrounding people;
– healing of past traumas which alter the expression of the life of the being and interfere with the various ways the other pivotal centres of the person function;
– order in the way one functions so that the actions taken go in the direction of the growth and fulfilment of the person.

To progress along these three axes, personal commitment is paramount.

The manifestations of growth in individuals and in their lives

How can we recognize that persons are changing, particularly in the growth of their being? We have been able to observe many tangible signs of this growth, both in the inner lived experience of people and in their behaviour. Some examples follow.

Growth manifested by the very sensation of growing and the happiness derived from it

Depending on the time of life, the sensation of growing is more or less perceptible. Most of the time the growth one experiences is measured only after the fact. Individuals observe that they have changed in comparison with their past. However, there are periods of strong emergence of the being, where the sensation of progress is significant. These are very rich periods in awareness, in adjustment to the ways one functions, in the actualization of one's capabilities and in creativity. They propel the person forward. These moments can give way to latent periods, which often times occur when previous growth sequences are integrated, and when inner maturing in preparation for a new step of development takes place. Conversely, individuals can also experience the sensation of regressing, with the reappearance of dysfunctions from which they thought they had been freed. In particular, this is the case when the need of a pivotal centre has not been taken into account sufficiently (a need for physical rest, an affective need, a need to stimulate the being …), or when past sufferings have been awakened.

The sensation of growing and progressing is accompanied by a sensation of happiness, of being truly alive. Becoming oneself certainly provides one of the most satisfying forms of happiness that a human being can experience.

Note : This subjective and occasional perception of the sensation of growth is not to be idealized when all goes for the better, nor dramatized when one falls once again into old ruts or stagnates. It should be decoded with intelligence and integrated more as a whole in the history of the long process of growth of the person. Outside witnesses, such as a growth accompanist-educator or a counselor in helping relations, can be a valuable help for this overview and the succession of "highs" and "lows" inherent in all human growth. They help one to remain realistic, not giving way to discouragement in face of the slowness with which the capacity to exist emerges or the time it takes to resolve some dysfunctions.

Growth manifested through increased awareness

The phenomenon of growth finds expression in a developing knowledge of oneself and of external reality, knowledge which is gradually acquired through experience. The person's field of awareness is modified, broadened, enriched, deepened. One becomes more lucid. Some psychological sensations are more distinct, more precise, more condensed, stronger, richer in content. Delicate sensations are perceived more frequently. Thanks to the experience and analysis of sensations, what was an inkling becomes a certitude, habitual at first, then unwavering. One develops the self-confidence and self-assurance to affirm one's riches and limitations.

Growth manifested through a new relationship to reality

Starting from their own experience and from what they have seen in others, in events, and in their environment, individuals form their own representation of reality. This experience, especially that from early childhood, leaves traces felt as positive or negative in their relation to this reality. These people may have reacted to painful aspects of reality by using mechanisms which have altered their relation to reality even further (mechanisms of flight, refusal, doubt, the "fixing" of reality to suit themselves, or by exaggerating certain aspects of it, by minimizing or even hiding other unbearable aspects, etc.).

The growth of persons is expressed by a healthier and more adjusted relationship to reality, which is perceived, received and accepted much more as it is. Little by little, one lets go of the power that one has tried to exercise over this reality to make it what one would like it to be. An attitude of healthy humility (understood here as an acceptance of reality) is developed. One becomes free to adapt one's behavior or make choices, to no longer put up with reality but to become allied with it, in both its pleasant and frustrating aspects.

Growth manifested through the development of capabilities of action and commitment

Growth in both self-knowledge and self-confidence causes changes to one's essential course of action. This growth is manifested through actions which are more efficient, more fruitful and more in harmony with one's being. This is the case even for recurrent, necessary or compulsory actions. People see a sense of responsibility developing in what they are and what they do. From this a strong commitment grows. They become more enterprising and more creative in the axis of their "essential course of action". Their profound aspirations, instead of remaining short-lived wishes, are concretely materialized. They become more and more capable of assuming the existential solitude which is inherent in everyone.

Growth manifested through progression in autonomy with regard to others and through improved relationships with them

The human growth process is measured by the development of

one's capacity to relate to others as an autonomous, unique and therefore different person. Individuals become able to exist in face of the people around them in faithfulness to their deep conscience rather than in conformity to what is expected of them. Moreover, this internal freedom brings an openness to others, an attention to them, to their aspirations and needs, as well as a deeper understanding of their experiences.

The outlook one has on others changes. One becomes more tolerant, more receptive, less judgmental. One recognizes, to some extent, that one is concerned with the successful life of others and that one is equipped with gifts likely to serve that cause. The growth process of an individual manifests itself through this passage from the exclusive preoccupation with one's personal good, to a decentralization of self. What follows is the development of a perception of the collective dimension and a search for the common good which is in the best possible harmony with the good of each person.

Growth manifested through increased openness to a Transcendency

As we have seen[*], with progress, people become aware that they will not find in either themselves or in arts or sciences a satisfactory answer to the questions they ask, notably on the subject of the meaning of their existence, death, or the reason for certain events. They discover another facet of reality which is irrational, invisible, metaphysical, but nonetheless a part of their own life. The limited universe of their own individuality, as well as visible rational and objective reality, are no longer enough for them. Observation has shown that some people experience an openness to a Transcendency very early in childhood. This openness is amplified during the course of their life, with an increasing interest in a quest for the Absolute, which leads them further. One then discovers an interaction between personality growth and a developing relationship to a Transcendency.

Negative or difficult religious experiences can hamper this openness.

[*] Cf. p. 60.

The paths of a growth journey

A person's growth journey can be considered to follow three main paths. These are the solidity of the being, affective maturity and docility of the "I" to the deep conscience. *"The personal growth journey is accomplished through a simultaneous and converging progression on these three paths".*

Several stages mark out the journey along each pathway.

The solidity of the being

This path relates to the growth of the "rock of being" and the freeing of its alienations. Individuals feel more and more solid foundations being developed within themselves, upon which they can rely to conduct their life and put a proper perspective on events, others and turmoil in their own sensibility. More confident in themselves, these people gradually develop the capacity to hold their own in life and in front of others.

We have identified three stages in the progress along this pathway :
– the stage of almost total alienation to others, to influences of the sensibility, to ambitions of the "I". Not having established their own references, individuals lead their life and make their decisions by conforming to the people around them, the cravings of their sensibility and the aims or principles of their "I";
– the stage when reference to one's own habitual and unwavering certitudes starts. An internal solidity appears with the emergence of the "rock of being". Now more solidly based, individuals are less subjected to the pressure of events, others and their own drives. They start to affirm themselves as a subject and to make free choices;
– the stage of inner freedom and solidity. At this stage, inner references and the deep conscience have been sufficiently experienced and brought into awareness so that individuals can feel their strength and solidity, making them more autonomous in relation to others and masters of themselves.

The path of affective maturity

This is the path of growth of unconditional love, that love for others which emanates from the inner self. As a consequence, it is the path of healing of an unhealthy need to be loved, which makes one egocentric, selfish and dependent, aggressive, distant or non-existent.

Three stages mark this path :

– because their need to be loved is very strong, individuals practice possessive love. When they happen to give, it is not gratuitously, they expect a return and experience painful frustration when nothing comes to pass. When they are not appreciated, they suffer a lot;

– individuals begin to be able to perform acts of gratuitous love. They are progressively decentralized from themselves, opening up to the reality of others, to their needs and welfare. They learn to accept more easily the inevitable affective frustrations;

– the unhealthy need to be loved has disappeared. Individuals are able to accept that someone might hold negative feelings toward them. Their sensibility is not indifferent to these sentiments, especially when the relationship has a high emotional content, but this no longer conditions their own affective investment. The normal need to be loved remains, helping to promote growth and bring happiness. Unconditional and universal love develops.

The path of docility to the deep conscience

The "I" can have many "masters": duty, outward appearances, perfectionism, power, assets, knowledge, the recognition of others, etc. The path of docility to the deep conscience corresponds to the choice of the "I" to make the fulfilment of the being its very first preoccupation, progressively abandoning its own projects and/or enslavements. To attain this docility, the "I" must be attentive to the being and its aspirations, decode its messages, submit to the invitations of the being and finally, activate those things that are conducive to what is good for the being and the overall person.

We have noted four stages in this itinerary of growth in docility :

– the "I" pays no attention to the being. It lets itself be led by other "masters", or just "does its own thing". It is obedient to others, to its own principles, to conventions, etc., but not to the being, of whose very existence it is sometimes totally unaware;

– the "I" begins to pay attention to this deep zone, either spontaneously or under the impulse of a manifestation of the being (reflex of being, event of being, imperative of being ...). It perceives aspirations coming from the being which do not leave it indifferent. At certain times, this life of the being influences its important decisions;

– the "I" starts to become faithful to the being, experiencing the profound satisfaction of making important decisions in keeping with the deep conscience. The "I" willingly gives up its views, ambitions and projects, or its sensory gratifications, to move in the direction of invitations from the being;

– as fidelity mounts, thanks to choices it makes, the "I" gradually reaches a state of spontaneous docility to the being and its proposals. Fully and without resistance, it takes its place to serve the fulfilment of the being and the person.

Simultaneous progression on these three pathways leads to maturity and a harmonization of one's personality. The person becomes unified. This journey of growth, reconstruction and orderliness liberates energy, allowing individuals to invest fully in their "essential course of action".

Growth factors (means and attitudes)

As we have seen in the paragraph on the "mechanism of growth", the phenomenon of growth results from the conjugation of at least three main factors: a natural occurrence, linked to the dynamism of growth inscribed in the being; the functioning of the other pivotal centres serving the fulfilment of the being; and the collaboration of an environment. This amounts to saying that, in large measure, growth is a process which takes place naturally, so long as it is not contradicted or thwarted by individuals themselves or the people around them; but growth can also be consciously accompanied and even promoted through a way of living and being, derived from choices and attitudes. The nature of human beings is the power to use their freedom in order to contribute to their own growth, therefore to their own humanization.

When botanists observe what is most conducive to plant

growth, they observe, among other things, not only the role of factors such as light, humidity, temperature, humus …, the role of genetic factors, but also the role of the gardener. They also note that "hardships", such as cold, dryness and wind, can help to reinforce the resistance of the plant, on the condition however, that these "hardships" do not surpass a certain threshold, etc. From their observations, they can derive the laws of growth of vegetation.

It is the same thing in the field of psychology. By observing human beings one can isolate constant factors which promote their growth. There are two different and complementary types of these factors. There are, on the one hand, means to take in order to progress, and on the other, certain inner attitudes to develop in order to facilitate this growth and conform to the changes which that implies. The means refer to the "how to" become oneself and grow and the attitudes refer to the "how to be" in order to journey toward one's fulfilment. Even though attention may have to be concentrated primarily on a specific means or attitude at certain stages of the journey, these means and attitudes are to be used together. They constitute a sort of personal "control panel", allowing a quicker diagnosis of where certain stagnations in the journey can originate, therefore making the management of one's growth more efficient.

Six means for progressing

The following means can be used to collaborate in the construction of one's personality :

— *Having life-giving relationships*

As we have seen, people have no direct power over the growth process of their being.[*] However, they can exercise their intellect, their freedom and their will to create a human and material environment for themselves which stimulates the life of their being and the actualization of their potentialities. Because it is a priority for growth, this means is recommended. *"Life-giving relationships are the bread of growth"*[38]. In other words, they are essential "nourishment" for those who wish to grow.

[*] Cf. p. 64.
[38] FPM *"Growth Guide"*, p. 14, 1994.

— Living and acting in harmony with one's being

One's personality structure and harmonious evolution are certainly dependent on the original genetic makeup and the socio-cultural environment in which one is immersed. But they also depend on the way one lives, makes decisions and performs one's daily actions. The decisions and actions one takes are never neutral with respect to the process of growth: either they allow the being to affirm itself, to become consolidated, so that one becomes more and more oneself, or they hamper the being, distorting the personality or reinforcing distortions already acquired.

— Becoming deeply impregnated by the important realities of the being

Everyday life does not lend itself to frequent contact with the inner self, to refocus oneself on it, "steep" in it, find new strength in it and become one with it. Life has a tendency to externalize people, depersonalizing them in favor of gregarious behaviour.

This third means emphasizes conscious contact with one's being and becoming impregnated with what is constitutive of self at that level: one's identity, one's "essential course of action", one's "bonds of being", one's relationship to transcendent realities, one's life's motivations. This is an in-depth movement of interiorization to get in touch with the live sensations of those aspects of self or those realities.

— Healing from past sufferings

Driven to exist, people sometimes come up against internal resistance, fears, doubts or mental blocks. Such personal hindrances to the natural movement to actualize the potentialities of one's being indicate the presence of wounds from which it is important to heal.

— Knowing oneself through analysis of one's lived experience

Personal growth does not occur without progress in self-knowledge. In fact, it is self-knowledge which makes individuals progressively pass from an original state of total unawareness, lack of differentiation and dependence on one's instincts, to a state of maturity, characterized by self-awareness, clear-mindedness on the motivations for the actions taken, and the conscious exercise of one's freedom ...

Because of the primary role past experience plays in the growth of persons, in the development of their freedom and their personalization, the tool of analysis is of paramount importance in PRH psycho-pedagogy.[*]

— Living according to the wisdom of one's body

From one point of view, the body can be considered as a "sage" who knows and delivers messages the intellect can only perceive through its intermediary. To achieve harmonious progress, one must listen attentively to its messages.

Five fundamental attitudes for progress

Implementing the means described above greatly facilitates the growth of the being and the overall person. But growth can be made even easier if at the same time the person develops certain interior attitudes. These are ways of being and working on oneself which are particularly favourable to self-knowledge and the mobilization of one's energies in the direction of one's evolution. Thanks to these inner dispositions, one progresses more quickly and is led further and more firmly on one's growth and healing journey. Here is an explanation of these five fundamental attitudes, with a commentary for each:

— The will to know oneself

This attitude is basic to every growth journey since there can be no growth, as we understand the term, without development of self-awareness. The will to know oneself involves first of all, deciding to know oneself, and then actualizing this will through action, notably by setting up means which will enable this knowledge to take place (for example, "to shed light on oneself through analysis" by putting one's analyses down in writing). This is an attitude of the "I" which calls upon both free and voluntary functioning.

— An openness to inner reality

To know oneself truly, one cannot avoid direct self-observation and a methodical analysis of what one lives internally and the

* Cf. p. 48-49

behaviour which ensues. For a person to realize this self-discovery, the "I" must open up to the inner world with the sensations, emotions, desires, resistances, sentiments, thoughts and fantasies, which inhabit it. The breadth of this openness of the intellect can vary. It can be selective, letting only certain "inoffensive" sensations filter into awareness. It can close itself to certain unknown realities believed to be destabilizing and a source of doubt or even suffering.

– A taste for truth about oneself
Persons who want to know themselves and get to their inner reality will discover truths about themselves that will modify their field of consciousness. This might consequently lead them to more or less important changes in their way of living, of perceiving themselves, of existing with others ..., which could at times be uncomfortable. There are many ways that the "I" can react to this awareness of truth about oneself :
– at the level of the being, it can concur with this inner taste for being true and recognizing reality such as it is, even though it might not suit the individual and might perturb the sensibility;
– the "I" can also dodge this reality, for example: by seeking to justify it, by minimizing it, by overvaluing it, by censuring it, by looking at it only superficially, by leaving it vague in order to eliminate or dilute any of its disturbing aspects.

For it to be healthy and solid in its foundations, the personality must be constructed starting from the honesty of the intellect with respect to the reality experienced by the person. The taste for truth is the driving force behind self knowledge, turning the person into a researcher.

– Humility with respect to oneself and before others
One can recognize that reality is just as one discovers it to be (attitude of truth about oneself), but not accept the fact. The attitude of humility in face of oneself consists in progressively letting go of what one would like one's life to be, or to have been, and accepting the truth as it is, or was. This attitude of humility applies just as much to the acceptance of one's riches of being, as to the acceptance of one's wounds and their consequences, or the

acceptance of one's past or one's current stage of progress.

This attitude of humility before others consists in showing oneself to others such as one is, with one's riches, weaknesses and limitations, accepting things as they are at the moment, without locking into this image or letting oneself be locked into it. This attitude toward others is made up of authenticity, simplicity and congruency, not seeking to present an image other than what one is really living. This does not mean that one has to divulge everything about oneself to just anybody. It is only good sense to reveal only those aspects of oneself that one feels in good conscience have to be revealed.

Personal growth speeds up considerably when progress is made in practising this attitude. In fact, *"A paradox exists: no change is possible without first accepting the present situation"*. Humility frees one from waging an internal combat against some aspects of self. It opens the door to self-reconciliation and a quality of existence where nothing is denied, where all one's inner lived experience has a right to exist, where one can exist in public simply as one is, freely.

– The determination to progress

This attitude is characterized by a very fundamental motivation: the desire to live, to be oneself, ever more oneself. While the will to know oneself is a phenomenon linked to the "I", the determination to progress begins at the level of the being and the dynamism of growth therein. It is an irresistible force which pushes forth toward a blossoming of self, toward an "enhanced being". This force overcomes resistance, shatters fate and brings about important changes in the course of one's journey. Without the emergence of this attitude, in order to grow and change the person is condemned to voluntaristic efforts which are often exhausting. The emergence of the determination to progress gives individuals the sensation of an inner "motor" which constantly spurs them on in every way they can advance.

Obstacles to growth

Having covered what fosters the growth of persons, let us look at what hampers it. Two types of obstacles can thwart the natural movement of growth in persons, one external and the other internal to the person.

Obstacles linked to external factors

The thrust of growth can be inhibited, even arrested, by surroundings that are harmful, disapproving, expecting a lot from the person, perfectionist or conversely, not stimulating enough, etc. It can also be affected by difficult life conditions such as malnutrition, noise, overwork, unemployment, promiscuity ..., for example. In these conditions, energies are channelled more to face difficulties and survive, rather than to self improvement.

Obstacles linked to internal factors

These can be numerous and often escape the awareness of those who experience them. Most of the time they are the expression of dysfunctions in one of the pivotal centres of the personality. This is especially true of the "I", because of its particular role in the growth process.

Among these internal obstacles, the self-image to which one holds, because it has become familiar, is certainly very important. One has organized one's existence in coherence with it, and most often it is the starting point for one's decision-making process. There is a sort of internal resistance to seeing oneself otherwise and showing oneself in this way to others. Because of this reluctance one does not change, remaining a prisoner of this self-representation, and what it allows or forbids to live.

To these obstacles to growth, linked to one's self-image, whether it is positive, negative or overvalued, one can add the influence of negative concepts of human nature. How can one hope to change when one has learned that humanity is fundamentally evil, selfish, jealous, dominating, ruled by instincts ...? Moreover, this anthropological concept has many examples to substantiate it.

Other dysfunctions of the "I" that slow down growth, include voluntarism, flight from reality, self-doubt, alienation to the ideas of others or to one's own principles, negative brooding about oneself, etc.

Other internal obstacles one can encounter are a superficial lifestyle, very externalized, with no time taken for internalization which would facilitate the emergence of the being. This way of living is often coupled with a lack of depth in motivation to progress and contentment with a life where the sensibility is relatively peaceful.

Growth requires, to a measurable degree, that the strength of the body can actualize that for which one is made.

Wounds of the sensibility also play a preponderant role in these hindrances to growth. Wounds block the life of the being and bring about the dysfunctions which have just been mentioned. When persons heal from the traumas which handicap them, not only do these wounds no longer stop them but they have enriched them with an experience which can help the growth of some aspects of their personality that would not otherwise have been developed in the same way. For instance, once healed, people who have not received enough attention to what constitutes the core of their being, can develop a quality of presence to others in their essential selves, by the very reason of the suffering they have endured. It will have sensitized them to the importance of having this type of outlook on others.

Evolution of the place of others on a growth journey

The place and role of others has already been mentioned several times, and presented as part of the fundamental elements of the personal growth journey. While the importance of the human environment may be a constant throughout the life of a person, changes in the place others take in this growth process can be noted. This change is neither automatic nor general, however, but dependent on the level of humanization of the human environment and the person's own choice of autonomy.

In the early years of life, others occupy an irreplaceable and essential place. Children learn from others what human beings are all about and how they function. They tend to identify with the models surrounding them, absorbing through osmosis the values and behaviour patterns of those people. With the experience of this identification, the children themselves will then develop the potentialities which correspond to those of their own being, instinctively leaving behind those which do not match their own personality. At that time, their significant others (those from whom they expect recognition and love) hold an essential place. Approval or disapproval of their tentative behaviour will have an influence on the way they will grow, either in or out of harmony with their being.

During adolescence, others are considered differently, depending on whether or not they exercise authority, and also on the power of influence they are given to have on and by these young people. Their presence is necessary for the teenager, but the relationship is often ambivalent. Adolescents still refer to adults to some extent, but at the same time they reject those external standards, seeking to experiment with their own or test those of their peers. In fact, at this stage of life the influence of the peer group has a tendency to replace parental influence and reflects more or less positively on the growth process, depending on the case. The place of others is less essential for adolescents than for children, but the growth process of young people is still very marked by outside influences and the acceptance or rejection of their "steps of existence" by the people around them.

In adults, the place of others on the growth journey is modified. The progression toward autonomy puts it in a different perspective in comparison with the earlier years of life. One can exist more easily without this dependence on the attention of others and assume a form of solitude. Moreover, one can distance oneself from those who are harmful, something which a child cannot do. Having said this, the place of others remains important for more than one reason:

– as we have seen, the human environment occupies a special place for stimulating the being, which is an essential source of the growth process;

– this environment can also constitute a milieu which is conducive to the healing of past wounds. Certain quality relationships contribute to an in-depth restoration of potentialities which have been blocked by old traumas caused by harmful relationships;

– finally, the place of others allows one to live one's essential potentialities in the service of others. Participating with others in collective advancement like this gives meaning to one's life and greatly stimulates growth.

The place of others in the process of growth tends to diminish in importance as progress toward maturity takes place, in the search for the satisfaction of personal needs of a psychological nature (recognition, love, security ...). One comes more to terms with oneself and thus has less recourse to others. However, the importance of the place of others in the growth process is accentuated by the possibility they offer of actualizing one's potentialities. In other words, with age and maturity, the growth process takes place more by doing what one was meant to do to serve others than by receiving compensation from them.

Note : It is not easy or obvious for everybody to accept the fact that others can have a place in one's growth journey. Some people encounter opposition. Thus, some have a tendency to feel guilty in their relationships with others when their own personal growth is concerned. They accuse themselves of "using" others to their advantage, judging themselves to be selfish and sometimes going so far as to forbid themselves all relationships from which they benefit. They may even oblige themselves to entertain difficult or often harmful relationships under the cover of altruistic intentions.

In such cases, it is necessary to clarify what one is doing. Here are a few possible clues to understand this phenomenon:

– this guilt can go back to a moralizing education where the Good rested in a permanent focus on the search to satisfy the needs of others and on self denial. We have seen[*] that this form of education could explain many dysfunctions. Reference to the deep conscience rather than the socialized conscience helps to restore balance;

– it could be that through this guilt persons are expressing discomfort in face of a harmful psychological dependence from which they are unable to extract themselves. It is desirable at some point during one's journey to not take comfort in these alienations but rather to aim for autonomy;

– this guilt is often rooted in ignorance of the laws of human growth. In order to acquire the necessary strength to approach the phase of self-decentralization, a growth journey always begins with a phase of self-centeredness which requires a distancing from others. Cutting corners does not help to speed progress;

– stimulating human relationships will always remain a necessity if the being is to emerge

[*] Cf. p. 115-116.

and individuals in turn are to bring their potential riches to others. In other words, there is nothing selfish or blameworthy in seeking in other stimulating people what one needs in order to be oneself. The objective must be to give back, when the time comes, whatever those relationships have revealed or activated that can help others to exist. If they respect the freedom of others, these relationships offer those people the possibility of giving the best of themselves, and therefore are a source of growth for them as well.

The different stages toward maturity

Although individuals have their own personal journeys, personal growth moves according to a specific chronology. This movement begins at conception, driven by the dynamism of growth which is present at the level of the being. At birth, it is mainly the body, including the five senses, which develops.

As it matures physiologically, the baby starts to react to its surroundings, it babbles its first syllables, handles objects within reach and thus gives shape to what will become words, games or acts. The "I" of the very young child thus starts to awaken and develop. It is the beginning of numerous apprenticeships. This blossoming of the child can either be encouraged or thwarted by the surroundings. If it is thwarted, wounds are produced which will handicap the process of growth.

A stage comes in the development of the body and the intellect of children when the being manifests itself as well as the deep conscience. They have personal aspirations and actualize some of them (deciding by themselves, playing, entering into relationships, communicating, giving pleasure, creating, imagining ...). Their instinct of being can already guide some of their choices. Thus begins the adventure of becoming themselves, of liberating the potential of riches they have, and of learning to actualize them in harmony with their deep conscience.

With adolescence, a new stage is lived toward the personalization of the subject. Young people start to leave behind the landmarks which had so far guided them and go in quest of new guidelines, their own. Through the choice of their studies, their work, their state of life, their commitments, a whole essential part of themselves can surface and begin to be actualized, giving rise to new potentialities and faith in themselves and their possibilities.

In order to become adults, individuals must become aware, at some point in time, that they can be actors in their own evolution and that they must commit themselves to the two paths of growth and healing.

Where growth is concerned, individuals approaching the adult stage seek to become aware of their identity. Progressively they commit themselves in line with their "essential course of action". "Essential bonds" emerge. Their aspiration to exist is very evident through all their achievements.

Once the foundations of their personality has emerged sufficiently, these individuals start to blossom.

As we have seen, this growth process can be halted by the presence of past wounds. Also, persons aiming for adult maturity will have to embark on the path of healing of past wounds in order to rediscover their capacity to exist as they feel in conscience they must. This stage can vary in duration depending on the case. An in-depth transformation occurs, the pivotal centres of the personality are progressively put back in order. The compensatory functionings due to the non-existence of the being gives way to normal ways of functioning. The persons gradually become unified around their being which can then fully exist and continue to reveal all of their riches.

Thus, the phenomenon of growth is manifested throughout the existence of the person, at least as long as the functioning of the "I", the sensibility and the body allow it. Growth is inseparably linked to the good functioning of one's faculties that are associated with these pivotal centres, even if those faculties are limited.

"Impairments" in the personal growth process: the phenomenon of wounds and of non-existence

To describe these "impairments" which happen in the process of growth, we must go back to the two foundations of the growth process: the aspiration to exist and the satisfaction of the need to be recognized, in one's right to be oneself. From there, we will examine the phenomenon of wounds when one does not obtain this recognition and is therefore thwarted in this fundamental aspiration to be oneself. The phenomenon of non-existence in children will then be treated as a consequence of this non-recognition of the right to exist such as one is.

The aspiration to exist and the need to be recognized

Children are born with an irrepressible aspiration to exist. This naturally drives them to grow in the axis of the personality which is in germination in them, and which characterizes them. But just as strong in them, is the need to be recognized in this aspiration to become who they are, mainly by their significant others (their mother, father, brothers and sisters, teachers, playmates, etc.). They need to be recognized in their right to exist such as they are, especially in their core of self, and they need to feel they will not be abandoned. This is more essential for them and their growth process than receiving affection, which is beneficial to them, of course, but which can be granted while their needs for recognition and affective security are lacking.

This test of recognition is passed when children feel that their life is precious in the eyes of those dear to them and they are received with joy. They must feel that their significant others are ready to invest in their success because they believe in it, because they feel that the child can become someone worthwhile, likely to bring good to others. Children will thus feel they have a place, an importance and a role in their universe, with space offered for them to actualize their aspiration to exist. Their need to be recognized is also satisfied when they profoundly feel that what they are and what they are trying to communicate in their own way, interests others, is seen, heard, understood, respected, appreciated. Moreover, children need to be received and accepted with their limitations taken into account. People should not expect something from them which is beyond their reach.

The sensation of being recognized is awakened by the thousands of verbal and non-verbal messages they receive from their surroundings. Children read into the way their parents or close ones look at them, the tone of their voices and the content of the words addressed to them, the care that is taken of them, etc. They read not only how much their right to exist such as they are is recognized, but also how much their personalities are perceived to be profoundly lovable. It is through a consistent way of being and of doing with them that makes them feel recognized and loved. Certainly this feeling can disappear momentarily when their significant others frustrate them in their needs. This can happen when the attention of their significant ones is taken up by another child, for example, or when they are unavailable at the time a need to be heard is manifested, or again when they are angry with them. When they occur only occasionally, these frustrations do not plant deep doubts in the children. Their latent feeling of being recognized and loved is restored as soon as the others explain their behaviour, recognize their tactlessness or error and excuse themselves. Children then learn that others are not always fulfilling, that they also have their limitations and weaknesses. They must therefore not count only on others for their well being. This experience fosters the healthy apprenticeship of autonomy.

Thus, inasmuch as their need to be recognized is adequately met, the children's personality grows harmoniously. The difficulties of life keep on testing their sensibility but they see no long-term manifestation of malicious intent or hostility on the part of the people around them. They are assured the recognition, love and protection of these people, if need be. They do not have to protect themselves abnormally in order to exist as they are, even though they must take the people around them into account, adapting the natural rhythm of their own existence to respect the existence of others as well.

The phenomenon of wounds

Here, the concept of wound means a psychological trauma, which most of the time has happened in childhood, and has reached the nervous system, altering the normal functioning of the person. A wound does not necessarily imply pain. In fact, some wounds are really felt painfully in the body and the sensibility, while others are repressed, anaesthetized, encysted. The person may not be aware of their existence. Yet, they are present in a kind of memory, said to be "organismic", recognizable by the dysfunctions they generate.

Not included in this concept of wounds are the more superficial and transient sufferings which assault the sensibility. In such cases, the personality has not been deeply affected. Physical traumas, however, may have generated deep insecurities.

In the majority of psychological wounds, the search for causes turns up a direct link to a major frustration of the need to be recognized such as one is, described above. Children are really very vulnerable. It takes only one important person who refuses them the right to exist such as they are on a long-term basis for a wound to be created. This hinders their aspiration to exist, and because of this, provokes an "impairment" in their growth and the harmonious construction of their personality. The more people there are who do not recognize them, particularly their mother, father, a close adult or a brother, sister, the deeper and more serious will be the wound. This will also be the case if the non-recognition affects essential aspects of their being. At times, it is the whole child who is rejected. It could be said that the great majority, if not all human beings, carry wounds and therefore disharmonies.

We note that some wounds occur in adulthood, in various contexts of life and in particularly difficult relationships (dismissal, unemployment, divorce, assault, accident, war, etc.). However, these wounds, while they are very painful, are less serious than those produced in childhood because the adult defense system is more advanced than that of children. Adults are better at protecting themselves psychologically against external assaults. They can put things in perspective and understand them more objectively. They are more capable than children of standing on their own because their existence no longer depends solely on the recognition of others. Because of this, they have less need to repress what they feel.

At times these psychological traumas in adulthood occur in an already wounded area. This explains the magnitude of some disproportionate reactions and also the difficulty in distinguishing between what comes from childhood wounds and what is the product of current wounds.

How is a wound produced?

A wound is in some way the consequence of two factors: an external wounding factor and an internal responsive factor proper to the person. In other words, the same causes do not produce exactly the same effects. It all depends on the subjective state of each person.

Included among the external factors likely to create a long term wound in children, the following can be noted :

– words. Words of rejection, condemnation, negation, mockery, irony, suspicion, blackmail, jealousy, depreciation, overvaluation, comparison, insults, falsehoods, slander;

– gestures. Gestures of violence, of scorn, of rejection, of disrespect for the body;

– actions. Actions of tyranny, vengeance, territorial violation, excessive punishment, sexual perversion, abandonment, destruction of emotionally precious objects;

– attitudes. Attitudes of indifference, of contempt, of domination, exploitation, overprotection, too much responsibility, exaggerated expectations, doubt;

– an environment. Environment of conflict, destruction, sadness, repression, rivalry, insecurity, guilt, prohibitions, judgement, suspicion, outward appearances, solitude;

– an event. The death of a family member, the birth of a little brother or sister, an accident, the separation of parents, serious illness, suicide …

To potential sources of wounds one can also add: the refusal of an unwanted pregnancy; the proximity of another child, more lively, more attractive, or one who requires more attention or care; identification of one's existence as causing the unhappiness of another, etc.

All those factors reach the children, sometimes in the mother's womb, in their thrust into existence. Children feel more or less consciously and painfully that their life, what they are, their behaviour, or simply some aspects of themselves are neither recognized nor accepted, never mind appreciated. This is how the phenomenon of non-existence makes its appearance.

The phenomenon of non-existence in children

The phenomenon of non-existence is manifested through an internal defense system which prevents children not only from feeling their aspiration to exist in areas where they are not accepted, but also from using their capabilities. Children "introject" the rejection of their existence and the guilt of not being as others would wish them to be.

"Non-existence settles in because children continuously see their right to be themselves being rejected. They are not accepted as they are".[39]

It can sometimes happen that non-existence appears immediately at the time of a trauma of non-recognition, but most of the time children struggle to be recognized. They demonstrate the injustice they feel, crying out their helplessness in face of expectations they cannot satisfy, demanding their right to be loved just as they are. They send all sorts of messages to shout their inner suffering at not being accepted as they are. But if the people around them do not understand their distress, if nothing changes, if they are reproached for their show of emotions, then their existential quest will lose its intensity. They will progressively feel the pointlessness of their efforts and cries and enter into a form of despair at not being able to exist as they are, because they cannot be heard and understood in their vital need for recognition. A break in communication with these significant others becomes firmly established. A defense mechanism is put into place to eliminate the pain.

In fact, seeking to be oneself and not being recognized in this existence is such an intolerable and at times destructive suffering for children, that their psyche, in a reflex for survival, prefers to capitulate and repress its fundamental aspiration to exist, rather than feel this indescribable wound. *"The failure of this first attempt to exist, at this age in childhood when one is still very vulnerable, leads to profound doubt of both oneself and one's capacity to be recognized, esteemed and loved"*.[40] This is how a negative self-image is generated.

In most children, an instinct for life urges them on not to let themselves be completely destroyed. It leads them to compensate for this non-existence at the core of self through the use of deviant forms of existence, just to glean a few substitutes for recognition. Depending on their personality and surroundings, children use different means to continue living:

[39] O.N. *"The Aspiration to Be Oneself – the Need for Recognition – the Phenomenon of Non-Existence"* p. 6, 1991.
[40] *"The Aspiration to Be Oneself and the Phenomenon of Non-Existence"*, p. 6, 1992.

– The most common means is "rebounding" in the attempt to reestablish a balance. Not recognized in their essential selves, children rebound by developing potentialities which are appreciated by the people around them and correspond to these persons' expectations. For instance, they will do well in school, becoming recognized through a report card that makes their loved ones feel honoured, or else they will train for success in sports if they have talent in that area and the activity is pleasing. Others will exaggerate their potentialities for obedience, kindness, willingness to help, generosity, humour, their manual skills, their intellectual or artistic gifts, etc.

– Some children or adolescents, more or less conscious of adult flaws, have reacted to the non-life forced on them by revolting, by quasi systematic opposition, by deviant behaviour (lies, stealing, drugs, running away ...) or nonconformity. They unconsciously reestablish a form of justice by being themselves a frustration to the people around them.

– Other children exercise a sort of pressure on the people from whom they expect recognition and love, as if to force them to be aware of their existence. This is the case, for instance, with children who use illness, failure or their fears, to attract the attention of adults, whether it be their pity or just their worry, simply to prove that they are not totally inexistent in their eyes.

– Children can also find a middle range to their non-existence by compensating elsewhere for their frustration with the people who offer them recognition. They turn off as soon as they are in contact with harmful surroundings, but light up wherever they are seen and appreciated in the depth of themselves.

It is to be noted that some children, in all likelihood more fragile psychologically, fail to compensate in any way and develop mental symptoms, cutting themselves off from a reality which has generated an anguish they cannot bear.

The "impairments" to growth which constitute past wounds are not irreparable. Human beings have within themselves the power to heal these traumas and their behavioural consequences. This will be seen in the next chapter.

Before closing this chapter on the phenomenon of growth, let us review the essentials in diagram form (Cf. diagram p. 177).[41]

– A foundation - The past
Children arrive on earth equipped with a network of potential-ities which aspire to live, and with constitutional limitations.

They meet two types of surroundings which influence their development: stimulating surroundings which recognize and appreciate them with their potentialities, encourage their actual-ization and accept their limitations; harmful surroundings which do not see the best in them, do not accept them, do not love them as they are, or else do not stimulate them to be "themselves".

These harmful surroundings wound children in their funda-mental aspiration to exist. They are at the root of a painful past and the phenomenon of non-existence.

– First level - The realities
In the person who has become an adult, we find two types of realities :
– potentialities, whose birth was facilitated by frequent contact with stimulating surroundings;
– deficiencies, resulting from the inadequacies of detrimental sur-roundings and hence from the painful past of the person;

– Second level - Aspirations and needs
Potentialities give birth on the one hand to aspirations which impel persons to actualize their potentialities and, on the other hand, to normal needs, whose satisfaction is necessary for the growth process of the person (the need to be recognized, loved, to have a place, to be believed, to be encouraged, etc.).

The deficiencies give birth to "deficiency needs" characterized by the disproportionate expectation of their satisfaction and by the extent of the frustration if nothing ensues.

– Third level - Interior movements
In the subjective lived experience of the person, aspirations and needs are felt as interior movements which can be classified in three categories:
– aspirations produce "straight arrow" movements which expect

[41] O.N. *"Aspirations and Needs"*, 1992.

no return and which impel persons forward to live according to who they are and according to that for which they are made;

– normal needs generate "bent arrow" movements which are directed at others, but to get something back. There is an expectation. This is related to growth;

– there are also movements that manifest a strong expectation and an insatiable thirst to be fulfilled. These are movements born of "deficiency needs" One looks to others to satisfy one's deficiencies.

– Fourth level - The overall interior lived experience

The different drives cited above coexist within oneself, often in some confusion. It is important to learn to untangle them in order to know what is at the root of one's actions.

– Fifth level - Actions

Actions are released starting from this inner lived experience where the three types of interior movements are mixed together: "straight arrow","bent arrow" and drives born of deficiency needs. Understanding one's actions starts with a clarification of the respective part played by each of these different interior movements.

Summary Diagram

This diagram may be read from top to bottom to understand the origin of the actions one takes and the interior movements one feels. But it can also be visualized from the bottom up, in which case it offers a key to understanding the process of growth.

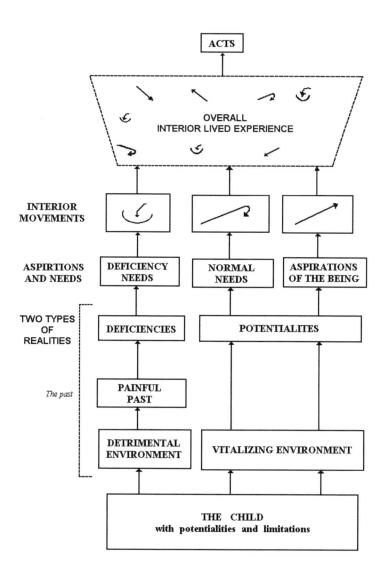

Chapter 6

The phenomenon of healing past wounds

Past wounds which have not been healed are harmful to proper functioning. They hamper the actualization of riches of the being, sometimes to the point of maintaining it in a state of under-development. They upset the objectivity of the intellect, distort its perceptions, provoke dysfunctions such as alienation, voluntarism, cerebral functioning or the different lethargies of the functions of the "I". These wounds clutter up and interfere with the sensibility. They take a lot of energy from the body. They alter relationships with oneself and others, and are themselves the origin of wounds caused to others. In short, their presence in the human psyche is harmful as much for the persons themselves as for the people around them.

A process of healing is therefore necessary to unblock one's aspirations, encourage the growth of the being, reduce the negative consequences of the wounds and allow individuals to live harmonious lives. Experience proves that it is possible to heal wounds, depending on certain conditions.

The term healing is given a very precise meaning in PRH Psycho-pedagogy. First of all it will be defined, then the following items will be covered in succession: the phenomenon of non-existence in adults, the necessary conditions for healing to take place, the way in which the process of healing takes place, the obstacles to healing. The chapter will end with a paragraph which examines the way to manage the healing of a painful past.

The concept of healing at PRH

In a growth journey, healing is understood to mean the phenomenon of the progressive restoration of the capacity of individuals to exist in areas where the actualization of their potentialities was hampered because of the presence of wounds. To heal is to rediscover one's capacity to exist in harmony with one's being and one's deep conscience.

The healing process, like that of growth, is part of human nature. It can be encouraged or checked. An analogy can be made with physical wounds, even deep ones, which tend to heal by themselves naturally, but which also require care to facilitate this healing and avoid complications. In fact, underlying this phenomenon of healing one finds the latent aspiration to exist at the core of self and the latent need to be recognized in this essential of self. In the innermost depth of self, while the aspiration to be oneself may be vexed and repressed, it remains; while the need to be recognized and loved may be frustrated and anaesthetized, it awaits satisfaction. As long as individuals are alive, their being tends to actualize itself by seeking, sometimes in devious ways, the recognition and love which they need to exist. It is this dynamism of growth of the being which makes healing possible. This dynamism is always present in all persons, even the most wounded.

Thus, the healing of past wounds is :
– the result of the sudden appearance of the dynamism of life at the level of the being of the person, an appearance that renders more and more intolerable the defenses which prevent one from truly existing and more and more enviable the fact of being oneself,
– the result of a determination to heal and thus of a decision to take the necessary means.

Note : concerning the term "healing" :

The term healing frightens some people who understand it to mean the notion of an illness to treat, and who therefore dread being viewed as "sick people". Let us say straightaway that in the PRH psychological approach, the phenomenon of healing is integrated into the growth process of which it is a constituent part. The term "healing" has been retained because it well represents the notion of a wound which has bruised the person, and evokes the notion of restoration to a state of health and proper functioning.

It is necessary to distinguish between persons living dysfunctional lives linked to traumas of the past, which are embarrassing for them or the people around them, and persons suffering from mental illness (disabling neuroses, psychoses ...). The fields of psychopathology and psychiatric treatment do not come under the competence of the PRH approach.

Paradoxically, in others the term healing arouses a sort of fascination. They wish to heal at all costs. Healing almost becomes the goal of their existence and is no longer ordained to growth. The aim of self-help as practised in PRH psycho-pedagogy is not primarily to heal but to exist and to grow; neither is it primarily to eliminate suffering, but to stand up to the difficulties and hardships that one encounters. Healing comes as a fruit of the emergence and growth of the being and the commitment of the "I".

Note : concerning the possible comparison of PRH to a form of psychotherapy:

The term psychotherapy has greatly evolved in the past few years. In the past, it was reserved to the field of psychopathology and to everything pertaining to the treatment of serious psychological problems and mental illnesses. Today there is a tendency to group together all the methods that bring well-being to people, under the term psychotherapy. (Cf. the quotation by Edmond Marc mentioned at the start of this book p. 35). This extension of the definition of psychotherapy rightfully raises the question of how education systems for personal psychological development, such as those of PRH, relate to psychotherapy. It appears important to us that the two approaches not be confused. They certainly have points in common (among others, work on the axis of healing, the beneficial effects of the psychological lived experience of individuals ...), but they also have differences which make them particular, some specific characteristics of which are :

– related to objectives (personal development in education systems, healing in psychotherapy);

– related to the type of population concerned (persons displaying different degrees of turmoil);

– related to the methods used (educational workshops and helping relationships aimed at integrating the results of the workshops on the one hand, and on the other hand, the use of transference, dream interpretation, hypnosis ...);

– related to the modes of intervention and to the areas of competence of the contributors (the educator is not involved in a relationship with the "client" in the same way as a psychotherapist is. The educators use pedagogical tools allowing for self-education and act as mediators between the clients and themselves; in the case of psychotherapy, the transferential relationship which is established is the main factor in the process of evolution of the client. Moreover, persons who follow education systems can address themselves simultaneously to different educators, whereas psychotherapy requires working with only one therapist);

– related to theoretical references, which are also coloured by the characteristics of each approach (in an education system such as that of PRH, the accent is placed on a theory of psychical structure viewed from the dynamism of growth of the person; in psychotherapeutic approaches, the accent is placed more on the theory of unconscious intrapsychical conflicts and their symptomatic manifestations ...).

From these differences, specific forms of training ensue for educators and therapists.

This comparison reveals one of the differences which distinguish André Rochais from Carl Rogers. André Rochais established himself more in the field of psycho-pedagogy with a set of pedagogical tools to help him (PRH education), aimed at giving people knowledge about themselves which would allow them to take their life in hand. Carl Rogers situated himself more in a psychotherapeutical approach (Counselling) using relational interaction to help individuals restore a healthy relationship with themselves and others.

The phenomenon of non-existence in adults

This phenomenon is very prevalent and yet, paradoxically, few adults are aware of it. Childhood wounds have been forgotten for the most part. Deficiencies have been compensated for by other means of receiving recognition and appreciation (different forms of social success), or other forms of gratification (intellectual, spiritual, artistic, physical, recreational, possessions, commitment, etc.). Because of this, individuals may have the impression of existing, at times even feeling happy and good about themselves. They easily attribute their behavioural disharmonies, which could alert them to the presence of wounds of non-existence, to their character, to circumstances or blame them on others or the way society functions. In other words, adults unconsciously perpetuate the initial repression and justify it to preserve some consistency.

Consequently, many people are unaware that they could have a richer and more unified inner life and a sounder, more harmonious and more fruitful existence. They are content with living superficially, not suspecting or rarely so, that deep down, their true personality suffers from being condemned to a non-existence or a partial or peripheral existence.

And yet, the phenomenon of non-existence, whether it be total or partial, can only be detected by those who agree to (or at times are made to) question their life to put it back on track. Observation has made possible the identification of many signs of this wound of non-existence. These are grouped under the expression "disproportionate and recurring reactions"[*].

As we have seen, these exaggerated reactions, ranging from aggressiveness to inhibition, are reproduced in analogous circumstances, in the face of the same persons, or the same type of situation. They have a link with a past wound. Individuals experience a phenomenon of projection, finding themselves in some way confronted with their past "aggressor" or in the presence of the traumatic situation, which had been so wounding. This transferential situation explains the disproportion and the recurrence. The past wounds are there, encysted in the sensibility, and are awakened when current situations are analogous to the initial situation. Establishing the "composite sketch" or describing what triggers such reactions, helps to make the link with the person or situation of the past which triggered the wound.

Here are a few examples of disproportionate and recurring reactions:

– *Excessive attachments*

In the previous paragraph we recalled the existence of a phenomenon of transference which happens when a person from one's surroundings awakens negative sentiments in oneself which are in fact addressed to an offending person from one's past.

Another form of transference is produced with respect to men or women whom one hopes will satisfy needs which were deficient in childhood. This comes out as an emotional fixation, in other words, as an excessive attachment to these persons. When one is close to them, their receptiveness, understanding and esteem rekindle the right to exist such as one truly is. The aspiration to exist is awakened with force and the tyrannical need to be recognized is concentrated on this potential source of appeasement for the suffering caused by the deficiency. An affective overinvestment

[*] Cf. pp. 104-105.

is then produced on these persons who lavish their attention, their listening and their kindness.

These manifestations are not easy to manage in an interpersonal relationship. On the one hand, the person has exaggerated expectations and attempts at possession, with intolerable frustrations and an impression of being rejected, since the other will never be able to fulfill the deficiency. On the other hand, persons who induce this attachment must face the psychological pressure exercised by the other and must learn to reconcile their own needs with those of the other party.

If these situations are clearly understood and well managed, they can contribute to growth.

– The fear of no longer being loved. Fear of rejection

When individuals have not been recognized in their childhood, they are imbued with emotional insecurity and self-doubt. Having reached adulthood, they are anxious with people who love them or by whom they wish to be appreciated. They doubt that the latter can, in fact, love them or be interested in them, or they doubt that this love can be long-term. They are afraid of not being or no longer being accepted. They fear rejection and abandonment, at times going so far as to anticipate this rejection or abandonment and they themselves bring about the rupture of some relationships.

These fears and doubts indicate the presence of a wound of non-existence.

– Feelings of frustration

Human beings have many needs and many aspirations, more than they can satisfy. They also experience frustration very early in life. If these frustrations remain within the limits of a certain threshold, as uncomfortable as they may be, they can be a motor for certain potentialities to develop. Human beings are equipped in some way to assume these inevitable dissatisfactions.

However, when fundamental needs have been denied or seriously frustrated during childhood, a wound has been suffered which makes the person intolerant to frustrations in adulthood. These disproportionate reactions can be manifested under the form of revolt, demands, aggressiveness or a more or less significant state of depression.

– A feeling of guilt[*]

This sentiment can be awakened very easily in some people. They blame themselves for everything that goes wrong around them. They feel at fault the moment others manifest negative sentiments. They judge themselves to be the cause of unhappiness in other people. They reproach themselves for some of their own sentiments or needs. Sometimes this guilt feeling appears without any objective reason.

Underlying this feeling of guilt there is a wound of non-existence. Persons who were not recognized or loved as children, have either unconsciously introjected the guilt of not being what they should have been to have their needs satisfied, or they have felt guilty for being harmful to the people around them.

– Other manifestations of non-existence

Wounds of non-recognition and non-love can also be manifested through the following :
– certain disproportionate and recurring reactions of a psychosomatic nature (insomnia, hypersomnia, fatigue, headaches, gall bladder attacks, ulcers, skin disease, stomach pain, etc.);
– habitual recourse to compensation (activism, day-dreaming, drugs, alcohol and food abuse, sexual turmoil, overspending, waste, chasing after material success, social notoriety, etc.);
– an inability to accept one's solitude;
– a feeling of emptiness, an absence of meaning to one's life, a loss of the taste for living, anguish;
– a feeling of powerlessness allied to despair, etc.

Identification of these different symptoms of wounds of non-existence in adults opens the way which will lead, little by little, to the painful cause of these dysfunctions.

[*] Cf. p. 88

Essential conditions for healing

It is true to say that all human beings have the potential to heal their wounds. One must add, however, that certain conditions have to be present for the process of healing to begin and in fact take place.

A first condition: the awareness of having been wounded

It is indispensable that individuals perceive and identify the ill-being, the disharmony and disorder in themselves and their behaviour, as being the result of a wound of non-existence. This awareness is not easy to come by for many people. They reassure themselves by choosing to justify their maladjustment and "empty" moments with all sorts of arguments. They avoid asking themselves questions on the inner origin of these dysfunctions. Moreover, the compensation offered by social success and pleasures of all kinds can very well mask the fragility of a personality which was unable to be constructed on the essential of self. Thus, it is necessary that one day such people become aware of the disproportion of some of their reactions and question themselves on the inner origin of these reactions.

A second condition: to have the necessary strength

Persons must have sufficient energy and physical health to confront their painful past. To do so, the life of the being must have been awakened and they must find solid inner support to be able to let go of their protective defense mechanism and rediscover the original buried suffering.

A third condition: to be motivated to heal and consent to the time required to do so

To engage in the task of healing one's past, in order to live a better and more enhanced life, requires true determination. Individuals can be content just to restore their equilibrium after the "shock" of their disproportionate and recurring reactions. They can also organize their lives to avoid situations or people who awaken these turmoils. To choose not to flee and to seek the deep causes of one's disharmonies in order to heal requires strong motivations. These can be strengthened when the aspiration to be oneself grows and the fact of not truly existing or of being hampered in one's life becomes more and more unbearable.

A fourth condition: to get help

Most of the time, wounds of non-existence have been produced through harmful relationships. The process of restoration requires in the first instance that individuals experience beneficial, stimulating and reassuring relationships, followed by a helping relationship to accompany them in their healing process.

Thus, the healing of past wounds is possible in persons who are aware that they must heal, are motivated to do so, have the necessary strength and are supported by competent help. Individuals who cannot meet all of these conditions can nonetheless develop the potentialities which were not hampered. They can learn to live with the consequences of that painful past which suddenly appears in disproportionate and recurring reactions.

The healing process in individuals

Neither children nor even adolescents are able to exist and to display the dreadful suffering caused when they are not being recognized and loved. Even though they may grumble, children do not have sufficient psychological strength to let themselves feel the suffering which strikes them in the core of self. In a survival reflex, they repress this suffering and capitulate before their aspiration to exist.

In adulthood, the healing process consists in *"reliving the original suffering and daring to exist at the very core of the reactualized suffering, at the same time facing up to the image of the person who denied the right to exist. This is not a physical face to face meeting, but an internal face to face ... In other words, it is a question of doing as an adult, with the inner strength that one has developed, what one was not able to do as a child because one was too weak"*[42].

There are many stages to the healing process, which can span over the course of many years, depending on the nature of one's wounds and the actualization of the conditions for healing (Cf. § on the essential conditions for healing p. 186).

[42] O.N. *"How to Heal from Non-Existence"*, pp. 2-3, 1992.

The stage of becoming aware of the origin of one's dysfunctions and putting one's suffering into words

At this stage, it is a matter of identifying the disproportionate and recurring reactions, symptomatic of past wounds which are still active, as well as the physical sensations and feelings which are produced at the very moment the disproportionate reactions are triggered. In fact, these reactions and sensations relate to something which happened in the past. While one is well in contact with these living sensations, it is important to turn to the past and ask the following questions:
– When did these reactions begin?
– Who could have triggered them?
– What could have happened?

It is only gradually that recollections will reappear in the field of one's awareness, establishing links between today's reactions and past traumas. These recollections of wounding events or situations are strongly coloured by the subjective lived experience of the person. It is a question of the perception the person had of this event or situation and not of the objective reality of the facts.

During this stage, it is important to distinguish between what is a product of reflection or logic and what comes from enlightenment emerging into awareness, as a result of analyzing sensations. By itself, this enlightenment can make individuals progress in self-comprehension and therefore toward the solution to their problems.

The fact of expressing what they feel and what they are becoming aware of, to someone who knows how to listen and knows this process of healing, helps individuals in their search and restores communication with that buried past. In the presence of someone in whom one has confidence, individuals see their defense mechanism being slackened. They can venture further in the analysis of the deep causes of their turmoils. The verbalization of one's lived experience is already an act of healing, for it interrupts the process of repression, unlocks the feelings of guilt, introduces enlightenment and puts one into a relationship. In other words, it makes one exist.

Stage of reliving repressed sentiments

The exploration of the past starting from sensations present at the time of disproportionate and recurring reactions, gradually leads individuals, not only to rediscover the circumstances of their wounds, but also to feel the repressed sentiments which were in them at the time the wounds were suffered. Slight and fleeing at first, these sentiments become clearer and more intense. Past feelings are relived as are the reflexes recorded in the nervous system (trembling, upset stomach, nausea, etc.). Usually, these feelings occur at two levels: the level of refusal, rejection and aggressiveness toward the person or persons who caused the wound; and the level of supplication, the complaint lodged to obtain recognition of the right to exist which was initially denied.

During this stage, individuals learn to let go of their defense mechanism and fears. They also get used to letting themselves feel their past with its original intensity.

The stage of the evacuation of pain

A time comes in the healing process when feelings and sensations linked to past wounds are sufficiently awakened, and individuals are solid enough to abandon themselves to revisit these sensations. Now, the sense of security of a helping relationship allows this evacuation of the relived pain.

At this stage, individuals have to consent to relive completely the sensations awakened in their body and sensibility through the reminiscence of that painful past. By letting their sensations take on their full volume, individuals liberate the emotional charge which is present there. The body can then shake with sobs, sometimes start trembling or become stiff with tension. Individuals rediscover in their flesh the pain which they were not able to express and evacuate at the time, as well as the nervous tensions experienced by the body to protect the being.

In other words: *"It is not by throwing off one's suffering that one heals. Nor is it by denying it, nor dominating it, nor sublimating it. One heals by existing at the very core of this suffering that one lets unfurl in successive waves. It is in rising again, straightening up and standing upright that the process of healing is released and propagated"*[43].

Becoming aware and analyzing the experience lived during the

---

[43] O.N. *"How to Heal from Non-Existence"*, p. 11, 1992.

evacuation of pain is an integral part of this stage, with a view to integrate this lived experience into the evolution of the person's self-image.

This phenomenon of evacuation of pain is sometimes very intense. Once the emotional content is exhausted, individuals are calm, even though they have a sensation of fatigue. They perceive that a renewal of life and a liberation have taken place. For one and the same wound it often requires many evacuations of pain before the pocket which contained that pain is emptied. In each sequence, individuals go to the very bottom of the content accessible to them for liberation at that time.

The stage of re-education

When individuals have not been able to exist such as they are at the core of their being, they put compensating ways of functioning into place so as to have a certain impression of existing. They also protect themselves through defense mechanisms in order to avoid reliving traumatic situations. These ways of functioning are like "bad habits" of behaviour which these people have adopted. Even after evacuating their pain, individuals can rediscover these "bad habits" which in them have become second nature. Establishing order in their ways of functioning is therefore necessary, with the contribution of the faculties of the "I".

It is a matter of learning to decide and to live one's actions in harmony with the being. In other words, the process of re-education does not reside solely in the mobilization of the will to fight these dysfunctions, but also requires letting oneself be attracted by both the good feeling of existing in harmony with one's deep conscience and the fact of actively progressing.

There are many aspects to the task of re-education :
— "on the spot" awareness of a dysfunction. For instance: "I am in the process of alienating myself to what that person wants", "I am in a voluntaristic spin", "I am trying to justify myself", "I am using imaginary functioning", etc. To facilitate this awareness, attention to physical sensations can be helpful (tension, malaise, desire …);
— the mobilization of one's energies in order to decide to change one's way of functioning. This requires an effort of the will which,

in order to be successful, assumes that the individual has sufficient energy;

– engaging in a good way of functioning which will leave individuals at peace at the level of their deep conscience.

This task of re-education can start as soon as the growth process is begun. It is painstaking at first, as are all apprenticeships, but it soon gives deep satisfaction to the individuals, who experience their life changing, and the joy of living becomes more intense.

The process of healing has been described here as something which is linear, with a succession of stages. In actual fact, these different stages are superimposed and interconnected at all times during the process.

A few criteria to recognize the healing of past wounds

The healing of past wounds occurs progressively during the course of this long process. Certain criteria make it possible to verify that the healing has taken place :

– disproportionate and recurring reactions disappear. Individuals are no longer controlled by impulses beyond their control and regain mastery over their behaviour. They no longer project on today's people the feelings or intentions of persons of the past. Their relationships are generally improving;

– their essential selves, previously hampered by wounds, can exist and blossom. Individuals realize that nothing that makes up their being has been destroyed. They rediscover their being as one rediscovers an innocent child, with all its freshness, its simplicity, its thirst for life, its beauty and also its vulnerability. They dare to live and affirm themselves such as they are, including in face of the persons who wounded them in the past or people of a similar nature;

– one can recall the past peacefully and talk about it. The suffering has disappeared. There is no more bitterness, aggressiveness or depression. The wounds have been healed. The scars remain and will remain, engraved in the person's memory, but the after-effects no longer hamper their progress, because from now on, the person can better manage them, without falling prey to them.

Obstacles to healing. Pitfalls

There will be resistance which slows down the process, even stops it, as well as pitfalls which must be avoided. The healing process cannot take place without coming across them. Here are few of the most frequent obstacles and pitfalls.

Curbs and obstacles

These are generally related either to a lack of motivational maturity or to dysfunctions introduced during the healing process. Included are the following :
— lack of motivation. The determination to heal from past sufferings is fundamental to launching oneself on this sometimes long and difficult process. As long as individuals do not feel strongly motivated, they do not really get underway;
— fears. These fears can be of all kinds: fear of hurting, fear of being destabilized and not being able to find one's equilibrium, fear of showing oneself as vulnerable, fear of ridicule, fear of the time it will take, fear of questioning an idealized parental image;
— principles. "One doesn't give in", "men don't cry", "one is old enough to settle one's own problems", "where there's a will, there's a way";
— the secondary benefits which one draws from these wounds. Complacency in the role of victim. The attention received from the people around because one is not well;
— guilt. Individuals are ashamed of what they are experiencing. They feel guilty of holding a grudge against their parents. They feel guilty for having problems;
— being content with restoring balance when one is perturbed, without attacking the causes of these turmoils;
— impatience, voluntarism and their corollary, discouragement. Wishing to be healed "by the sweat of one's brow" then, when this method fails, believing that one will never heal;
— idealization of the healing of one's past. Believing that this work of healing will solve all problems, or eliminate all suffering;
— detachment from reality by minimizing or conversely, dramatizing disproportionate and recurring reactions;
— apprehension about the consequences of one's own change on

the people around them, family or professional life, when one is not ready to accept them.

The pitfalls

They are often related to the way individuals look at healing :
– believing that healing comes from satisfying deficiencies. This is a very frequent pitfall since it is an instinctive human reflex to seek satisfaction for what one has missed. There is a tendency to invest in anything that might ease the anguish caused by the lack of something essential. Deficiencies, however, cannot be satisfied. Needs which have hardly been satisfied reappear with the same strength as before. However, one can free oneself from the suffering related to these deficiencies. The disproportion of those particular needs disappears;
– believing that healing consists solely in relating current symptoms to past causes;
– believing that one is healed by a "settling of accounts" directly with the people from one's past;
– believing that one can heal by oneself, without the help of others;
– confusing the evacuation of a pain with letting oneself be submerged by painful sensations. The fact of letting oneself feel one's pain is not enough to free oneself from it;
– believing that healing is to no longer have needs, or to no longer feel pain.

Managing the healing of a painful past

Healing from a painful past requires time. The length of time depends on several factors: the scope and depth of one's wounds, individual potential (one's life forces, motivations, degree of acceptance of reality, etc.), the strength of one's defense mechanism, and also on the possible help coming from others. During that time, individuals can manage their healing process, that is, take up their share of responsibility so that this stage of healing is handled as efficiently as possible, by avoiding the pitfalls along the way.

Starting the process of healing past wounds on a solid foundation

It is not at the beginning of an exercise in self-knowledge that one begins a healing process. Neither is it when one's life is unbearable and one is afflicted by all sorts of problems or suffering. The healing stage occurs :
– when the being is sufficiently emerged and its life faces up to the resistance related to the presence of wounds;
– when persons are sufficiently developed in the analysis of their sensations to reach the depth of their lived experience, beyond symptoms;
– when persons have sufficiently clarified their motivations to engage in a task of healing which will be long and exacting;
– when persons are ready to be helped by somebody who is competent;
– when persons live the fundamental attitudes described in the chapter on the growth process.

Working simultaneously on growth, establishing order and healing

It is important never to lose sight of the fact that, in the process of healing of past wounds, the objective is growth. Thus, on a growth journey :

"There is an interdependence among growth, establishing order and healing.
– If sufferings are to become unencysted, life must be sufficiently liberated and strong.
– All evacuation of pain is accompanied by a revival of life.
– The work of establishing order and of reeducation allows to liberate further the strengths of the being and the desire to exist.
– When persons cannot advance on their healing journey, they must look to their axis of growth or their axis of orderliness and reeducation"[44].

A methodical personal task

On this road to healing, individuals can advance at random as sensations are awakened. They can also perform their work of healing methodically. In this case, it is a matter of pursuing:
– a methodical exploration of one's past in order to better identify what has happened, the wounds received, the way one

[44] O.N. *"The Aspiration to Be Oneself – The Need for Recognition – The Phenomenon of Non-existence"*, p. 13, 1991.

reacted to them and the mechanisms which were put into place to compensate for the wound of non-existence;

– an in-depth observation and exploration of the current after-effects of this painful past, notably the analysis of disproportionate and recurring reactions, the defense mechanisms, the tyrannical needs which are awakened in face of certain people;

– an acceptance of all of that past and its consequences.

This personal undertaking is very useful in preparing for the helping relationships during which pain will be evacuated.

The relationship to others during this stage of healing

Two types of persons become important during this healing process. These relationships may have already been present, but they are even more conscious at this stage.

– The first type: helping and stimulating persons. The relationship to these persons greatly fosters the revival of repressed needs linked to past wounds. In fact, by receiving today something that was lacking in the past, individuals are awakened, not only in their aspiration to exist, but often at the same time, to the suffering of not having received it as children. Moreover, the competence of a helping person allows quicker access into these unconscious zones of self, which are almost inaccessible by oneself. This help also serves to supply the necessary explanations on the growth and healing journey, which are often disconcerting to those experiencing it. The relationship to these helping persons evolves during the course of one's growth process and inevitably include a distance-taking phase.

– The second type: individuals (a boss, a colleague, a spouse, a child …) who, through their behaviour, their words, their tone of voice …, awaken the "aggressor" from the past. First of all, the work of healing opens up relational problems, which makes the relationship to these people difficult. It is only gradually that one is able to differentiate today's person from the one who caused past wounds. The reactions with respect to these people include an unjustified aspect. They can in turn provoke the same type of disproportionate reaction in the one who is felt to be the aggressor if that person's sensibility is touched in a wounded zone. The suffering and the reactions thus escalate. Therein lies the source of numerous interpersonal conflicts. The same person may alternately or simultaneously be felt as being fulfilling and frustrating. There is no long-term positive transference.

It is a joint effort between the work of life at the core of the person and personal work that lead to an in-depth restoration of one's personality and give access to the freedom of being oneself. Wounds are not what is most profound in a human being. In the course of this healing process, one experiences that the positive foundation of oneself becomes more and more liberated and is in a position to continue blossoming.

Chapter 7

The meaning of life

This theme will not be approached as a philosophical reflection on the meaning of life. Rather, it will be in keeping with what is proper to the PRH approach, which is the analysis of the lived experience of people from the point of view of their growth. Our experience has shown us that the meaning of life, the way one questions (or does not question) oneself on this subject, and the way one answers certain fundamental existential questions, have an important influence on the growth of persons. Here the term "meaning" is considered in two contexts: the reason one exists and the direction one's life is taking.

Three ways to envision the meaning of one's life

Depending on the people, on their stage of development and also on the sectors of life concerned, there are three different ways of envisioning and experiencing the meaning of life. Each of these three ways of envisioning the meaning of life can coexist with some of the main characteristics of the other types.

Meaning proposed by the surrounding environment

From early childhood, there is the meaning of life as proposed explicitly or implicitly by the surrounding environment. This meaning is based on the values found in that environment.

Examples : In some families, one learns that "the meaning of life" is to have a career, to achieve material success, to leave something to the children ...; in others, it is to militate, to defend causes, to be committed ...; other circles advocate that the meaning of life is to take advantage of everything life brings in the way of satisfaction and pleasure ...; conversely, others submit that the meaning of life is a duty to accomplish, work to do, perfection to attain, self-denial to seek ...; still others convey a meaning of life considered as self-fulfilment, as a never-ending process of growth, etc.

Sometimes, persons infer from the people around them that life has no sense, that it is absurd, that it is not worth living, that it is only a succession of trials crowned by death, considered as nothingness.

Experience shows how much these conceptions of the meaning of life, received at a very early age, influence and even condition the choices and actions of someone later on. Even as adults, people remain sensitive to the meaning of life pervading their surroundings.

The meaning that individuals give to their own life

There is the meaning that individuals themselves give to their own life, their decisions and actions in order to justify them or provide a reason for being. It is the meaning that they would like or wish their life to have, that guides their behaviour. It emanates from an ideal or from beliefs created to satisfy certain needs. It is a meaning that answers to rational logic, to a project or an ambition, as well as deep aspirations.

Examples : some people give meaning to their life by sacrificing themselves for others, by taking up an occupation, a state of life, a responsibility. The reasons they give for their choices include necessity, the needs of others, the interpretation of external signs or events, etc.

This meaning given to one's own life is resolutely logical, a label that a person tends to apply to life to give it coherence and value. It is true that meaninglessness, incoherence and absurdity cause anxiety and are therefore unbearable for human beings. They will therefore justify their existence by attributing to it a meaning which they justify with reasons that are legitimate in their own eyes. The mechanism of self-justification, which prevents individuals from perceiving and adhering to their reality, can be recognized here.

If individuals could stop to analyse their feelings thoroughly, they would very probably sense, on the one hand, deep aspirations signalling to be heard and developed, integrated into their lives, and on the other hand, signs of this need to justify their existence.

Note : In this phenomenon of meaning that one gives to life, one sometimes finds the origin of existential crises which some people experience, although seemingly balanced and well engaged in their life. Certain events tell these individuals that what constituted the meaning of their life up until now, is collapsing. They can no longer rely on dependable certitudes to decide and to live. They are destabilized by profound doubt. This is a passage, certainly painful, but beneficial to the attainment of a higher level of maturity in which the being takes its leading place in the personal growth process and the meaning of life is received rather than sought.

The meaning of life coming from a deep intuition

A third way of understanding the meaning of life differs from the previous two. This meaning of life is neither imposed nor willed, but comes from within the person. It appears in the field of awareness only after the fact, while the awareness of the meaning of life which has been instilled by the surroundings or the one which has been self-imposed precedes its actualization.

It is a deep intuition which asserts itself progressively until it becomes an unwavering certitude, a sort of unifying thread, stamped with coherence. This thread goes back to the dawn of the person's life, marking it along the way. This intuition emerges especially when individuals reexamine their existence, the significant facts in their life, their actions taken, their expressed potentialities, their manifested and actualized aspirations, the essential relationships they have formed. Through their life's history individuals become aware, that one or more very basic aspects of their personality have emerged or tried to emerge quasi-permanently. (This is an example of the phenomenon of the "instinct of being" which unconsciously drives individuals toward the fulfilment of their potentialities.) By going over their life like this, they see how much the meaning of their life has been directed to the actualization of those essential traits of their personality, and how the meaning of their life calls them to continue in this direction. In fact, it is their commitment on this path that provides the sensation of the meaning of their life, as well as its direction.

In other words, the meaning of life emanates from the manifestation of the identity of individuals, of their "essential course of action", their essential bonds and the growth of these realities. This sense is permanent, even though it is expressed with different subtleties at different times in one's life. It colours all actions. It resists the storms of life. One cannot question it without denying oneself.

A link can be seen between these three conceptions of the meaning of life and the three types of moral conscience discussed in the chapter on the deep conscience. The socialized conscience corresponds to the meaning of life received from others; the cerebral conscience corresponds to the self-imposed meaning of life; and the deep conscience corresponds to the meaning of life received from the inner self as the fruit of one's experience. Giving different meanings to one's life, like referring to different consciences, has a bearing on the personal growth process.

Meaninglessness in one's life

As a corollary to what was presented in the preceding paragraph on the three ways of conceiving the meaning of life, a feeling of meaninglessness in one's life shows a dislocation of the person in relation to one's being and the path of one's "essential course of action". Individuals make decisions, take action and sometimes live their lives in the opposite direction from what the dynamism of growth of their being invites them to do. A feeling of discomfort ensues which can go so far as to put one at odds with oneself, accompanied by a sensation of uselessness or failure, even of absurdity of one's existence. This incoherence with the meaning of life – to be oneself and to realize that for which one was made – can generate mechanisms of justification in order to ease the resulting psychological pain. It is not easy to admit a feeling that one's life has no meaning. Now, before change can take place, this feeling of meaninglessness has to be recognized.

The lack of meaning in one's life can also appear through events whose meaning is not understood, which even seem to be absurd: the death of a child, an accident which handicaps one for life, an epidemic or earthquake which devastates a population, etc. Faced with such events, observation shows that some people manage to deal with them without being deeply shattered. Life retains all of its meaning. But for others, it is a disaster, life no longer seems worth living. In the latter case, the meaninglessness of the event is transferred as a meaninglessness of life. These people probably had been relating the meaning of life to an understanding of what happened to them or to a succession of favourable events. In fact, as long as the meaning of life depends on preserving favourable life conditions, the risk of meeting up with meaninglessness remains, for unfavourable circumstances can always arise. However, what can help persons to live through these seemingly absurd trials, is to have established their meaning of life on the being, in other words, on the fulfilment of essential internal realities. External conditions can certainly change but since it is not established on these external conditions, the meaning of life remains.

This phenomenon of meaninglessness is aggravated when the person is surrounded by people who present life as being absurd or evil and where nihilism rules, destroying all hope. In such cases, when senseless things happen they confirm the beliefs of the milieu and close the person off in a sort of fatalism and hopelessness.

Some fundamental questions on the meaning of life

Many, if not most people, are confronted and bothered, sometimes haunted by fundamental questions touching the meaning of life. These questions emerge at one time or another, often on the occasion of circumstances such as the birth of a child, the death of a loved one, in face of suffering, a turning point in life, an important encounter, the search for a way of life …

Everyone formulates in their own way the content of the questions they have about the mysteries of life and death, of growth, of each person's place on earth and among others, of God, etc. :

– Can one continue to develop throughout life? Is the being within the person bottomless, infinite, immortal?

– Is there life after death? Is death the end?, a passage? a metamorphosis?, a beginning?

– What is the meaning of these few decades that most human beings spend on earth? Does each person have a place to occupy and a role to play in the whole that forms humanity? Is humanity itself moving in a direction that would give meaning to each human life?

– Is God a reality? a projection? a compensation? a myth?

– Etc.

To find a meaning to life that is "comprehensive", full and fulfilling, people have to situate their life in an ensemble which goes beyond them: Humanity, Life, the Cosmos, God ...

Science, philosophy, religion and various cultures undeniably bring answers to these questions. Nevertheless, these answers remain "the answers of others". They satisfy children, especially if they echo certain intuitions which, often very early on, are already present. Adults, however, need to discover their own certitudes, their own answers, capable of satisfying both their reason and their need for coherence. These certitudes must also be capable of translating the profound intuitions of their being on this subject. The fundamental questions on the meaning of life then lead to a process of inner questioning which brings gradual progress toward an increased clarity on the mysteries of Life. Persons thus form a system of beliefs, of faith, starting from this interaction between their intuitions, the review of their reasoning, the beliefs of the people around them, scientific data, revelation (in the case of religion), etc.

It is obvious that the big questions relating to the meaning of life cannot be answered exhaustively and definitively. Reality cannot be captured in the perception of a single moment, as broad and deep as that perception might be. Also, the person's belief system must be in constant evolution and must be communicated to others with all the modesty and respect imposed by the limitations of the human intellect in face of these transcendent realities.

The role of the quest and the discovery of the meaning of life in the growth of persons

The growth of persons may be considered from the point of view of their progress in questioning the meaning of life and also from the point of view of the evolution of elements of an answer to this quest for meaning .

– In their early years, individuals do not ask questions about their life and its meaning. They are content to live in osmosis with whatever is acceptable in their milieu.

– They reach a phase of maturity and humanization in their growth journey when their first questions appear: "What will I do with my life? What is the meaning of my life? Why am I living? Is there a place for me in this humanity? …"

– A third phase follows, with the first elements of an answer and the genesis of a personal faith in certain certitudes perceived as truths.

– A fourth phase brings a perception of the meaning of life and a free and conscious commitment to the path which one feels is one's own.

In the process of growth, several important roles can be attributed to the quest and the discoveries concerning the meaning of life and the great existential questions. Here are some of them.

A driving force in the personal growth process

The very fact of asking questions on the direction one's life should take and the meaning of life itself, engages individuals in an exercise on themselves which stimulates them to go beyond ready-made answers. This places individuals in a dynamic of research, driving them to take actions which have meaning. Moreover, the fact of making discoveries, notably on the very meaning of one's life, releases important energies. People know where they are going and why they are going there, which is very stimulating for the growth of their potentialities. Growth in itself takes on meaning.

A role of personalization

Because the meaning of life is imprinted directly on their identity and "essential course of action", this research puts individuals in touch with their own sensations and intuitions concerning who they are and for what they are made. This results in a progression in personalization and autonomy in relation to the thought processes of the people around them.

A role of unification and solidification of the personality

The gradual discovery of the meaning of one's life and the ability to situate it in the broader field of humanity and Life itself, helps greatly to unify one's being and behaviour. The emergence of deep certitudes brings greater internal assurance, basic serenity and faith in life.

A role of awakening to the sense of responsibility

The fact of putting words to the meaning of one's life, and the place it has in the whole of humanity, awakens a sense of responsibility with respect to what life offers. A requirement to value all that one has received propels people to invest where their "essential course of action" leads them.

***

The question of the meaning of life has always haunted humankind. Thus, at the close of this 20th century, with all the upheavals brought about by the unprecedented evolution of Humanity, it seems that profound questions are being raised about everything that until now has given meaning to life, notably in the most developed countries. There is a loss of meaning, a loss of guidelines, undermining these prosperous civilizations.

The consequences of this phenomenon merit our greatest attention :
– they are alarming as much for individuals as for groups: not only states of depression, exponential consumption of psychotropic substances (medication, alcohol, drugs), suicide (the major cause of mortality in young people in a number of developed countries), but also the proliferation of sects, of fundamen-

talism, of forms of violence and terrorism …
– conversely, this loss of meaning of life conveyed by the environment can incite some people to seek out the meaning and objective of their existence. The renewal of certain forms of spirituality, recourse to the social sciences, studies conducted in business enterprises on values and ethics, the development of humanitarian action, and so many other things, translate in their own way this quest for meaning.

Today humanity is confronted with an important challenge. Its vitality, health and capacity for creation and innovation, its continuity, all depend for a great part on the way it will honour this quest for meaning.

Chapter 8

The person in order

The explanatory system of the person in the process of growth which we have just covered leads to a perception of the "ordered" person. We will now describe the goal individuals tend to achieve when they set out on a growth journey.

Let us say first of all, that the "order" discussed here has nothing to do with an acquired state of permanent equilibrium, nor with immutability. It is not like a room, perfectly arranged, each item with its permanently defined place, where all movement would be destructive of that "established order". On the contrary, the order in question here cannot exist except in association with change, creation, evolution, everything that comprises both dynamism and innovation, but also renouncement of former acquisitions, destabilization, agonizing indecision and discomfort. It is the orderly interaction of the pivotal centres of the personality that best foster harmonious functioning and growth of the person and therefore of groups and society as a whole.

The normal and the abnormal

Researchers in psychology have often been confronted with fundamental questions such as: what is normal or ordered in a human being and what is abnormal, even pathological? Should the normal be evaluated in relation to quantitative criteria (what the greatest number of people are living can be perceived as normal;

the exception, as the abnormal), or to qualitative criteria (all that is harmonious can be felt as normal, and all that is disharmonious as abnormal?) What is harmony? What is psychological health? Can one be healed of dysfunctions, or are they organic? What is an ordered personality? What is an accomplished human being? ...

By observing people who were less wounded in childhood and people who have been healed from past traumas, as well as studying individuals from the point of view of growth and the five pivotal centres, it has been possible to specify criteria for normalcy in the way individuals function and distinguish these from what is ab-normal. (Functioning ab-normally does not mean that the person is abnormal). This distinction between the normal and the abnormal is paramount, because it generates a lucidity about oneself and about the possible changes that can be made. As long as people live without guidelines, unaware of their confusion or illusion, they stagnate. They have the impression that they are normal and even comfort themselves with comparisons to those who live in a similar way. The observation and study of people have brought to light characteristics of the mature and healthy adult on the way to self-accomplishment, a person whose way of functioning is normal or ordered.

In general, one can postulate that normalcy for an individual, is to exist in harmony with what one is at the level of one's being, in harmony with the deep conscience. What is normal is to grow. The personality then develops harmoniously, in line with one's original potentialities. As a corollary, the abnormal includes all of one's ways of functioning, all of the behaviour patterns which deviate from the person's path to existence, are not in harmony with the deep conscience and hamper or stop the natural growth pattern.

The progress of individuals toward adult maturity, in which the pivotal centres of their personality function normally, is a very gradual process which often takes place at the price of a struggle. It is so easy to let oneself be taken in by instincts, desires or ambitions, without any concern to be in accordance with the being.

It feels so comfortable to fit in to what is being done in one's surroundings, to appear to be rather than to be. One can find so many benefits in being unaware or "half-hearted" in life, instead of confronting the reality of one's problems or simply the reality of one's immaturity.

Choosing to become oneself, to affirm one's uniqueness, to make one's own way, to grow, is an exacting task, especially in social contexts which are not very open to these values, even critical of them. Seeking to live an ordered life requires determination.

Having said this, each victory won, each progress recorded, each stage of growth surmounted brings increased life and additional motivation to pursue one's Way, plus a taste for happiness. In fact, to be oneself, faithful to oneself, to function harmoniously, rewards one with so much essential pleasure as to put all the difficulties and frustrations that this progress entails into perspective.

The characteristics of the ways of functioning of persons "in order"

The characteristics of the ways of functioning of adult persons are the following :
– They are fully aware of their riches of being and their limitations. Their personality has a solid foundation on which they can lean to affirm themselves such as they are. They can face life's turmoils even though they may be sorely tried at times.
– The path of their "essential course of action" is more clearly defined. Individuals thus put into action the essential of themselves with more and more efficiency and productivity for society. Their essential bonds gradually appear, fostering the actualization of their "essential course of action".
– Once it is established, the relationship to a Transcendency becomes more alive, confident, free, exacting and blossoming. Individuals are brought to their peak with dynamism and determination. They experience a profound serenity in face of the newness of Life. Their existence takes on meaning.
– The deep conscience, more and more enlightened by the lucidity of the "I", becomes the reference by which they conduct their lives. Individuals become more faithful to their conscience and more confident in their deep intuitions. They open their own furrows in spite of the inner solitude that this entails, sometimes including incomprehension on the part of the people around

them, and therefore suffering, but also profound peace and internal freedom.

– The "I" enters into a healthy relationship with the reality it perceives, accepting things more and more as they are. It is active and obedient to the deep conscience, clearly governing individuals on the path for which they were made to exist and be creative. They become more and more aware, humble and free, in a word, unified.

– The sensibility is gradually freed from interference, from encysted sufferings, notably those which hampered the actualization of the essential potentialities of the person. The life of the being has a tendency to irradiate the deep zone further. This produces more harmony in the reactions of the sensibility and in the general behaviour of the person.

– The body is perceived as a friend, a faithful reflection of internal life. It externalizes the life of the being. Individuals increasingly get to understand its messages, its needs and its limitations and take them into account more spontaneously, relying in some way on the wisdom of their body.

– The relationship to others is open, tolerant, respectful. At the same time, its demands are fitting and stimulating and it is authentic. Persons can develop close relationships while remaining free. They are capable of loving whomever crosses their path, not to say that this is always easy, particularly with those who do not return the favour.

– The relationship to the material environment, the lifestyle and nature, is peaceful, respectful and creative. Individuals satisfy their needs in moderation.

Thus, ordered persons are those who :
– have become unified around the being;
– base their life on the actualization of the being;
– refer to the being and to the deep conscience;
– answer the needs of other centres (the "I", body, sensibility) in harmony with the being. These individuals thus function normally, according to the dynamics of their profound nature.

"This normal way of functioning depends on :
– the degree of life and emergence of the being. The higher the degree,

the more this way of functioning is habitual.

– the degree of healing of the past, because past wounds, even though they are not conscious, cause interference in the person, disturb the normal way of functioning and give birth to disharmonious ways of functioning."[45]

One can also say that the normal way of functioning depends on the degree of humanization of the human environment into which individuals are inserted and the quality of the relationships which ensue.

An accessible fullness of existence

Having arrived at the adult stage of their progress and actualizing that for which they were made, individuals experience *"a fullness of existence which keeps on increasing"*[46]. Because their innermost aspirations are in the process of being realized, individuals are internally fulfilled. In fact, a human being is not fulfilled by arriving at a static human perfection, an immutable order, or an idealized state of happiness where all suffering is absent. These fantasies are not fulfilling, the most they do is to help one flee from an unacceptable reality. What really fulfills people is :
– to feel the best of themselves existing;
– to perceive the deep meaning of their existence;
– to experience their bond with a Transcendency;
– to progress in the actualization of their "essential course of action" and journey with people associated with them in this actualization;
– to feel that they contribute, in a modest way, to the advancement of humanity.

In other words, what fulfills, is to grow and to foster growth. Therein lies the fullness that a human being can experience.

"Naturally, at the beginning of the journey, one does not savour this sensation of fullness except in fleeting moments. But it is enough to have tasted a bit of the real happiness of being oneself, so that the memory remains and nostalgia becomes established, motivating one from within to pursue that Way."[47]

This fullness of life, experienced by those who place their prior-

[45] O.N. *"Summary of the Functionings"*, p. 2, 1984.
[46] O.N. *"Living Oneself in Order"*, p. 9, 1984.
[47] O.N. Idem p. 10.

ities in the growth of their being, coexists with the inevitable difficulties of life and the sufferings inherent therein.

"Stripped of the armour which in the past one had concealed for protection, one is more sensitive and therefore, to a certain extent, suffers more but is touched less deeply, only the sensibility is reached. The being is not shaken."[48]

Education as a means of establishing order in the person

This description of the individual in order may seem idealized to many people. This is so much the case that the majority of human beings function normally only on occasion and many abnormal ways of functioning are "standardized" and even valued in certain circles (intellectualism, activism, perfectionism, voluntarism ...). Only persons who were just slightly wounded or who have healed from their wounds of non-existence function normally most of the time. Their dysfunctions are rare and of short duration. They usually live in obedience to their conscience. Such persons are relatively rare.

In fact, most people do not even suspect that a better life could be theirs. Many have made efforts to improve and have become discouraged because of the lack of results. They doubt the possibility of growth and justify their dysfunctions as traits of character, even as a necessity, saying, "one must have a few faults", or else they blame others. These failures can be attributed to their lack of know-how in that area of their growth. Some people, wounded at their very core, say they do not believe in what they call "pipe dreams". They are satisfied to conform, as best they can, with the behaviour proper to their surroundings, or else they are in constant rebellion against society. For them, existing as they are awakens too much fear or too much pain, so they unconsciously repress their fundamental aspiration to exist.

To become oneself, to be healed from what prevents one from being oneself, to live harmoniously and gradually accede to a fullness of life, is something which can be learned. This apprenticeship is available to everybody. It requires an acceptance of the collaboration of others, because becoming oneself is an adventure

[48] O.N. Idem p. 10.

which cannot be undertaken alone. That collaboration is the role of education systems and growth accompaniment. It is the role of all educators, who should have received this education themselves as an aid to becoming true adults.

Part Three

Applications and extensions of the PRH explanatory system: social dimensions

One of the fundamental aspects of humankind is its social dimension. People are established in families, often in conjugal units, in groups, in a given society, with its culture, its political and economic systems ... Individuals carry within them this social dimension which includes belonging, interdependence, relationships, constant interactions, group awareness, aspiration for the success of the society and many other aspects.

In part three, we will examine three topics which relate directly to this human social dimension: the group, the couple and the education of children.

These different realities, in which interactions among individuals are found, will be observed, as were other realities in PRH psycho-pedagogy, from the point of view of growth.

Chapter 9

The group

The group is an ensemble of individuals in interaction. It is a social entity in itself with its own characteristics, which present analogies with those of individuals.

– Temporal characteristics: the group has a beginning, a life span, an end.

– Ontological characteristics: the group has an identity (linked to the profile of its members, its size, its internal culture, and the objectives it pursues, etc.). It has its boundaries (there are those who are part of it and those who are not). It has its raison d'être. It is more than the sum of the individuals who comprise it.

– Structural characteristics: the group has its way of functioning. A hierarchy exists with one or more leaders, often many categories of members having specific roles, and being able to form sub-groups. Methods of assembling are defined (frequency and duration of meetings, meeting places). More or less formalized interactions are established among members, with group phenomena such as the feeling of belonging, a system of values, influence, power, tensions and conflicts, etc.

Different group categories
(task group, life group)

Two categories of groups can be distinguished: task groups and life groups.

The first objective of a task group and its members is to accomplish something together. People are gathered around the work to be done. This is generally the case in business enterprises, unions, educational institutions, associations, etc. In these groups, a certain life together exists, but it is related to the tasks to be done.

The first objective of a life group and its members is to live together. This is the objective pursued by families, community groups, and to a degree, nations. These groups also have tasks to do for the common good and the satisfaction of each member, but it is not their first objective.

Personal aspirations and needs, and group life

People join groups to realize their potentialities and also to satisfy both their normal and "deficiency" needs. The aspirations and needs of members of a group constitute a *"key to understanding group phenomena"*[49]

The phenomenon of belonging

The choice of belonging to a group is conditioned by the degree to which its members can expect their aspirations and needs to be satisfied. They will maintain their affiliation as long as their potentialities can be realized, which means, as long as they can exist according to their being and on the path of their "essential course of action", and as long as their normal needs or "deficiency needs" are sufficiently gratified. They leave the group if it fails or ceases to let them actualize their aspirations or when it frustrates them too much in their expectations.

The phenomenon of values

Every group has its system of values, that is, a system which ranks what is essential, what is important to the group and what it seeks to promote or defend.

Note : The word "value" can cover many shades of meaning:
– the notion can be defined as value "of itself" (all that is of a nature to foster personal growth and the humanization of society), or value "for oneself" (all that is important to the person, such as one is, without reference to personal growth) ;

[49] O.N. *"Aspirations and Needs – A Key to Understanding Group Phenomena"*, 1991.

– moreover, these values can be:
  • values that are homogeneous with the being;
  • values which emanate from "deficiency needs", principles or projects;
– a value homogeneous with the being can actually be either the expression of a potentiality, or the satisfaction of a "deficiency need". For instance, love is a value which can be
in harmony with the being and its expression is then authentic, appropriate and respectful of others. But it can also seek to fill a disproportionate need to love and be loved, in
which case the expression of this value is excessive and not well adapted to others.
The common point between these different values is that they are perceived subjective-
ly as a good to be sought or defended.

The objectives of the group can include values that attract individuals and mobilize their energy. The *modus vivendi* of the group
also reflects certain sought-after values. The sensibility of each
person to some values rather than others also conditions one's
belonging to a group. This can be explained by the correlation
between the deep aspirations and/or the needs of individuals, and
the values of the group. The values guiding relationships within
the group are in keeping with the aspirations and needs of the
individual members.

The phenomenon of influence
"*They have influence who answer to the aspirations and needs :*
• *of the group as a whole, or;*
• *of a part of the group, or;*
• *of a particular person.*"[50]
Through who they are and what they do, people with influence
provide others with the possibility of satisfying their own aspirations and needs in the group. In return, the group members offer
their confidence and give them a power they hold only insofar as
the group is satisfied in its aspirations and needs. This power is not
related to rank. However, influence can be diverted from the good
of individuals and the group. It can be turned to other purposes
by using manipulation or demagogy.

The phenomenon of tensions and conflicts
The source of tensions and conflicts has a direct link with the
phenomenon of aspirations and needs. In fact, when a person's
aspiration is thwarted in a group, it generates increased tension

[50] Idem p. 6.

between that individual and the group or a member of the group. Also, when a personal or group need is manifested, but not taken into account, this produces tension with the group or with the group member toward whom these expectations are directed. The tension is greater if the need in question is a "deficiency need". Handling these tensions, which are inevitable even in a group with strong cohesion, instead of denying or minimizing them, avoids having them degenerate into conflicts.

Factors for group efficiency and harmony

These factors are numerous and varied. Of equal concern are:
- the definition of objectives and strategies;
- the definition of the roles of each member;
- the necessary material means;
- the motivation and commitment of each person to implementing the action plans.

Let us look at a few fundamental factors which have an influence on the performance of a group and the climate therein. What makes a group progress in the achievement of its objectives and in the harmony of its relationships, is:

The capacity of each of its members to exist
A group is much more efficient and vigorous when its members are aware of their being, including its riches and its limitations, and have liberated their capacity to be themselves. They then enrich the group with their human resources. They become competent and efficient actors at their own level. This is all the more true if the position they occupy corresponds to their "essential course of action".

This assumes that those who are responsible have sufficient knowledge of the members, pay attention to their development, are able to be themselves as leaders and are also personally sound. Members who dare to exist need to have people in charge who are mature, capable of listening to them and taking them into account, without alienating themselves to them. This also assumes an organization where partnership is developed in hierarchical relations and in relationships. Before all this, choices in terms of education are indispensable in order to facilitate the personal growth process of the group members. As we have seen, knowing how to be oneself can be learned. The principal fruits of this learning are maturity of behavior and the capacity to actualize one's riches.

The capacity for commitment

The efficiency of a group also depends on the capacity of everyone to be committed effectively by exercising all their powers, both formal and informal

In a group, one can exist by being content to do what those in charge demand, to accomplish the task for which one is being paid (in the case of companies, for example). Commitment, in addition to that, means taking initiatives to make the group succeed in the achievement of its objectives as well as in the good harmony of group life. Most of the time, group members hold powers far more important than they are aware of. They can speak, contribute their suggestions or be quiet, take action or remain passive, enter into relationships or remain in their corner, help someone or leave them to fend for themselves, let rumors run wild, even feed them, or stop them, etc. To commit oneself is to take responsibility. It is to be not only an actor but an "author" of progress in the effectiveness and humanization of relationships.

Two types of disproportionate and recurring reactions are very often encountered in the way individuals exist and become engaged in a group. Some people, undermined by wounds of non-existence, seem to be paralyzed in their relationship to others, not daring to exist in a group; others to the contrary, although wounded as well, experience an over-affirmation of self, existing "too much" and dominating the people around them. Both are cases of lost opportunity for group efficiency and healthy internal relationships.

The capacity to adapt

The capacity of members of a group to adapt is necessary in order to face the obstacles they meet, without losing sight of the essentials.

When one exists such as one is and makes a commitment, one

is necessarily confronted with external difficulties (different opinions, disagreements, the unexpected, material difficulties, time constraints, etc.) In face of these obstacles, one can be obstinate, exercise pressure and seek to dominate. Another reaction can be to abdicate, resign, capitulate, "give up" on problems. Or again, one can seek to adapt, in other words, come around to revising the original project in order to take into account the reality which presents itself. At times, wisdom and the good of the group make it imperative to go back on a previous decision.

Adaptation starts with an acceptance of the presence of the obstacle and forfeiting what one had expected to do. The next step is to seek and choose another solution, more realistic and therefore achievable. To be constructive for the group, this adaptation must not renounce something essential. If that were the case, it would no longer be adaptation, but self-denial. Some members may, in conscience, have to leave the group if the required adaptation constrains them to deny their personality in some essential aspects or suffer unbearable frustrations.

In order that these three ways of being: to exist, to commit and to adapt oneself, contribute to the optimal advancement of the group, it is necessary that the greatest possible number of people have integrated the dialectic necessary to the double action of being oneself and adapting. In other words, once those members of a group exist and commit themselves, it is important that they have, within themselves, a latent willingness to adapt if the situation requires it. On the other hand, if they must adapt, they must have within themselves the latent requirement to not renounce what their conscience dictates. This internal predisposition for authenticity and adaptation is a protection against pitfalls of domination and capitulation.

"This authenticity-adaptation dialectic is the most powerful motor existing for group advancement, because :
— the authenticity of each member enriches the group with all the riches of being of the members of the group;
— and the capacity for adaptation of each member oils the works, avoids the phenomenon of domination, avoids conflicts and maintains a climate of cooperation and partnership." [51]

[51] O.N. *"The Authenticity-Adaptation Dialectic"*, p. 3, 1991.

The capacity to manage tensions and conflicts

The three ways of being that have just been described find a direct application in another factor for progress and harmony in a group: the capacity to manage tensions and conflicts.

In a group, tensions are unavoidable. When life conditions are difficult, they increase. Tensions should be considered positively, as symptoms that are important to analyze in order to best remedy them. If they are well understood and well managed, these tensions can be useful indicators, since they often demonstrate that something has not been sufficiently taken into account. They generate changes and improvements. At times, it is important to accept a difficult reality, over which one has no direct control.

Conflicts arise from tensions that have not been taken seriously soon enough, or that one was unable to resolve. These conflicts hinder the advancement of a group. Their resolution uses up a lot of time and energy. It is therefore important to confront them as soon as possible. The ideal would be to prevent them from happening through good interpersonal relations, sound management of each one's contribution and clarity in the objectives and plans of action. This could be done by a system of internal communication, allowing the expression of dissatisfactions so as to remedy them as soon as possible, and by creating opportunities for periodic adjustment.

The following are a few basic principles that can help to manage these tensions and conflicts:

– To aim at preventing conflicts by giving serious consideration to displayed tensions and responding suitably to legitimate expectations.

– To examine the situation in order to define the real problem. Behind the discontent, the criticisms, the demands, the movements of aggression and violence, the strikes, one must know how to read frustrated aspirations and unmet expectations. To discover just solutions that will appease tensions and contain conflicts, requires that one get down to the real causes, beyond the factors which triggered them.

– To communicate. In order to do that, to seek to understand the point of view of others by trying to put oneself in their place, trying to feel what they feel, without moral judgement on what they are experiencing. For fruitful communication, it is indispensable that the sensibility of the antagonists be sufficiently appeased. In communicating and attempting to understand, to beware of interpretations of the experience of others or readings which make one disconnect from the reality of others. To be wary also of imaginary functioning which could easily make things worse.

– When the problem is sufficiently clarified, to seek possible solutions which, without completely solving the problem (and that is not always possible), would bring about an improvement and a step toward a more satisfactory solution. Following the authenticity-adaptation dialectic mentioned above, will help to achieve this.
– The common good leads to the respect of both the good of individuals and the good of the group in a balance which must always be sought.

Note : The directors, managerial staff and people responsible for a task group or a life group can profit from a good study of the explanatory system of the person in the process of growth such as developed by PRH. Because of their responsibility, the consequences of their behavior in their relationships are important and can have an effect on the social climate and the efficiency of groups they are leading. Their education in human relations, in order to learn to listen better, to analyze better, to diagnose better, to react better ... is proving more and more to be a major asset.

The role of groups in the growth of persons

As we have just seen, the growth of persons through the contribution of their riches, is a growth factor for groups. Conversely, group living can be a powerful accelerator of personal growth for the individuals who make up the group. It offers a privileged place of actualization for each one's potentialities. But this assumes that certain conditions be met, among which are the following :
– that the objectives of the group allow the members to live the best of themselves;
– that the persons responsible not be solely focused on the task at hand, but also concern themselves with planning satisfying work-

ing and life conditions for the group, and concern themselves with individual growth;

– that the members of the group have liberated their potential and have acquired sufficient internal freedom and affective maturity to exist such as they are in depth, without molding themselves to the standards of the group;

– that all members have developed an awareness of their personal responsibility for the common good.

***

Group living can be a regressing factor for its members when the objectives or the common life rules do not lead to the good of individuals or when the individuals do not live ordered lives. Energy then becomes dispersed, and the group quickly becomes inhibitory even destructive of the personality of the people who compose it.

However, if the conditions cited above are assembled, life group liberates an energy incomparably more stimulating for growth than if one remains alone, or if one has only interpersonal relationships. A sort of synergy is then produced among the members of the group, making everyone more efficient and more creative and rendering the group itself particularly fruitful. In those conditions, the group becomes a privileged place of growth and fulfilment for individuals, particularly in the social and creative dimensions of their being.

While group life can be a stimulant for the growth of persons, this is not its only purpose. In fact, groups themselves play a primary role in the humanization of society. Their entire raison d'être is to contribute to the advancement of humanity, which they serve that much better when the synergy described above is lived in their midst.

Thus, groups possess an obvious potential for personal as well as for collective development. They constitute a fundamental lever for the progress of humankind.

Chapter 10

The couple

On the one hand, this is a very broad subject and there is no question of claiming to cover it completely in this chapter.

On the other hand, observation of the actual experience of couples has led PRH to formulate some hypotheses, notably on what brings the couple together. However, these hypotheses must still be verified and compared to other explanatory systems, before they can be retained. Many couples have reacted favourably to these hypotheses during educational workshops, adding that they have provided effective help on their life journey, particularly in times of crisis. This justifies serious consideration of these hypotheses, which should continue to feed research in this area.

The "bond of being of a couple"

The notion of "essential bond" or "bond of being" has already been mentioned in the chapters on The Being and on Relational and Affective Life. The bond of being of a couple is specific to the case in which a man and a woman unite and embark on a commitment to live together and create a family.

The bond of being of a couple constitutes a particular aspect of the being of a person. It can be recognized from the sensation of not being complete without the other and consequently, of not being able to live one's life to the full without the other. Each member of the couple can, to some extent, exist and be fulfilled alone. This is a proof of their autonomy, indispensable if a true relationship is to exist. Experience shows, however that, related to each other, united to each other, interacting with the essence of each other, individuals find a dynamic of existence and self-revelation in their potentialities which allows them to go much further in their own fulfilment than if left alone.

Thus, the two commit themselves to each other based on a strong intuition :
– that they will become more fulfilled in who they are and in that for which they were made;
– that together they will be able to follow an "essential course of action" which will give full meaning to their life and be helpful to society;
– that they will form a united, happy and fruitful couple.

The bond of being of a couple is a living reality for both partners which can only exist in reciprocity. It is a locus in which one feels profoundly united to the other in essence. While all couples speak of mutual recognition, some will go so far as to claim their unwavering certitude that they are "made for each other".

Note : On the basis of that last observation, some people extrapolate, introducing a notion of predetermination to this fact of a couple's bond of being. This determinist, even fatalist concept of human phenomena ignores a given of human reality which everyone can observe for themselves, that is, the freedom with which people guide their life based on the choices they make. In our opinion, it would be more accurate to say that in every person there exists a capacity to start a couple. Before it can be actualized, this capacity is often seen as an aspiration to commit one's life to someone, to form a couple, to start a family ... Everything leads us to believe that the bond of being of a couple is born of the two-fold condition that there be a meeting with a person with whom one sees the possibility of a long-term life together and that both partners adhere freely to a mutual commitment. Then, thanks to this recognized and accepted emerging bond, the initial capacity is actualized through this commitment.

A few characteristics of this bond of being of the couple:
– This bond joins the partners of a couple in the entirety of their persons, particularly at the level of their being. What characterizes a couple's bond of being is not simply an affinity at the level of the sensibility. Nor is it merely physical attraction, common interests,

or even some similar aspirations or things to do together. It is a bond that people feel as constituent of their being from the time they mutually choose each other, and which involves their entire selves. Thus, faithfulness to the other is at the same time faithfulness to oneself, one's being and one's own conscience.

– Because it is part of the person, this bond is therefore alive and in constant evolution. Thus, during the course of the couple's life, the bond is consolidated, becomes more profound, reveals itself with multiple facets, is solidified. The growth of the bond depends on the degree of emergence of the being of each partner. But this bond can waste away to become almost inaccessible if one does not take care of its growth and if the relationship is left to become bogged down in the turmoils that assail it.

– Underlying this bond is a feeling of unique and profoundly committed love.

– This bond is felt as long-lasting. Many couples have a feeling that their bond is so essential, solid, resistant to trials or to simple daily wear and tear, that it is indestructible.

– A couple's bond of being is characterized by a feeling of unity, of complementarity, of profound inner proximity, of a common outlook on life, and also an openness to the outside.

– The bond of being of a couple is unique, personalized. Every couple has its identity, as does each person. This identity is marked by the lived experience of the relationship (couples being characterized by their mutual tenderness, their complicity, authenticity, joy of living, dynamism, their mutual confidence, their interiority, etc.) It is marked also by shared or complementary action (investment in a relationship to children, in the reception of others, in common professional, political, and social commitments, etc.)

– This bond is fruitful, stimulating the growth of each partner. It is the base for building a family. Fruitfulness is also expressed through external commitments useful to society.

Two interacting realities: the bond and the relationship

It is important to distinguish two realities which are in constant interaction between the partners in a couple: the deep bond which unites them and the relationship between them.

The bond

The bond is what unites two persons through the being, that is, through the most essential in each of them. Like other realities of the being, the existence of this bond is not a matter of personal will. (A person will sometimes wish to forge a bond of being of couple with another, but because there is no reciprocation, no bond occurs. Conversely, there are those who meet someone who does not correspond to the idea of the mate they were expecting, but nonetheless recognize their bond of being as a couple). Thus, the bond appears. It exists. Both partners gradually become aware of it in the act of their meeting, of their keeping company, of their awakening to a profound love and mutual recognition. Eventually, the existence of this bond asserts itself strongly enough to become an unwavering certitude, giving support so solid as to permit a long-term mutual commitment.

The relationship

The relationship incorporates the individuals in all that they are: their essential selves of course, but also their "I", their sensibility and their body. It includes all the experience proper to these pivotal centres: their needs, their resulting expectations, their normal ways of functioning and their wounds. The relationship falls within the responsibility of each of the partners, who may or may not commit themselves to it, who may encumber it with their dysfunctions or seek to restrict them, etc.

"*It is obvious that there is permanent interaction between bond and relationship. It is because of the bond (felt as an inkling before becoming a certitude) that the relationship was formed. It is because the relationship is good that the bond can further develop, enriching the relationship. The latter, in turn, will renew the bond and so on and so forth.*"

It is absolutely essential to distinguish between the bond which unites the individuals at the level of their being and the relationship which they experience between them:
– *this distinction is particularly important when a couple is first*

starting and one can easily doubt the existence of a bond (about which there is little awareness) because of difficulties in the relationship (which are inevitable). The bond/relationship confusion keeps doubt alive, causes useless suffering and delays progress;
– this distinction also helps one to weather tensions and conflicts. One can dare to exist in the relationship (at the risk of upsetting it) without being afraid of "breaking off the bond". Such fear opens the way to the unspoken or to non-existence, neither of which bring anything worthwhile to the relationship;
– finally, this distinction clarifies exactly what must be "worked on": the relationship.

This latter point is fundamental. Just as one can say that the bond of being of a couple is a reality whose existence is beyond the control of individuals, one can also say that together, individuals have full control over the relationship, including its termination.

Four axes on the growth journey of a couple

The couple is a reality whose evolution relates particularly to :
– the personal growth of both spouses;
– the strength which comes from joint commitments or from individual commitments supported by the other;
– the emergence of unity between the two spouses and the resulting strength of their bond;
– the stimulation and harmony brought about through physical and sexual relationships.

These four points represent four axes on the growth journey of a couple. To nurture the growth process as a couple, is to progress along these lines. Let us review these points again.

Personal growth
This axis is fundamental and takes priority in the growth journey of a couple. It is a question of each of the partners becoming themselves, liberating their potential for love and learning to harmonize their existence and their growth with the other, without

denying themselves nor blending into the desires of the other, without distancing themselves for any length of time or shutting themselves off from the other, also without imposing themselves upon or dominating the other.

This search for harmony is a daily task. On the one hand there is self-affirmation and faithfulness to oneself in the couple (indispensable conditions if growth is to take place). This must be harmonized, on the other hand, with an adaptation to the partner, with that person's potential and limitations. There is always the possibility of preferring a peaceful relationship to growth. By definition, the latter makes people change, triggering reactions which always disrupt the harmony of a couple in one way or another.

It is normal to take one's spouse into account and to aim for harmony in the relationship. This leads to voluntarily making sacrifices, being flexible and amending one's method of putting into practice the means to growth. However, it would be abnormal and unhealthy for the couple were one (perhaps both) of the partners to bury their personality and give up on becoming themselves because it generates upheavals in the relationship.

Personal growth can be promoted by the spouse. Each partner can encourage the other through faith in the other's potentialities, through truthfulness and love, through well-adjusted demands, through agreement on outside help, through commitment to one's own personal growth journey, etc. (Cf. the paragraph on mutual help in the couple.)

Joint commitments

When a man and a woman recognize that they are made for each other, they often discover simultaneously (sometimes subsequently) that they have something important to live and to do together. There is a more or less conscious aspiration to be creative together, leading to something of a "life project": to have children and educate them, to set up a household, to commit themselves both to the same cause ... The experience of couples engaged in a common "essential course of action" shows the astonishing social creativity that a couple can produce when both bring to it the best of themselves.

The commitments taken together as a couple coexist with personal commitments. When those commitments, in which the partners each seek to actualize themselves, receive not only the blessing, but also the moral and concrete support of the other, experience shows just how much that can promote the accomplishment of the task, as well as the unity of the couple and the growth of each partner.

Frequently, however, the commitments of each person added to the commitments of the couple give rise to conflicts within the relationship. If these conflicts are not to cause trouble for the unity of the couple, it is important to take them seriously and analyze them. Necessary adjustments can then be made to such commitments and the way they are handled.

The unity of the couple

The unity of the couple comes basically from the bond of being of the couple which unites a man and a woman. In other words, unity cannot be created, it is not even an objective to attain. Unity is an ontological characteristic of that bond, a fruit of that bond which comes to maturity as one develops personally and within the couple. Having said that, it is apparent and consolidated only in proportion to the emergence of the bond of being of the couple and the degree of harmony of the relationship.

This unity is realized for each couple and for each partner in a personal way. It is expressed in areas which can be very different: unity of tastes and sensibilities, unity of bodies, unity of ideas, unity of action and commitment, unity through one's most profound self, unity of aspirations, of beliefs, etc.

Many expressions are used to describe the unity of a couple: the same outlook on life, partnership, inner togetherness, harmony, mutual and deep tenderness, an impression of being "welded" together, of being "molded from the same clay"... but there is also an "otherness" made up of exchanged and accepted differences, a source of complementarity and creativity.

– *A few characteristics of unity in a couple :*
– unity emerges with the bond, which means that it is generally perceived from the start of the relationship, when the individuals discover their bond;

– unity is felt as containing strength and stability, which are particularly apparent when the couple faces moments of hardship. The unity of a couple is not an ephemeral reality, dependent on the moods of each partner, but a stable and long lasting reality always in evolution;

– unity is accompanied by a sensation of being inhabited by the "presence of the other" in one's innermost self, whether the other is physically present or not;

– unity in a couple is also characterized by an intuitive understanding which perceives the innermost depths of the other, often beyond what each partner knows of the other's potential. This profound and intuitive knowledge is the source of faith in each other and their capacity to become what they are meant to be;

– unity in a couple is perceived as a source of fertility, life and love. It is a forward propellant, opening onto others and radiating over the people around them.

The particularly rich potential contained in the unity of the couple can be seen in these few characteristics, noted in couples under observation. Progress on this line of growth frees this potential and makes it work to their advantage.

– Distinction between unity and fusion

Couples often experience some ambiguity in the notion of unity, particularly at the beginning of a relationship. Unity is often confused with fusion. Fusion, which is often presented as the model to attain, means to be but one, to be the same, to eliminate all differences, to always be in agreement on everything and therefore avoid any source of potential conflict. In brief, it creates a "monolithic" entity where the partners blend into each other and give up any element of their personality which makes them different from the other.

It is not always easy to make the distinction between unity and fusion, because the sentiment of "being one" with the other is common to both of them. And yet unity and fusion are two phenomena of a totally different nature :

– *"Unity comes from the being. It results from a meeting between being and being. It gradually affirms itself because of a long-term, solid, fruitful, autonomous relationship which is open to the other, to*

others and is respectful of differences.
– Fusion comes from a wounded sensibility, that is, from deficiencies and non-existence (i.e. the inability to hold one's own, to lead one's life, to assume one's solitude as a human being in circumstances which can be more or less numerous)".

At first blush, fusion may be felt as fulfilling. Love of the other, often passionate, gives the impression that deficiencies have disappeared. This love is very stimulating at first, facilitating the birth of numerous potentialities.

But fusion quickly becomes a trap, in which one confines oneself and has a tendency to confine the other and the relationship. Instead of learning to exist according to one's personality, thus tending toward autonomy, the temptation can be great - especially if the deficiencies are serious - to seek to maintain this fused relationship. This situation will invariably provoke an eventual crisis in the life of a couple. This crisis can be an opportunity for growth if it is seen clearly, but it can be fatal to the relationship if the partners are not too aware of their basic unity and fail to call upon competent people to help them through this difficult time.

– *Attitudes which promote unity*
Some attitudes build, consolidate the couple's relationship and thus allow unity to manifest itself and be reinforced. Of specific note are :
– the attitude of truth to oneself and in the relationship. In fact, there is no consolidated relationship that can be constructed without the presence of this attitude of truth, which is a source of clarity, confidence and health in the relationship;
– the attitude of humility before oneself and in the relationship. Much stagnation in couples is due to a lack of acceptance of reality (one's own, that of the other, and that of the relationship) as it is. People often do not accept their qualities or their faults. They wait for the other to change, hoping for the relationship to be more fulfilling. An attitude of humility helps to remove these excessive expectations and the bitterness which they cause. It brings deep peace and disarms the defenses which cause stiffness and rigidity in face of the other;

– the attitude of determination to exist on one's own and progress in solitude. "*In a couple each partner is not there to carry the other, but to help that person grow, be fulfilled and march toward autonomy. Each one is not there to fill the other's deficiencies, but to help in healing them. Each one is not there to compensate for the other's frailties, but to help reduce them ...*" The attitude of determination to exist on one's own and progress in solitude, in faithfulness to one's deep conscience even though that might disrupt the relationship, lightens, enriches and stimulates the relationship, whereas fusion or dependence make it sclerotic;

– the attitude of determination to share one's inner experience. This determination is necessary to overcome the multiple resistances and legitimate reasons for not sharing one's lived experience. The relationship is "nurtured " because of these acts of sharing and withers when they no longer exist or are lacking.

The physical relationship and sexual harmony

The body and sexuality have an obvious influence on the growth of a couple, particularly on the personal progress of each partner (1st axis), their joint commitments (2nd axis), and the unity of the couple (3rd axis).

– *The physical relationship*

A true communication is established between partners on a daily basis through the intermediary of their bodies. Everything can become a "word", expressing most profound love for each other. It can be a smile, a look, a kiss, a caress, a gesture such as holding hands, embracing, walking side by side, but also in the way of dressing and grooming. The "friendship" which exists between the bodies constitutes a privileged path to reach this profound and unique friendship which joins each partner to the other.

The relation of bodies can also convey and at times even amplify personal or relational upsets. By paying attention to the messages of their own and the other's body, the partners can be alerted to an inner experience not yet brought into awareness. They can thus advance in full knowledge and understanding of each other beyond the words that are expressed.

However, each partner can have disproportionate reactions with respect to the other's body (excessive attraction or rejection), prejudicing this form of communication which is helpful to the growth of the couple. It is important in this case to heal the past sufferings which underlie these reactions.

– *Sexual harmony*

Human sexual life goes beyond the scope of the mere aspiration to procreate. It expresses important aspirations and it satisfies or attempts to satisfy multiple needs (normal or deficient): the aspiration to unity and the need to feel as one, the aspiration to give and perpetuate life, the need to touch and be touched, the need to be caressed, the need for warmth and security, the need to be kissed and held, the need to be wanted, desired, awaited, the need to relate by way of contact, the need to feel that one exists, the need for pleasure of the senses, etc. Some of these needs actually express deeper needs. For example, the need to be kissed may be the manifestation of a less conscious and more profound need for security or proof that one is loved.

Progress in harmony in this area of sexual relationships consti-tutes an axis of growth for the couple. Although the success of a couple is not solely or primarily dependent on sexual harmony (contrary to certain widespread beliefs), it is nevertheless a very important axis because of the consequences this sexual harmony has on the personal life of the partners and on the unity of the couple.

This harmony most often goes together with the overall harmo-ny of the relationship. It therefore requires time and advanced maturity before it can manifest itself in all of its richness and depth, and in some stability.

Sexual harmony manifests itself and is consolidated in the cou-ple through the quality of the exchanged love and tenderness as well as the attention given the other. It is also demonstrated by a blossoming of the whole person: physical blossoming through bodily contact and the pleasure it brings, psychological blossom-ing through the joy and stimulation which loving and being loved in this way provides.

Difficulties and disproportionate reactions can limit this har-mony, even compromise it. Among these difficulties are :
– difficulties in integrating the differences that exist between male

and female sexuality;
– past traumatic experiences which have left after-effects;
– ambiguities in sexual demands in which childhood needs or a compensation for non-existence can be unconsciously mixed;
– mental blocks, expressing a wound of non-existence;
– difficulty in mastering one's body, etc.

The help of a competent person can prove useful in understanding the origin of these difficulties and finding a solution for them.

Verbal communication in the couple

The best way for a couple to build along its four axes of progression is through dialogue. Without minimizing the importance of non-verbal methods (Cf. the paragraph on the relation of bodies and the sexual relationship), communication gains full meaning only through words which are felt, pronounced, heard and understood.

The content of conversations
The content of conversations can affect many fields of expression :
– the field of external realities. The partners talk about what they are doing, events, material organization, etc. without involving themselves personally in what is being said;
– the field of internal realities: they talk of aspirations, the essentials, intuitions, experience in basic commitments, needs, desires, wishes, sentiments, inner reactions, preoccupations, projects, etc.

The verbalization of these inner realities is fundamental if one is to know and truly get together with the other, to love that person and nurture the relationship. Communion between a man and a woman is the principal result of this deep sharing which awakens the being of each partner, making it accessible.

The form of verbal communication
The form of verbal communication is very important if dialogue is to take place and have the function of constructing the couple

and its unity. This is all the more true when delicate subjects are being treated.

Observation of couples has provided a few principles which can promote good communication. They include :
– to listen without interrupting until the speaker has expressed all he or she has to say;
– to listen by trying to understand and empathize in what the speaker is saying and experiencing internally;
– to listen while taking care to keep in perspective any biases on what the other says or experiences, by ridding oneself of preconceptions of the other and the relationship, by avoiding interpretations, projections, judgements, accusations … To listen by also keeping emotional reactions in perspective;
– to speak while taking care to facilitate the other's understanding (which assumes that one has a fairly clear idea of what one wishes to communicate to the other);
– to express one's wishes, needs, aspirations, keeping in mind a respect for the freedom of the other;
– to express what one feels one has to say in conscience and not wanting to match an ideal of "absolute transparency". To accept not having to say everything, and also that the other does not have to express everything;
– to share with the other what one appreciates in them, what helps the relationship … but also what is bothersome or hurtful.

The environment

The environment also counts toward fostering the success of the dialogue. This means the time of day, the place, the surrounding silence, the regularity of these communication sessions, and also the body's relaxation, the physical proximity to the other, etc.

Note that the human environment, especially persons competent in helping couples, can be of great help in overcoming a block or difficult communication. Experience shows that, when things are very entangled, it is neither healthy nor efficient to persist in wanting to resolve problems by oneself. The perspective and objectivity of a competent third party is often able to clear up misunderstandings held by two interacting upset persons.

Note : The phenomena of "the unspoken" and transparency in communicating on a one to one basis.

Two types of "the unspoken" can be distinguished:

There are things one keeps to oneself through fear and non-existence. These unspoken words prevent the relationship from establishing itself on healthy and clear foundations. This is a matter of dysfunctions which one must eliminate as soon as possible.

There are, furthermore, some things which are purposely felt as needing to remain unspoken. One feels that it would not be helpful or healthy, or else that it is not the time to express them. In that case, one's conduct is dictated by reference to the deep conscience.

Transparency is a sign of mutual confidence and a capacity to exist in truth and to receive the other's truth. If the ultimate goal is increasing transparency between the two partners, it is to be considered more as the outcome of the growth journey of the couple than as a given which is due or absolute.

Mutual help in the couple

The relationship within the couple contains a mutual help dimension whose realization appears under two forms: external help and internal help.

"External" help

This help has various modes of expression. It can be physical or material help (rendering a service, supplying something which the other person needs, giving "a helping hand", sharing in the duties that come with life together); or intellectual help (providing information, explanations, knowledge), etc.

This form of help is mainly concerned with things to do for, or with, the other. It can be a channel for expressing love for one's partner. It makes it easier to live together and achieve things which would be impossible, or at least more difficult, to do alone. Sometimes this external help also provides internal help: a feeling of support, togetherness, well being.

"Internal" help

"*This is everything that gives inner strength, that helps to better living as a couple with its responsibilities, and everything which helps one to progress on the road to growth and healing*".[52]

This help is lavished in different ways :

[52] FPM 45 "*Mutual Help in the Couple*", p. 1, 1988.

– in a way of being which is based on non-judgement, on acceptance of the inner lived experience of the other, on authenticity, kindness, respect, confidence;
– in a way of doing that adapts to the need of the other: listening, reflection, dialogue, advice, sharing of intuitions, encouragement, gestures of tenderness, etc.

This help form has its limits. One can be very helping at certain times, for certain types of problems, or in certain circumstances, but less so at others. This can be due to personal turmoil, or too much involvement in the problems of the other, or simply due to the fact that one does not have the internal availability.

When this internal help is possible, it is beneficial for each partner and for the relationship. Although less widespread in daily life than external help, this internal help is more important for the enrichment of the relationship. It stimulates the progress of growth and promotes commitment on the path of the "essential course of action". Moreover, this help form consolidates the unity of the couple. The fact of participating in a concrete way in each other's growth and hence in the success of their lives, greatly reinforces the bond which unites them.

Obstacles to life as a couple and to unity

A relationship will encounter dysfunctions. If they are not taken care of, they will wear it out, gnaw at it and deteriorate it, partially or entirely, temporarily or permanently. These obstacles hinder the development of the couple and hinder or even prevent their achievement of unity. For that reason, it is important to detect them and learn to remedy them.

There are signs that can indicate these obstacles. Serious dialogue becomes more rare. Misunderstandings appear. The feeling of love seems to become blurred, giving way to distancing, to resentment, suffering, aggression, a feeling of injustice. Dysfunctions proliferate. Confidence ends up being impaired as well as the pleasure of sharing one's life with the other. One can go so far as to no longer see the meaning of life as a couple, were it not for the presence of children. In spite of good will and attempts, any hope of finding solutions to all these difficulties gradually fades. Separation can then seem to be the only outcome to what has become a hell. Statistics attest to the fact that many couples give up at this point.

Egocentricity

What is seen at the root of these dysfunctions in the couple's relationship, is the presence of egocentricity, that is self-centeredness, which can go so far as shutting oneself off. Egocentricity moves in the opposite sense to the relational. The latter is characterized by openness to others and the interest one has for them, empathy, the gift of self to others, making one's riches available to help them become themselves. In egocentricity, one counts only oneself and tends to impose that as the reference in the couple: one's own ideas, perceptions, value system, wishes, desires, needs, beliefs, ways of doing, growth, problems, etc. Egocentricity finds its origin in deficiencies suffered in childhood, which makes one very concerned with receiving, or in ideological conceptions or cultural habits (the quasi institutional domination of man over woman, for instance).

This egocentricity is manifested in many ways. This has already been touched on when discussing relational difficulties.[*] It is reviewed here to give illustrations in the life of the couple. Among the most frequent manifestations of egocentricity and also the most harmful to the couple's relationship, one can name five egocentric mechanisms or movements:

– *Imaginary functioning*

Imaginary functioning is released by something which touches the sensibility. The persons start to reason, to interpret, to embellish or to dramatize reality or possibly to "create" it from nothing. They shut themselves off in this false perception of reality without being aware of it and act or react in all sincerity with respect to their partner starting from this false viewpoint. With such a base, communication can only be problematic.

* Cf. p. 140

– The mechanism of possession

The mechanism of possession is released by a need which impels one to take from one's partner whatever can satisfy that need and ease the inner tension provoked by it. Individuals are not content to receive, but help themselves, scorning the other's freedom. They tend to consider the latter as an object which they can dispose of as they please.

– The mechanism of domination

The mechanism of domination is released when partners, for one reason or another, wish to impose their will or views on the other, pressure them, exercise a power over them, monopolize them, "educate" them. This domination on the partner can be exercised in many ways: harshness, threats and sometimes violence, logic and persuasion, tears, muteness, blackmail, the game of seduction, manipulation, etc.

– The attitude of appropriation

The attitude of appropriation is a state in which individuals set themselves up before the partner and the relationship, seeing themselves as "proprietor" of the other, able to dispose of them as they wish. They will use possession or domination if the other manifests a personal desire which does not meet with their own wishes.

– Disengagement or resignation

When a person decides to live with another as a couple, there is commitment. This commitment means common action (the responsibilities of life together, children ...). It also means helping the other to become themselves and to actualize that for which they have been made. The attitude of disengagement is produced when one of the two partners goes their separate way in relation to life as a couple or in relationship with the other. One leaves the other the responsibility of facing alone, certain things which in fact require the participation of both parties. This type of resignation can be partial or whole. This attitude appears mainly when individuals do not get what they want through possession or domination.

These egocentric movements and attitudes are contrary to the attitudes mentioned in the paragraph on unity. Those are: truth (in imaginary functioning particularly, one disconnects from reality, reality of self, reality of the other, reality of the commitment); humility (one does the opposite in the movements of possession and domination); and the attitude of determination to exist on one's own and progress in solitude (egocentricity keeps one in dependence to the other). To reduce this egocentricity which affects the relationship of the couple, it is therefore necessary as a person and as a couple to return to those inner attitudes which promote unity. That is the antidote to egocentricity.

The meaning of the couple

We have seen in the chapter on the meaning of life that persons gradually discover the meaning and the direction of their existence through :
– the discovery and development of their identity;
– their commitment to that for which they were made;
– the deep bonds they have with respect to persons with the same "essential course of action";
– their place and role in humanity, starting with the human microcosm into which they are inserted.

The same holds true for the meaning of this adventure for two which is the human couple. The partners can discover the meaning of the couple by gradually analyzing :
– their identity with the potentialities which characterize and personify them in relation to other couples, these potentialities being either traits which are common to both partners, or those which could be considered complementary;
– their common "mission", concerning a successful life together, concerning life with the children, their education and the response to their fundamental needs, and also concerning common action in society (for instance, actions aimed at social organization, at the response to social needs, at social improvements, at the humanization of society, etc.);

– their essential bonds, those held with other parents engaged in the same educational areas, who share a concern and common references on the education of their children; bonds which are held in common with other persons engaged in the same social activities;

– their place and role in groups in which the couple is engaged, and in humanity, situating the couple socially and bringing out its usefulness to the life and progress of humanity.

***

By progressively discovering the deep meaning of the couple in this way, each partner enters into a dimension which is often unsuspected at the start of the relationship. The awareness of that meaning consolidates the bond of being of the couple and reinforces its solidity, liberating an impressive potential of energy. It motivates and makes one responsible to work on the quality of the relationship with the other and for the implementation of common actions in daily life. Each becomes aware that the success of the couple goes beyond the satisfaction of personal aspirations or needs. This success brings about benefits which touch and have an influence on others and on society.

Thus, the human couple is a reality of an astonishing richness as much for the fulfilment of individuals as for the humanization of society.

Chapter 11

The education of children

The PRH explanatory system was developed through observation of the real-life experience of adults. The understanding of this experience has brought to light the determining influence of education on the personal growth process. In retrospect, this has opened the way to useful teaching on how to educate children in order to facilitate their personalization and social integration. The aim of these observations and reflections is to help parents and teachers better understand the real-life experience of their children, or children in their care, to learn how to act with them, and for what purpose on a long-term basis.

Parental ideas on the education of their children

Whether they are aware of it or not, all parents hold deep-seated ideas on education to which they refer instinctively to educate their children. These innermost ideas form a frame of reference which brings together numerous elements gained through their own experience, the experience of others, and current theories. Some of the constituent elements of this frame of reference which can be isolated are :
– recollections of how their own parents and teachers treated them or their brothers and sisters, in specific circumstances, at various stages of growth and faced with different problems. These recollections influence them. They have a tendency to reproduce

what has been good for them, and to avoid what hindered them, without asking whether it is suitable for their children;

– principles, rules and methods, judged to be useful and good, which one tries to apply with one's children;

– ideas, theories, images, stereotypes and judgements, either handed down or self-made, on what is a human being, a child or a teenager and on how they grow, how to educate them. Thus, depending on whether one has a mainly positive or negative image of the human being, one will not use the same teaching method. In the first case, the priority will be to accompany the children and have faith in their potential; in the other case, there will be insistence on correcting what doesn't work and acquiring new models of behaviour;

– objectives and ideals forming references as to what children should be, should do and should become;

– sentiments related to one's own life and the influence of the environment. These can be happy family experiences, an abundance of happy memories, but also fears or guilt feelings, which influence one's dealings with the children;

– the parental frame of reference also includes "deficiencies" which show up as hesitations, doubts, questioning. One doesn't know what to think or do. There can also be confusion in the minds of parents, based on contradictory elements in their own references. (For instance, parents may hear on the one hand that it is not a good thing to punish a child, and on the other, that a child who doesn't receive a "good licking" once in a while will later become a delinquent).

This entire background often determines the educational activities of parents. They must be aware of it if they are to give the children a lucid education, adapted to them and their needs, and question any ways of doing which go against the growth of the human personality. Certain ideas, theories or principles can be good in themselves but sometimes prove to be untimely to what the children would need to receive at this precise moment in their life.

Thus, while it is necessary to know one's frame of reference, to soundly question it and to enrich it by reading, reflection and discussions, it is just as important for parents and teachers to learn to decipher the profound intuitions which emanate from their being. These are often remarkably wise and relevant and one can rely on them. One must also learn to distinguish these profound intuitions from other "voices" one may hear, (for instance, "voices" that say: "what will others think?"; "ideally, what should the child do?"; "what do people expect?"; "what has always been done in the family?")

What does "to educate" mean?

From the observations and experiences PRH has been able to accumulate to date on the subject of persons and their growth, here is how one could summarize what it means to educate children :

"Educating children :
— is helping them become what they are;
— is helping them find for what they are made;
— is helping them take their place in society".

In this concise formula one finds major highlights of the PRH explanatory system. The growth of the being is perceived as the development of potential riches which aspire to emerge, but whose actualization at the service of society depends to a large extent on whether the environment in which the children find themselves is helping or not and whether or not they are allowed to occupy a place in it.

The role of parents and teachers in the personality development and social integration of children

"So that their aspiration to exist may develop and bear fruit, children need the help of their mother and father. They cannot yet exist by themselves in this world where they have landed. The road to adulthood is long. It will be some time before they are solid enough in their being to engage autonomously in the Adventure of adult life and take

their place in the human Caravan.

Parents must therefore :

— help their children to become themselves;

— prepare them for life in Society;

— accompany them in their growth.

In brief, they must respond adequately to what the children need from them".[53]

In other words, the role of parents first of all, but also to some extent the role of teachers, consists in paying attention and taking into account the normal needs of children and seeking to satisfy them in a fitting and adjusted way.

Note : By fitting way, we mean a way which corresponds effectively to what these children need today to become themselves; by adjusted way, we mean a way of answering the needs of children which is neither excessive nor insufficient, and which takes into account the concrete situation including the limitations and needs of the parents.

Among the most fundamental needs to which parents and teachers must pay heed and must help to satisfy in the best possible way, one can note:

"— *the need for recognition;*

— *the need to be loved for themselves;*

— *the need for security;*

— *the need to be treated as children and not as mini-adults;*

— *the need for learning:*

— *the need to be "oneself".*[54]

Note : Parents themselves, in their own childhood, have not always had all these needs satisfied. This often brings them to overcompensate with their children so that they, in turn, will not experience the same suffering. This often leaves them unable to meet the needs of their children. Not having received, they don't know how to give, because their potentialities have not been able to germinate. Faced with the fact of their educational deficiencies, parents often have a tendency either to feel guilty or to make their children feel guilty for having these needs.

To get out of this rut from which few parents escape, it is important that they first learn to recognize their own deficiencies, (which often makes them able to abandon an ideal-

[53] O.N. *"Aspirations and Needs and Educating Our Children"*, p.4, 1988.

[54] Idem, p. 4.

ized image of their own parents and see them with their flaws). It is important also to learn to recognize humbly the residual consequences which these deficiencies have left. This recognition is fundamental, first of all for parents, because one cannot grow if one has not "landed" on the solid ground of reality such as it is. It is also fundamental for their children so as to best shield them from the guilt of asking something which the parents cannot give. (Children unconsciously think that, "if they do not give, I'm at fault for asking). Once this truth is established, it is necessary to learn to accept the reality of these deficiencies and their consequences (Cf. the attitude of humility described on p. 161.). Finally, parents can seek to surround themselves with persons who can make up to a certain extent for their deficiencies and bring to their children some elements of the responses they need in order to grow.

Having deficiencies does not make parents guilty but, when they cannot do it themselves, they are responsible for providing their children with the essentials, even if it is through intermediaries.

It is to be hoped that solidarity is developed between the parents, and among parents and teachers. It is necessary for the good of the children. Yet they must have been able to free themselves from the guilt of not being "perfect parents" and to have learned that a "good mother", or a "good father" is first of all a person who is just as able to recognize and share riches as to recognize and accept weaknesses and deficiencies, doing their best to limit the consequences on their children. The latter cannot achieve their own humanity, made up of riches and limitations, except in the presence of people who have learned to live with theirs.

The role of parents in meeting the needs mentioned above can be listed as follows:

To recognize the being of the children

The education of children consists in helping them to become who they are. This implies that the primary goal of the educational milieu is to guide the children to the knowledge of who they are at the level of their being, and help them actualize their potentialities and take into account their limitations. Children begin to know themselves only through the image that is fed back to them, mainly by their parents.

Thus it is important that the parents learn :
– to see, recognize and accept the riches of being of their children, and to appreciate them for their own sake (and not only in relation to the current value system);

– to give them sound feedback, by showing the happiness they feel for what their children are, without enclosing them in an idealized self-image;

– to figure out their potentialities through their desires, their projects and their aspirations, all of which they communicate in their own way; and

– to give up the dream of "perfect children" and the expectations entailed by that dream, which are a source of internal conflicts in children.

This recognition of the being of children by their parents is fundamental if the children are to give themselves the right to exist as they are and be happy. As we have seen, continued absence of this recognition or even worse, the rejection of children in their identity, causes wounds of non-existence.

To provide and communicate gratuitous love to the children

For children to develop with a normal self-image and thus attain a healthy relationship with themselves and others, they need quality love from their significant others. This is the love that proves to them that they are "loveable". The role of parents is thus to lavish this gratuitous love which emanates from their being, a love full of tenderness and affection, a love which is respectful and manifested through gestures, looks, tone of voice, time devoted, words and personal attention. This love for the children is also filled with goodness in the face of problems or sufferings, and tolerance for their errors and hesitations.

In order to love like this and express it, parents and teachers must liberate their deep affectivity. Children who feel loved gratuitously in this way by their mother and father, and not simply because of the satisfactions they bring, store a strength, an emotional security, in their psyche. They also receive a reference which awakens their own capacity for gratuitous love and trust in human love.

To offer security

Children are vulnerable, not yet having within themselves the physical and moral strength, nor the intellectual capacity to protect or help them face outside dangers. They are totally dependent on others for the satisfaction of their psychological needs, which are as vital to them as food and drink. Insecurity quickly takes hold in children when they perceive negative sentiments, conflicts, depression or anguish, in a family milieu from which they expect everything. The fear of not receiving their life needs, even of being abandoned, reaches them like a death threat and can paralyse their life force.

Thus, they expect this material and affective security and the protection they need from people around them, mainly their parents.

The role of parents is first of all to be aware of this extreme vulnerability of children and take it into account in their relationship with them. At the same time, they should not use threats or let their own insecurity weigh the children down. Their role also includes an adequate response to the physical and material needs of the children and protection against dangers. They have to enfold children emotionally so that they are assured that they can count on their parents and will never be abandoned. Furthermore, since much of the feeling of security or insecurity is transmitted through osmosis, it is incumbent upon parents to work on their own insecurity in order that they influence the psyche of their children as little as possible. This task starts with the recognition of the insecurity which causes one to set certain standards or to be hyper protective or dominating at times. Finally, parents can play an important role in helping children conquer or heal their insecurities, notably by inviting them to verbalize their fear instead of repressing it, by receiving them calmly with their fear and, when possible, by helping them to find what could restore their peace.

Through these adapted responses to their security needs, children start to develop a whole trust in life, in others, and in themselves, as well as a basic solidity.

To adapt one's demands to the maturity level of the children

It often happens that parents have disproportionate demands and behave as though their children were reasonable adults, capable of taking care of themselves, of succeeding on the first attempt, of being responsible, understanding, respectful of other people's property, autonomous ...

But children need to be asked for no more than they can deliver, to be accepted in their hesitations and their mistakes. They need requirements that are proportioned to their stage of development. To make them want to take short cuts and to expect too much from them is not good for their growth and can incite a feeling of guilt.

Parents have a role to play to accompany each child's rhythm of growth, respecting the stages of that growth by accepting that there will be moments of regression or letup. They must also concern themselves with awakening the children to the responsibilities of their age. This accompaniment requires patience, understanding and stability especially in the case of teenagers, whose contradictions, blunders and inconsistencies often offend the logic and sensitivity of their parents.

All human beings have the right to their childhood, their adolescence and their youth. It is under these conditions that they will become real adults.

To carry out training in the various forms of "learning"

In order to one day assume their responsibilities as adults in society, children, adolescents and young people have a lot to learn in the four areas of knowledge: knowing-how-to-do things in as many areas as possible, so as to assume one's practical life, take up a career and be autonomous; knowing-how-to-be oneself, which promotes the potentialities of the person through the integration of universal human values (to be true, tolerant, open, realistic, just, etc.); "knowing how to live" which allows one to feel at ease, alone and with others, because they respect the same rules and have the same relational guidelines; and finally, knowledge, which brings recognition of culture in general, awakens curiosity of the mind and enriches inner life through contact with everything that makes up the universe, from the infinitely small to the infinitely large.

Note : In this training, it is usual to think about :

– everything that can help children to fend for themselves in life (learning to speak, read, write, calculate, etc.);

– sexual education, by speaking with them about physical changes, sex differences, boy-girl relationships, the desires and sensations they experience, the way babies are born etc., knowing that the way this learning is carried out is as important as the content itself.

– On the other hand, importance is less frequently given to learning how human beings function and how to live in order to be happy.

Very early on, for example, parents or teachers can initiate children to the discovery and analysis of what they are experiencing: the ideas that come to mind, judgements they make of their peers, the momentary desires that they want to satisfy right away, at any cost, the needs of their body, their innermost heart, their innermost conscience which dictates what is right and not right to do etc.

These rudiments of psychology, which make "the diagram of the person in the process of growth" (Cf. p. 56) understandable to them, can help them: to make their decisions and develop a reference to their deep conscience, to differentiate what is essential from what is not essential, to take into account the needs of their overall self, etc. Moreover, this training awakens the interest of children in knowing themselves and initiates them to a self-discovery method which will serve them throughout life.

When one sees how early in life behavioural aberrations start and how long it takes to restore what deforms a personality, this form of training provides a preventive pedagogical path which deserves some attention.

In all areas of training, parents have a role with their children to transmit to them their own knowledge, notably all that can be useful or which can interest them in their slow ascension toward their autonomy and their encounter with the world.

This transmission is made in various ways: through example, children learn by observing and copying; through osmosis with their surroundings; through knowledge and the explanations their parents or teachers provide.

The way in which these periods of training unfold has an important influence as much for the integration of this knowledge as for the parent-child relationship. During the course of these apprenticeships, in the way one goes about it, children experience a response to the needs for recognition, being loved, being secure, being considered as a child and not as an adult. In other words, to respond adequately to the learning needs of the children is also to respond to the fundamental needs examined above. Thus attitudes of patience, acceptance of the time it takes for this learning to be acquired, of kindness, flexibility, openness to dialogue, of adaptation and pedagogical creativity, all make these periods productive and often very stimulating, for the children feel the love of their parents through and beyond what they teach them. It is not rare that these moments are engraved for life in the memory of the children and that, having in turn become parents, they create them spontaneously with their own children.

Thus, with the passing years, the children inherit this immense "capital", endowing them with knowledge that is indispensable if they are to actualize their potentialities and therefore become themselves and establish themselves in society.

To encourage personalization

When choices have to be made, parents are often tempted to influence their children in a way that corresponds to their own expectations, what suits them, their value system. Nor are occasions lacking to address the children collectively, thus clipping the wings of their personal characteristics. It is also common practice to compare one's children with the children of others, or to compare them among themselves, by filtering out along the way the choice of "model" desired. It is not easy for parents to accept that their children be "themselves", persons in their own right, at times radically different, unique, capable of making choices and orienting their life in other directions. But children need to be encouraged in this otherness and personalization in order to construct an identity that is their very own.

The role of parents will be to accept this otherness and to facilitate it. Here are a few examples. Emphasize in front of the children their own characteristics; refer them back to themselves and what they feel is best for them, then respect their choices; as much as possible and where help seems necessary, help them to realize these choices; encourage them to be "themselves" rather than conforming to what is expected of them, or to such and such a model, etc.

When they are perceived as unique and reassured in the sense of their personality, children will slowly gain confidence in who they are. Then, when the time comes, they will set the objective of becoming themselves on their own initiative by daring more and more to affirm themselves including in their own differences. In this way, all individuals are called progressively to become persons with their own originality and unique internal reference.

To locate, understand and help manage the sufferings of the children and heal their disproportionate and recurring reactions

The preceding paragraphs have explored the normal needs of children, important for their growth, and the way the parents could play a role in satisfying them. In this paragraph we shall examine other needs of children, "deficiency needs" which can manifest themselves very early in children, and the role of parents when faced with these needs.

At the end of Chapter 5 on Growth, we have seen how "deficiency needs" are born, along with the psychological wounds which accompany them. These wounds are inevitable, they are part of the human condition. In fact: *"Neither the great love that we can have for our children, nor our will to educate them in the best possible way, protect us from educational blunders. It is so easy to become polarized by one child to the detriment of another. It is so easy to be absorbed by work or more rewarding activities than the education of children. There are numerous pitfalls to divert attention from this major task which is the education of those we have brought into this world"*[55]

Furthermore, *"one must also take into consideration that the family is not an island,*
— there is the children's relational environment: the school, with friends and teachers, the street, various groups of which they are members;
— there is the social environment and everything which enters into the mental universe of children through television and the various media;
— there is the factor of heredity;
— finally, there is the freedom of the child, the teenager, the young person"[56]

One can also add the traumas related to special circumstances (difficult labour, accident, bereavement …). All of this must be taken into account by the parents if they are to accept the fact that their children have wounds, without feeling guilty about it, and determine the origin of these wounds.

Some parents can contribute to the healing of their children, even though they may have been the authors of those wounds. We

[55] O.N. *"Children's Rights with regard to Their Parents"*, p. 4, 1988.

[56] Idem, p. 4.

will limit ourselves to a few fundamental points :

– The first thing, is to take the situation seriously and diagnose the sufferings of the children, whether or not they originate in a past wound. The suffering of children can take many different forms. These can include tears, aggressiveness, despair, jealousy, and also inertia, self-effacement, lies, insomnia, psychosomatic reactions, etc. The expression of suffering is always a sign that something is happening within the child, a bit like a signal lighting up on a control panel. Often, the message is easy to decode, the cause and effect relationship easy to establish: the child is tired, frightened, upset because of a frustration, a bruise, etc. But sometimes, this suffering seems enigmatic, without apparent reason, without any obvious relation to an older trauma. It can be transient or lasting or it can be recurring. Being diagnosed as "capricious", or even a "temperamental child" burdens the latter with a judgement of guilt and fails to seek out the cause of the behaviour.

The role of the parents is first of all to receive the manifestations of their children with understanding and kindness by listening to them talk about their pain. Thus, it is not a question of consoling them, nor of minimizing their pain ("it's not serious"!), but on the contrary of facilitating the expression of the suffering (without however falling into the "interrogation" trap), so that it will not be suppressed. It is the evacuation of the pain in a favourable emotional climate which will gradually allow children to be appeased.

Eventually, when it is necessary and the situation allows it, parents can act on the cause if the latter is external to the child.

– The second thing is to pinpoint the children's disproportionate and recurring reactions. The suffering probably takes root deeper than in the annoyance which provoked it today.

In this case, the role of parents consists in seeking to understand where, in the past, the root of that suffering is located, to help the children be aware of it and, if possible, help them evacuate the past pain.

To do that, they must listen to their children from the best of themselves, that is with patience, understanding, and without judgement. When one has some intuition on the origin of the suffering, one can suggest it to the children by asking questions, leaving them to verify if the hypothesis echoes their sensations.

The important thing is to let the children express their real-life experience by themselves, going to the bottom of what they feel is the cause of today's suffering. They must feel accepted in what they are experiencing.

This requires that the parents hold off on their reactions to what the children are saying, for it could involve them or alter the facts. The important thing is to neither react nor justify oneself during the time the children are trying to communicate their real-life experience. It is only when the children are appeased and feel understood by the people around them that they can open up to an explanation of events which differs from their own.

The evacuation of a past pain is not usually done in one operation. Children will have to pursue the expression of their real-life experience on the occasion of other disproportionate reactions. Parents can then once again help their children by agreeing to listen to them and receive them with their reactivated suffering.

Finally, let us note the amendment function that an attitude of truth and humility by the parents can have when the latter are involved in the sufferings of their children. Parental errors, blunders or limitations may have altered the parent-child relationship. Accepting to recognize them in front of the children who have suffered them helps the latter to rid themselves of guilt and puts the relationship on the road to recovery.

***

To conclude this chapter on the education of children and on what is required on the part of parents, let us stress a few important points :

— *Concerning the difficulties parents have in responding to the needs of their children*

In view of the survey we have just made of the fundamental needs of children and what that implies by way of responsibilities for parents, the latter might be tempted to get discouraged and legitimately ask themselves if the role isn't beyond their reach.

Must all of those needs really be satisfied in order for one's children to not be wounded? Faced with this question, here are a few points for reflection :

– In educational matters, wounds of non-existence are only provoked if the children's threshold of tolerance to frustration is frequently overstepped. This threshold varies a lot depending on the individual. Therefore, it is not occasional frustrations that profoundly wound children, but a situation where their needs are almost constantly frustrated and they are not allowed to live and express their needs.

– Besides, the fundamental needs of children do not necessarily have to be satisfied as soon as they are expressed, and this for two reasons. On the one hand, parents are not always willing or able to satisfy them. They have their own limitations. It is important therefore to receive the suffering caused by the children's frustration and let them know that their need has been heard and will be considered as soon as possible. On the other hand, paradoxically, one must realize that seeking to fulfill the children and protect them from all frustration is not constructive of their personality. In fact, so long as the frustrations stay within their tolerance level, reaction to displeasure participates in the personal structuring of children and in their sound insertion into reality.

It is good for children to hear their parents quietly refuse some requests, explaining the reasons for their refusal. This will help them to not feel guilty and not consider the outside world as solely fulfilling. That would not prepare them to live in a world where things do not happen as and when one would wish them to. Moreover, from the non-response to one of their needs they can develop the creativity to seek other means, other sources of life and happiness.

– The way parents react to the dissatisfactions of their children goes a long way, either to limit the normal tension provoked by frustration, or to exacerbate the request. Peaceful communication is essential if the children are to feel loved, even though one does not respond to their expectations.

– *Concerning the education of parents*
Parents cannot adequately respond to the needs of their children

and foster their growth except under a two-fold condition. They must be aware of the importance of those needs and must acquire a know-how as well as a more advanced maturity than their children. This maturity of the children's significant others is all the more indispensable as they advance in age and need to be accompanied by adults who are stable, loving and sufficiently available.

It is therefore necessary that parents have at their disposal education which is adapted to their needs, namely :
– training in the education of children, so as to be aware of what is indispensable for children to receive if they are to become themselves and integrate into society, and to acquire competence in matters of education;
– education in the life of the couple, in order to give parents a sufficient grounding in that area, allowing them to develop their unity and to face their difficulties as a couple. This will enable them to bring their children to an affective security based on that unity;
– education aimed at the personal growth of parents, so that they may acquire the maturity which is indispensable for leading their children toward their own adult life.

– *Concerning the role of society and its leaders*

To assume their role and to prepare new generations for the numerous challenges of tomorrow, the parents need to receive the necessary help from society. This help is three-fold :
– material help, notably for parents deprived of resources or having serious responsibilities (large families);
– help for training, schooling, extra-curricular activities;
– assured personal help for the basic forms of education mentioned above ...

Those who hold power in a society have an important responsibility to ensure that the needs of parents are taken into account and means are at their disposal to help them educate their children.

"The 'skill' of parenthood can be learned. We cannot be satisfied with what we have received from our own parents, when we are living at a time in which research on personal growth and education brings us very useful enlightenment.

Public authorities who are responsible for preparing the future, cannot lose interest in the family which is the basic unit of Society.

To care for the material well-being of families is indispensable, but we must go further and put into place a system which would enable parents to be competent educators."[57]

[57] O.N. *"Children's Rights with regard to Their Parents"*, p. 8, 1988.

By way of conclusion ...

Impacts of the growth
of persons on society

While it is not the objective of the book, this theme has been touched on several occasions in the preceding pages. It is obvious, of course, that growth, and the personal development which results from it, would have no sense if they did not open onto broader progress for the society in which we live: economic, social and cultural progress ... all of which are examples of progress in humanization.

From the beginning of the first chapter: "Overall approach to the person", we maintained that: *"PRH views humanity with optimism. It has faith in the capacity of humankind to evolve and find solutions to the problems it encounters; faith in its humanization. This faith is reinforced through observation of the depth of resources present in all human beings, and the fact of undeniable progress in the humanization of persons and groups. Society is in some way driven toward an enhanced-being. (...) The very relevance of PRH action with persons, couples, parents, groups and business firms rests on this faith in humanity and the progressive humanization of society. (...) In PRH, this commitment takes the form of an in-depth operation with those who wish to participate, to free the huge deposit of potentialities that they possess, to help them discover the meaning of their life, to educate their deep conscience, to heal the wounded areas of their personality, to equip them with the necessary knowledge to become themselves and to make their life as successful as possible, in relationship with others."*[*]

[*] Cf. pp. 45-46

This positive position does not rest on an arbitrarily selected initial premise. Through almost 30 years of observation we have been able to establish a close link between the growth of persons and the humanization of society. Contrary to widespread belief, personal education does not risk bringing about withdrawal into oneself, disengagement, individualism or even the egocentricity which at times has been attributed to it. Admittedly, this risk can show up at one time or another during a growth journey, but it is only a passage. The attentive "counsellor" knows that, in order to surmount this risk, one must go further, more deeply into oneself, to reach the social roots of the being. It is impossible, in fact, to become fully oneself without participating in the common good and collective advancement.

Whether it is a question of professional life, life in a group, in a couple, the education of children or urban life, there are numerous accounts testifying that work on oneself opens onto something larger, commits one to action, reduces distances between people, improves relations, makes one more creative and more efficient in all the areas of life in society.

This collection of happy and fruitful experiences should no doubt be told. This could be the subject of a second book, one which is already on our minds ...

This position, both positive and realistic, brings a hope that rests, in the words of André Rochais, on this *"deposit of potentialities and therefore of creativity which is latent in the innermost depths of every being"*, and in the possibility of putting this formidable human resource to work, allowing individuals to fulfill themselves.

At this depth, it is striking to observe that the movement of "centring on oneself" leads to an opening toward "more than self". This is undoubtedly because, beyond race, culture and religion, one reaches the shore of what is most "common" and most universal in all of humanity, the perception of a profound and true fraternity.

PRH is not alone in holding this optimistic viewpoint. The entire current of humanistic psychology testifies to this today. A thinker like Pierre Teilhard de Chardin, to quote only him, was able to affirm: *"The Human Being is essentially the same in all. One need only dig deeply enough into oneself to find a common base of aspirations and light*"[58].

We can hear André Rochais echoing this affirmation. In a text profoundly imbued with all of his discoveries on the aspiration to exist and the phenomenon of non-existence, he went from intuition to the affirmation of a certitude: "*Everything is there, in this sub-stratum of Humanity, in this sub-stratum of men and women of this planet, everything is there to form a more human world.*"

If such is the case, the growth of persons is not only one value to be recognized among others. It becomes "*the No. 1 value of a human society*". If taken really seriously, and on a vast scale, it would foster the crossing of a threshold: that of greater personalization and greater humanization of society.

By the same token, the various tools of in-depth education provided today in the world of the humanities are not only a personal means of living better, they offer a possibility of fostering this growth in personalization and humanization of society. "*The crossing of this threshold has become possible thanks to different in-depth educational tools which, like drills exploiting pockets of oil, allow us to reach the deposits of potentialities and creativity that we talked about, and bring to light all the riches of being on which we were sleeping without knowing it.*"[59]

This statement opens onto a wide horizon, and at the same time raises many questions …

Could we not transpose on a larger scale the methods which a minority of people have already started to use profitably to bring their potential into awareness and to actualize it, making the people around them grow to greater humanization?

Should it not be a priority to propose these methods to the leaders of society, whose powers and influence could have multiplying effects?

Behind the symptoms by which it is troubled, will our society know how to hear the suffering of the many people, particularly young people, who cry out in their own way their despair at living a life whose meaning they do not understand? Will it know how to bring new reasons for living, new guidelines, new means of seeking answers to the existential questions posed by individuals? Will it allow all individuals to discover who they are and that

[58] "*Comment je crois*" (Oct. 28, 1934) p. 118.
[59] O.N. "*How to Facilitate the Growth of Persons*", p. 13, 1991.

for which they are made? And will it know how to provide persons with means to fulfill themselves, means which already exist?

What a Humanity we would generate if everyone had within their reach the ability to discover the riches contained in their being, to be able to actualize the best of themselves and perceive the profound meaning of their existence and their actions!

What appears to be a dream can be tomorrow's reality ... It is up to today's men and women to work and take the means for the world to have a future; that this future be inscribed in the hope that lives in the heart of all human beings, a hope that, from the beginning of time, opens the way to a progressive humanization of our world.

Afterword

In the beginning we said that PRH psycho-pedagogy always liked to think of itself as being at the service of what is most human in individuals. In that sense, we hope that this work has been useful. But in matters of knowledge about human beings, we know that only that which allows advancement and a true transformation, a mastery of one's life, in the sense of authentic growth, is useful. We are aware that to inform is not to form and even less to transform ... That is why this work will have a limited reach if, for the reader, it remains only a theory which is added to other acquired knowledge.

The theoretical framework referred to in these pages was born of experience, and in constant interaction with a clientele, made up not only of PRH "educators", but also of participants in our educational workshops. The part they played in the discoveries which this work has tried to put across can never be stressed enough. From the start, under the impetus of its founder, André Rochais, it was the pedagogy experienced in these workshops that was recognized as the first element of transformation and advancement. It was always less a question of teaching others than of making them discover and experience that which, in their inner selves, animates and impels them to fulfilment.

Today as always, this is the raison d'être of all PRH educators throughout the world and the main objective of the educational workshops and other pedagogical methods offered by PRH.

CLAUDE ROUYER
President, PRH-International

A brief presentation of the PRH Organization

The origins of PRH psycho-pedagogy and its explanatory system have been described in the introduction and first part of this work.

They were developed within the framework of the "PRH Organization", the objectives and methods of which are outlined here.

The PRH Organization offers to anyone who so wishes a set of educational methods which can :
– facilitate the experimental and progressive discovery of the PRH explanatory system,
– and help to draw from it everything that is relevant to one's daily living and various commitments (personal, professional, relational, educational …).

In all parts of the world where they have been introduced, these methods of education, using an original pedagogy, have proven to be particularly effective.

In fact, since 1970, when the "Personnalité et Relations Humaines (PRH)" Organization was first constituted in France, PRH education has not stopped spreading throughout the world. Today, PRH is established in some forty countries, from which more than 300 educators spread the PRH education to some 20,000 persons each year.

Among the educational methods offered by the PRH Organization, workshops occupy an essential place.

These workshops can be grouped in four cycles :
– the "Self-knowledge" cycle, which explores and studies in depth the way the constituent elements of the personality function and the interactions among them;
– the "Group Life" cycle which, combined with the preceding cycle, treats of relational living in a group or business firm;
– the "Couple and Education" cycle, which clarifies the PRH explanatory system as it applies to the relationships within couples and to the education of children;
– the "Training in the Helping Relationship" cycle, which is addressed to anyone who, through their profession or activity, may have to help or accompany someone in their difficulties or their growth.

Each workshop is constructed in the form of a serious exploratory search related to the theme of the workshop. Self-observation tasks are proposed to the participants. Sharing follows the personal work, and this is then completed with commentaries taken from the PRH explanatory system.

But PRH education is not limited only to workshops. It is extended through the possibility of accompaniment (individually and in groups).

PRH-International, with headquarters in Poitiers, France, and the various PRH National Organizations, are the only agencies authorized to diffuse PRH education within their territory. They are at the disposal of anyone who wishes to experience the PRH psycho-pedagogy and receive information on its educational methods. These can be offered to them in their own country or in one nearby.

Glossary

A semantic analysis of the PRH vocabulary shows different tenors of meaning :
– concepts used in the meaning normally found in classical dictionaries (e.g., "truth", "indecision" ...). Such words do not appear in the glossary;
– new technical words (the "I".);
– common concepts which are used in a particular sense ("to exist", "affectivity", "deficiencies" ...);
– concepts used in other schools, but with a meaning specific to PRH ("ideal self", "unconscious", "transference" ...);
– concepts or expressions used metaphorically ("rock of being", "encysted suffering" ...).

This glossary contains words and expressions used in PRH psychopedagogy. Some are specific to the PRH explanatory system, others, of common usage or proper to some other school, appear here because they are given a specific meaning in PRH.

Ab-normal : Said of conduct which is disharmonious, maladjusted. The term is used without judgment as to the normality of the person.

Activity (or an Action) : Term used to designate what persons do in life and their commitments. "Activities" actualize the potentialities of a person.

Actualize : To implement (e.g., one's potentialities).

Adherence to a sensation / adherence to one's inner lived experience : Action of the intellect which gets into contact with one's inner lived experience in order to analyze it correctly.

Affective life : Evolutionary area in the life of a person where the movements "to love" and "to be loved" are experienced, as well as the various other sentiments one experiences.

Affective maturity : State of psychological evolution where persons have liberated their capacity to love gratuitously and let themselves be loved, because they have healed their principal affective wounds.

Affective relationships : The relationships in which feelings between persons occur, whether these feelings be positive or negative.

Affectivity : That which designates the entire field of the aspiration to love and the need to be loved.

Alienation to others : A way of reacting and/or behaving which subjects a person to the will and expectations of others.

Analysis : The use of the intellect to explore a sensation so as to bring its content to awareness.

PRH Analysis :
– Specific method of deciphering one's interior world, particularly psychological sensations with which one is imbued.
– A text which expresses the content of the psychological sensations explored according to this method.

Aspiration : Phenomenon felt by a person in the form of dynamism and impulse, expressing the interior movement of a potentiality of one's being which is seeking to manifest itself.

Aspiration to become oneself : Visceral desire to live and be oneself. Corresponds to the most fundamental, deepest and earliest dynamic in a person.

Authenticity-adaptation dialectic : Inner process of behavior adjustment, which harmonizes two attitudes seemingly contradictory: an attitude of affirmation of self, of one's truth, one's existence and an attitude of adaptation to others, (considered as openness and respect for the other), as well as taking the situation into account.

Autonomous centre : Said of the pivotal centres of the person which have an existence and way of functioning relatively independent in relation to one another. For example, the "I" constitutes an autonomous center since it can, in any event, function without referring to the being. By the same token, the being and the deep conscience are autonomous centers in the person since they can operate in an imperative manner.

Autonomy :
– Capacity to be in relationship with others, in a free and authentic manner, without alienating oneself (as opposed to "isolation" where persons cut themselves off from others).
– Stage in the growth journey of persons, characterized by the acquisition of an inner freedom and the development of their capacity to exist as they are in their innermost depths.

Axis of one's essential course of action : Main thread which symbolically links the important choices of activities in which the

person has become engaged. Instinctive at first, this axis is gradually revealed as it tends toward a way of investing one's energies and potentialities in a more and more specific, personalized, fruitful, significant and fulfilling course of action.

Being (one's) : Primary pivotal centre of the person, forming the foundation from which one's personality emerges progressively. Dynamic and positive in nature, this pivotal centre corresponds to the locus of identity, the essential course of action, the essential bonds of the person and one's openness to a Transcendency.

Being – unemerged : Aspects of the being which have not yet been revealed or actualized.

Bond of being : That which, at the level of their being, unites two or more persons durably and strongly in a common essential course of action.

Bond of being of a couple : That which unites a man and a woman at the level of their being, setting up the foundation of their commitment to share their life and start a family.

Bonds – essential (Cf. p. 277)

Certitude – habitual (at the being level) : Aspect of oneself or one's life about which the person is certain, in which one is confident, with which one has had experience and upon which one can depend. An habitual certitude can be put to question at times: in moments of trial or when faced with criticism from significant others, unlike an unwavering certitude (cf. "Certitude – unwavering).

Certitude – unwavering (at the being level) : Is said of a certitude at the level of being of which persons have such an experience that they no longer doubt this certitude, even during times of difficulty, criticism or failure.

Community aspect of the being : Aspect of the being which brings persons to encompass more than themselves by opening them up to others and to society.

Conscience – cerebral : Interior reference at the level of the "I" where are located the principles and rules that persons give themselves to conduct their life.

Conscience – deep : Considered as a pivotal centre, the deep conscience is a "locus of synthesis". It serves as an internal reference to discern what is in line with the inner being and its fulfilment. It also serves to assess the actions taken in relation to the overall growth of the person in a given situation (ie., in relation to their environment).

Conscience – socialized : Interior moral reference point constituted by the notions of good and evil, of permitted and forbidden, which are or were in force in one's surroundings.

Counter-dependency : Phase of one's growth journey toward autonomy characterized by rejection or distancing from those on whom the person was until then dependent or to whom she/he was alienated.

Core of self : These are the most essential realities of the identity of the person, of one's essential course of action and essential bonds. These realities are driven by a particularly strong dynamism.

Decipher a sensation : Steps taken by the intellect which consist in exploring and formulating the content of a specific internal lived experience. (Cf. analysis)

Deep Zone : That part of the sensibility which is in direct contact with and is irradiated by the inner being of a person. It is a zone of peace and harmony.

Defense system : The sum of means set in place by persons to alleviate past sufferings as a protection from wounds which still affect them or could still affect them.

Deficiencies : The sum of frustrated needs, generally from childhood or adolescence, which have created a psychological wound which appears in adulthood as disproportionate and recurring reactions when those needs are not satisfied.

Deficiency need/Ab-normal need : A normal need at the outset which, not having been sufficiently satisfied at a moment that was vital for the person, has become exaggerated and insatiable and consequently source of frustration difficult to bear.

Determination to progress :
– Interior strength which flows from the being of persons, impelling them to evolve, to improve, to adjust, to liberate the best of themselves.
– One of five fundamental attitudes which foster growth.

Discernment : Process of the intellect which, faced with a given situation, aims at finding the best decision or the least detrimental, in conjunction with the deep conscience and other pivotal centres.

Disconnect from a sensation / Lose contact with one's interi- **or reality :** To lose contact with a sensation during PRH analysis, notably when a person speaks dispassionately about a sensation, or reasons it out.

Disconnect from reality : Phenomenon of the intellect which loses direct contact (most often unconsciously) with external reality, projecting on it imaginary or distorting elements.

Disproportionate and recurring Reaction (DRR) : Phenomenon of the sensibility which, given similar circumstances, always reacts out of proportion to the circumstances which triggered it. These reactions can range from explosion, anger, aggressiveness or excitability on the one hand, to sadness, depression, dejection, flight, or even insensibility and suppression on the other.

Docility to the deep conscience : Attitude of the "I" toward the deep conscience, characterized by fidelity to perceived invitations, and commitment to the choices made in harmony with this deep conscience.

Dynamism of growth : Innate irrepressible strength which impels persons consciously or subconsciously to actualize their potentialities.

Educate children : Is to help them become who they are, to find what they are meant to be and to help them to take their place in society.

Emergence of being : Process of progressive awareness and actualization of one's realities of being.

Encysted suffering : Past psychological trauma which has been repressed but remains present in the nervous system where it is kept as in a protective cyst.

Environment : All that is exterior to persons and which directly or indirectly influences them and their growth: their human and material surroundings, their way of life …

Essential bonds : The totality of a person's bonds of being.

Essential course of action (Life-work) : That for which persons are made, their vocation, their life path, the type of action which corresponds to their most basic potentialities, allowing them to give their full measure and which gives meaning to their life.

Essential group : Group of persons, in relation with one another, who are engaged in the same essential course of action.

Evacuation of pain : Revival, awareness and exteriorization of a repressed psychological pain, which allows the body to free itself from an embedded tension and gives way to life's dynamism.

Event of being : Interior phenomenon, unexpected, particularly intensive and striking, which arises and imposes itself from the most profound depths of the person. Examples of events of being are: inner words, intuitive insights or very strong inner images.

Exist (To) : To stand up in who one is. To be affirmative and take action from the best of oneself, to live and actualize one's potentialities.

Faithfulness to oneself / to one's deep conscience : Inner attitude of a person free from former alienations, which consists in making one's own decisions and acting in consonance with one's being.

Frame of reference : The collection of ideas, theories, principles, norms, methods, projects and even memories which, consciously or not, condition persons in their way of being and acting.

Fullness of existence : Experienced sensation of giving one's full measure and achieving that for which one was made.

Functioning : The origin of an action, a behavior or an attitude resulting from aspirations or needs emanating from one of the four pivotal centres: being, "I", sensibility, body.

Functioning – adjusted / normal / peaceful : An act performed in response to a normal need of any pivotal centre, lived in harmony with the being, and adapted to the current situation.

Functioning – ab-normal : Hypertrophy or atrophy of a behavior, the origin of which, often unconsciously, is a wound from the past.

Functioning – cerebral : A way of using the intellect characterized by the fact that the person is no longer in direct contact with reality. Reality is deciphered through a filter of ideas, judgements, à prioris, theories or reasoning, rather than as it presents itself here and now.

Functioning – compensatory : Disproportionate method of satisfying deficiency needs in order to reestablish an equilibrium which has been jeopardized by the presence of a void, an inner deficiency or a state of non-existence.

Functioning – free : Way of living their freedom in which choices of persons are made in agreement with their being while taking into account external reality and the reactions of their own various personal pivotal centres.

Functioning – imaginary (also called imaginative functioning) : Exercise of the intellect, triggered by a movement in a painful or excited sensibility and characterized by a distortion of reality, which the person moderates or magnifies.

Functioning – instinctive : A way of satisfying a need, lived spontaneously without reflection or decision.

Functioning – sensitive : Impulsive behavior led by the cravings or repulsions of a person's sensibility.

Functioning – voluntaristic : Extreme and persistent mobilization of the body's energies, accompanied by internal tensions, in order to satisfy plans, ambitions or expectations which frequently spring from deficiency needs or an education strongly marked by the notion of duty.

Functioning – voluntary : Well-adjusted use of one's energies so as to accomplish what one has decided to do.

Fusion : Mode of partial or total

identification with another, where the personality of one disappears, stalls, or blends with the personality of another person or group, thus hampering the relationship.

Genetic makeup : That which is innate in persons, notably the constituent potentialities of their being.

Group : see 1) Essential group 2) Life group 3) Task group

Growth impairment : All of the things in the life of a person (traumatic events, psychological wounds) that have markedly thwarted the natural development of psychological growth and have constrained the person to a greater or lesser degree of non-existence.

Growth journey axis or growth axis : Direction in which persons have to progress to achieve maturity in certain areas of their life.

Growth journey phase or Growth phase : In the psychological evolution of persons, a phase of growth which takes place over a more or less long period of time. During that time they pass progressively from one type of inner lived experience and behavior to another type, which is more mature and more in conformity with who they are.

Growth journey : The path persons follow in evolving toward their maturity and fulfilment. It is comprised of a number of phases.

Growth relationship : Relationship in which persons address others to receive something which helps them in their own growth (recognition, listening, counselling, understanding, reflection, encouragement, etc.)

Growth :
– Dynamic of the emergence of the being through the awareness and actualization of one's potentialities.
– Overall development of the personality.

Healing of past wounds : Work on oneself which aims to restore the capacity to live and actualize one's potentialities, which until now have been blocked or curbed by the presence of past traumas.

Humanization of persons : Qualitative as well as quantitative development of human potentialities. This progressive development of what defines the human being aims at an "enhanced being" which is at the same time well-being.

Humility : Capacity of persons to accept their own reality as it is, no matter whether it reflects positive aspects, negative aspects or constituent limitations.

"I" : Pivotal centre where the intellect, the freedom and the will function. Its role is to govern persons in the growth of their being and toward an overall harmony.

Ideal Self :

– Image of the "better self" toward which persons tend and which corresponds to the potentialities of their being.
– Exemplary and utopic image of self, corresponding to what persons would like to be, based on their ambitions or social expectations.

Identity : Totality of personality traits (riches of one's being and limitations) which differentiate one person in relation to another. Permanent and fundamental characteristics of a person.

Imperative of one's being :

Inner drive which imposes itself on persons, impelling them with force to act from their being. This drive is to be distinguished from impulses of the sensibility or the "I".

Independence : A form of isolated relational self-sufficiency. (Not to be confused with interdependence).

Inkling (at the being level) : Non-verified intuition of the existence of a reality of one's being. In the process of the emergence of the rock of being, inklings are often the first inner manifestations of the presence of an aspect of one's being. Examples: inkling of one's capacity for creativity, inkling of suitability for life as a couple.

Inner freedom : Ability to make choices and to exist by giving priority reference to the dictates of one's deep conscience.

Inner lived experience : The sum of all psychological manifestations which occur in persons, whether they are aware of them or not. In the inner lived experience, one finds thoughts, images, sensations, sentiments, emotions, etc.

Inner reality : All of the psychological lived experience of a person at any point in time, whatever the origin of the experience.

Inner unity :

– Sensation experienced by persons when all pivotal centres occupy their rightful place and play their role at the service of their being.
– Interior state comprising harmony and deep peace.

Innermost depth of self : That which is brought to awareness at a given point as being the most profound reality of the person.

Instinct of being : Unconscious manifestation of the being which orients persons and makes them react toward the fulfilment of their essential aspirations.

Interior insights : States of awareness, often strong and unexpected, which emerge from deep intuitions, enlightening persons about themselves, their life, on decisions to be made or actions to be taken ...

Interior movement : Dynamic psychological phenomena, generated by the aspirations and needs of the person and felt in the sensibility. They can be externalized through action.

Interior order : Hierarchical organization of the psychological structure of the person, in which each pivotal centre occupies a place and plays a role in relation to the overall growth of the person.

Internal reference centre : Reference centre that persons consult for decision-making and to which they submit to act. The deep conscience is an internal reference centre.

Learning dependency : Provisional relation that persons experience in relation to someone who possesses a form of knowledge that they themselves need. There is a dependency because the learners cannot cope in that area on their own, but the dependency can coexist with an inner freedom with regard to the teacher.

Life group : Group of persons motivated by the choice of living together according to certain values and certain standards accepted by each of them.

Life-giving relationship : Any relationship which arouses the being of the person, stimulating it to exist and to grow. These life-giving relationships are indispensable to the growth of a person.

Limitation : Term of development of potentialities, resulting not from a blockage or disfunction, but from the natural constitution of the person. Potentialities can no longer develop beyond this threshold. (e.g. intellectual, artistic, relational limitations ...)

Lived experience : General term which evokes:
– subjective reality which is felt, perceived, brought into awareness at a given point (cf. Inner lived experience).
– the factual reality of the situation and the subjective reality of persons at a given point in their lifetime.

Locus of synthesis : Expression used to characterize the deep conscience which, taking the whole person into account, assembles the input of other pivotal centres into a decision making synthesis. In due time it evaluates the decision made or the action taken.

Love – dutiful : Affective expression rooted in principles and an altruistic ideal which are more or less voluntaristic, often devoid of true feeling.

Love – gratuitous : The expression of affective potentialities, unconditional and free of expectation of reciprocation.

Love – possessive : Affective egocentric drive which takes the other to oneself, to have and hold, in order to satisfy needs.

Manifestations of one's being : Forms of expression from the innermost being of the person, independent of the will and superficial desires. Some of these manifestations are: deep intuitions, the instinct of being, the reflexes of being, inner invitations, etc.

Mechanism : A "mini-functioning" which can be included in the broader functioning of a pivotal centre. For instance, the mechanisms of self-justification and self-depreciation are "mini-functionings" within cerebral functioning.

Need to be recognized : Fundamental need whereby individuals expect from their significant others the right to be themselves.

Non-existence :
– A person's internal defense system, tied to wounds of the past, which translates into a strong inhibition, even an incapacity to actualize certain potentialities and affirm oneself in one's relationships.
– Painful sentiment related to the inability to live up to one's aspirations because of a wound.

Normal need : That which persons expect to receive so that the different pivotal centres of their personality find a sort of equilibrium and satisfaction and, because of this, can fulfill the role of serving their growth.

Obstacle to growth : Interior resistance, disfunction (doubt, alienation, fear ...) or unfavorable exterior condition (noise, malnutrition, promiscuity ...) which obstructs the expression of the dynamism of growth of the person's being.

Openness to one's inner reality : Disposition of the "I" to be attentive and receptive to the realities of one's inner world.

Openness to a Transcendency : Ability to experience at the level of the being the presence of realities, which are at the same time constitutive of persons and cause them to sense a dimension of the absolute which surpasses them, calling them to an "enhanced being".

Painful past :
– In the life of persons, the painful past corresponds to the period when their main psychological traumas appeared.
– The sum of psychological traumas experienced in childhood and adolescence.

Periphery of self : The sum of those aspects of being for which actualization is not as imperative and essential, nor as meaningful as the actualization of aspects of the core of self.

Person in order : Individuals whose five pivotal centres function in consonance with their being, giving them a sense of inner unity, harmony in their personality and maximum efficiency.

Person in the process of growth : In speaking of humans, this expression emphasizes the dynamic of personality development. This is the angle from which the human being is observed in PRH.

Personality : The sum of traits and behavior which distinguishes persons and differentiates them from one an other.

Pivotal centre : In the PRH diagram of the psychological structure of the person, the pivotal centres correspond to the specific locations from which spring motivations to act. PRH anthropology distinguishes five pivotal centres: one's being, the "I", the body, the sensibility and the deep conscience. Each pivotal centre can function autonomously, in that it does not necessarily have to be in accord with the other pivotal centres.

Potentialities (at the level of one's being) : Innate and positive aspects of one's being, which tend to develop and to become actualized. Generic term indicating aptitudes, capacities, gifts, qualities, riches of being …

PRH Helping relationship : Specific method by which PRH counsellors accompany persons in their growth journey.

Psychological dependence : Relationship of alienation to another person or a group, which is characterized by the fear of being oneself, the fear of being judged.

Re-education : Particular phase of the growth and healing process, in which persons train themselves to take action consciously and voluntarily to restore or develop normal functioning in circumstances where disharmonious behavior had previously been instinctively released.

Restoring order in one's functionings : Work in the course of a growth journey, which consists in developing the normal functioning of the pivotal centres to allow each of them to occupy its full place, but only its own place, in consonance with one's being.

Riches of being : Components of the identity of a person which have a positive aspect and call to be developed and actualized.

Rock of Being : The sum of habitual and unwavering certitudes that persons have concerning their identity, their essential course of action, their essential bonds, their openness and/or relationship to a Transcendency. The rock of being is the solid base of an individual's personality, upon which one can depend to be and to act.

Self-image : The idea or representation that persons have of themselves, which generally provides a key-reference in determining their actions. This image can reflect more or less faithfully their real self.

Self-justification (mechanism of) : Phenomenon of the "I" which seeks to establish a coherence between actions taken and the image that persons have of themselves; or else between the actions or contemplated actions and that which would be or would have been reasonable to do.

Sensation – simply physical : Localized or diffused physical manifestations, whose origin, easily identifiable from a cause and effect relationship, notably with the environment, and is not related to the psychological life of the person.

Sensation with psychological content : Psychic message from within, which manifests itself in the sensibility and the body and which can be analyzed in order to understand its content and origin.

Solidity of being : Consistence, firmness and balance of the personality, related to the emergence and breadth of one's rock of being. This solidity is proven during the difficulties and trials of life when the person remains standing upright, grounded in habitual and unwavering certitudes.

Task group : Group of persons motivated by the accomplishment of an action to be conducted together.

Time of being : A pedagogical method used to foster personal growth, comprised of moments of deep interiorization aimed at becoming consciously impregnated with the realities of one's being.

Transcendency : A reality which is of the same nature as the being, and also sensed as being another reality. It is infinite, absolute, permanent and non-reducible to what persons are; neither to what they are living because of it nor to their awareness of it.

Transference : An often unconscious projection of a childhood lived experience onto a person or current situation, which alters the connection of that person or situation to the present reality. Transferences may be positive (one invests the person on which the transference is being made, with qualities that one would have liked in a significant person from their past); or negative (in which can be found the repressed negative sentiments experienced in relation to a person or a wounding past situation.)

Unconscious : Qualifying adjective which applies to inner phenomena which have not occurred within the purview of one's awareness, but which nonetheless influence one's behaviour. In PRH usage, there is no direct analogy with the psychoanalytical concept of the unconscious.

Wisdom of one's body : Expression meaning that all physical signs are messages to be heeded as one would heed the words of a sage. Indeed, these messages contain useful information for conducting one's life properly, by expending one's energy advisedly and without excess.

Wound : Psychological trauma, more or less serious and crippling, which follows a maladjusted answer, or the repeated absence of an answer to a fundamental need, thus handicapping the expression of the person's potentialities.

Wound of non-existence : Said of traumas which have affected the essential nature of persons and have engendered in them an incapacity to live according to that essential nature.

Table of Contents

The origins of PRH psycho-pedagogy

Psychological and pedagogical research at PRH

The phenomenon of growth

The phenomenon of
healing past wounds

The meaning of life

Impacts of the growth of persons on society

FORMATION PRH INC (Winnipeg)
Directory of PRH Educators

SHIRLEY DELISLE
34 Timmins Cresc, Apt 3
CHATHAM, ON N7L 4E1
Tel: (519) 345-8310

MARJORY McGUIRE
2704 Priscilla St, Apt 2
OTTAWA, ON K2B 732
Tel: (613) 596-8188

ANNE VERONICA MacNEIL
2287 Brunswick St
HALIFAX, NS B3K 2Y9
Tel: (902) 423-1383

MARGARET MARY O'GORMAN
2935 Richmond Rd, Apt 1001
OTTAWA, ON K2B 8C9
Tel: (613) 820-9791

PRH OFFICES
IN NORTH AMERICA

FORMATION PRH INC
BOX 53 ST BONIFACE POSTAL STN
WINNIPEG, MB   R2H 3B4   CANADA
Tel: (204) 237-4513

FORMATION PRH INC
44 RUE CLARK
SHERBROOKE, QC   J1J 2N2   CANADA
Tel: (819) 563-3033

ASSOCIATION FORMATION PRH
BOX 68073 - 162 BONNIE DOON MALL
EDMONTON, AB   T6C 4N8   CANADA
Tel: (403) 468-9435

PRH INSTITUTE - CENTRAL DIVISION
356 ARDEN PARK
DETROIT MI 48202 USA
Tel: (313) 875-1125

PRH INSTITUTE - EASTERN DIVISION
55 MOORE AVE
WORCESTER MA 01602 USA
Tel: (508) 756-0978

PRH INSTITUTE - WESTERN DIVISION
PO BOX 127
MARYLHURST OR 97036 USA
Tel: (503) 635-9018

ORDER FORM

"PERSONS AND THEIR GROWTH"

The anthropological and psychological foundations of PRH education

Please send me _____ copy/copies (at $25.00 per book) plus $4.00 when sent by mail.

Name _____
(please print)

Address _____

_____ Postal code _____

Enclosed in a cheque / money order for the amount of _____

Included (if you wish) is a donation of _____ to support this PRH venture.

Signature _____

Mail this order to: SHIRLEY DeLISLE
34 TIMMINS CRESC APT 3
CHATHAM ON N7L 4E1